THE ENTANGLED TRINITY

THE ENTANGLED TRINITY

QUANTUM PHYSICS AND THEOLOGY

ERNEST L. SIMMONS

Fortress Press
Minneapolis

Cover image © Thinkstock

Cover design: Erica Rieck

Library of Congress Cataloging-in-Publication Data is available

Print ISBN: 978-0-8006-9786-0

eBook ISBN: 978-1-4514-3857-4

The paper used in this publication meets the minimum requirements of American National Standard for Information Sciences — Permanence of Paper for Printed Library Materials, ANSI Z329.48-1984.

Manufactured in the U.S.A.

This book was produced using PressBooks.com, and PDF rendering was done by PrinceXML.

For Marti

CONTENTS

Acknowledgements

It has often been said that a work is never the product of a single individual. This present work is no exception. I am indebted to several institutions, mentors, colleagues, and friends, as well as leading thinkers in the field of theology over the centuries. I would like to thank Concordia College, President Paul Dovre and Provost Mark Krejci for providing sabbatical time as well as support for faculty writing retreats. The warm hospitality of Pacific Lutheran Theological Seminary and its president Phyllis Anderson as well as Dean Michael Aune and colleague Ted Peters who made the stay in Berkeley during my sabbatical quite productive and stimulating for both my wife and me. I appreciated the helpful input of Robert John Russell, founder and director of the Center for Theology and the Natural Sciences, as well as Sir John Polkinghorne and Ian Barbour, with the early configuration of this project. My religion colleague Roy Hammerling helped significantly with the historical chapters and colleague Hilda Koster made significant suggestions on the whole manuscript, especially in the constructive theology sections. My physicist/philosopher colleague Bryan Luther gave helpful guidance and correction in quantum physics. My mentor Paul Sponheim offered insight and wisdom on this project, as well as encouragement throughout the years and, along with my doctoral advisor John B. Cobb Jr., has nurtured and guided me in my vocation as a teaching theologian of the church. My student assistants Jeff Brown and Kristi Del Vecchio helped enormously as representative student readers and assisted with the formulation of discussion questions, key terms, bibliography, index, and endnotes. My wife, Marti, the love of my life for over forty-eight years, provided encouragement, support, and above all patience with this author, who was preoccupied by his work and not always as present as a loving spouse should be. It is to her that this work is dedicated. As always, any errors in this work are the responsibility of the author.

Introduction

He himself [Jesus Christ] is before all
things, and in him all things hold together.
–Col. 1:17

The doctrine of the Trinity is an exercise in wonder. It is drawn from the wonder of our own existence and the diverse experiences of the divine encountered by the early Christian community. That pluriform experience eventually gave rise to the doctrine of the Trinity as Christian thinkers attempted to coherently place the Christian experience of the divine somewhere between the pluralistic polytheism of the Greco-Roman world and the singular monotheism of the Jewish tradition. Christianity became a *pluralistic monotheism*, with all the contrasts and creativity that implies. Theologians of the church have drawn on the most sophisticated language and understandings of their time in their attempts to clarify and express that faith, and this task is no different today. It is precisely the continuation of this theological quest that this book will engage in as we reflect on the multiple ways the divine is present to human life for both meaning and hope.

The formative question of this study is: *What can the current scientific understanding of the natural world contribute to our reflection in a Triune fashion on the relationship of God and the world?* This theological question will be explored through the metaphorical appropriation of two central concepts in quantum physics: entanglement (nonlocal relational holism) and superposition with its resulting paradigm of complementarity. These concepts will be used to unpack for contemporary understanding the central expression of the Trinitarian mystery as the dynamic divine relationship of perichoresis.[1] Initially

---

1. I am indebted to Dr. Kirk Wegter-McNelly for first presenting to me, as one of his readers, the idea of connecting perichoresis and entanglement in his doctoral dissertation, "The World, Entanglement, and God: Quantum Theory and the Christian Doctrine of Creation" (Graduate Theological Union, Berkeley, CA, 2003), section 6.4.2. There he does not develop the idea at length but mentions it in passing and credits William Stoeger with raising the idea with him in private conversation. The dissertation has now be published as *The Entangled God: Divine Relationality and Quantum Physics* (New

1

appropriated by the Cappadocian Fathers from Greek categories, perichoresis is used to describe the "mutual indwelling" of the dynamic becoming of the Trinity. In this work, perichoresis interpreted as entanglement will be employed to affirm the unity-in-diversity that is the Christian conception of God.

The thesis of this study is that *perichoresis evolves within the Trinitarian life of God as entangled superposition, relating Creator and creation in mutual interaction, supporting a panentheistic model of God.* The immanent Trinity exists in simultaneous superposition with the economic Trinity and evolves within the entangled life of God with the creation. Entanglement gives metaphorical clarity to the manner in which panentheism models God's relationship to the creation, including incarnation and sanctification. Superposition and non-local relational holism provide physical metaphors for the whole within the parts in a way that illuminates a panentheistic model, in which the world exists in God and yet God is more than the world, being both in and beyond it at the same time. We will apply the model of perichoretic Trinitarian panentheism to the specific work of the three persons (hypostases) of the Christian experience of God.

Employing the theological method of correlation, this text is an exercise in constructive theology. It is divided into three parts: part 1, "Foundational Concepts"; part 2, "Trinitarian Development"; and part 3, "Science and the Trinity." Part 1 will define and develop the critical concepts of faith, knowledge, and theology. Part 2 will address the development of the doctrine of the Trinity from the biblical sources through the Reformation to contemporary expressions. This part will help the reader understand the origination of Trinitarian thinking as well as its historical development, with a view to contextualizing the constructive argument made in the final part. Part 3 summarizes ways of relating science and theology and important concepts in quantum physics before metaphorically appropriating them to elaborate the perichoretic nature of divine relatedness in a panentheistic Trinitarian model of God. This model is then applied to the historic functions of the Trinity in creation, incarnation, and sanctification.

York: Routledge, 2011). This excellent work is a much more detailed exposition of quantum theory (including equations) and entanglement than I am able to do in this introductory text. There in ch. 6 (220), he does briefly, referencing my earlier work, support the understanding of entanglement as mutual indwelling, leading to an enriched understanding of the Trinity. His overall focus, however, is on the relation of God and creation, not on the Trinity. He neither elaborates at length on the Trinity nor places it in a wider panentheistic model, which I am doing in this text. Both works, I believe, can complement one another.

As we shall see in subsequent chapters, human community builds on the dynamic, interconnected community of life in the creation, and this community in turn resides within the dynamic of the divine community of the Trinity. Divine community gives rise to creational and human community such that each interacts with and influences the other. The discoveries of the natural sciences in our time open up new possibilities of expression as well as understanding for this divine interconnection. Through the concept of entanglement (nonlocal relational holism), it is hoped that new light can be shed on the historic understanding of the dynamic interrelatedness of the divine life as that divine energy breaks forth into the entangled reality of the creation. The Holy Mystery exists not only in dynamic interrelatedness to itself but also to all that has come forth from the fecundity of that relatedness. It is the dynamic of this multifold relatedness that the doctrine of the Trinity attempts to express and that forms the beating heart of the Christian faith. This theological vision of faith sees life as existing in, with, and under community for both the divine and the human, for both the Creator and the creation. It is an empowering vision in which we see that "in him all things hold together."

PART I

Foundational Concepts

1

Faith

Fides quaerens intellectum
"Faith seeking understanding"
                    —ANSELM, *PROSLOGIUM*

The camel snorted and moaned gently as it made its way along the starlit gravel path. The Bedouin camel driver sang gently to his charge to keep him moving. As I gently rocked back in forth in the tight camel saddle, I gazed up at the desert night sky, moonless, with stars so bright, numerous, and appearing so close that one was tempted to reach up and pluck one down. As my gaze dropped onto the hulking, dark monolith that we were traversing, I saw fellow pilgrims, flashlights in hand, wending their way up the sides, looking much like a single strand of golden Christmas-tree lights cascading down a darkened canyon. We were clinging to the sides of Mount Sinai, and in the darkness time drifted away and we became one with the spiritual pilgrims of countless ages who had, since Moses and even before him, sought insight and solace on this mountain.

When we look up and gaze at the approximately three thousand stars that the naked eye can see on a moonless night, the questions inevitably come. Who are we? What is it all about? Where did it or we come from? And, of course, What is the meaning of it all? Mountaintops, especially at sunrise, cultivate such questions in the massive and yet delicate beauty of an apricot sunrise. These are quintessential human questions. They are the questions that inevitably arise as we contemplate our origins and become aware of our own finitude and mortality, the concrete awareness that we need not be. We are always pilgrims in this life. The wonder of existence has impelled philosophy, theology, and science for millennia. It is at the heart of the quote above from St. Anselm of Canterbury. We seek greater understanding. But while enhancing faith, understanding will never be a substitute for faith. Wonder always drives us back to the questions of faith, particularly the basic question, Why are we here?

1. Why Are We Here?

"Why are you here?" All of us have been asked, or have asked, that question of ourselves many times. As one of the most basic questions we can ask, every word is important. *Why?* The foundational interrogative raises the question of meaning and purpose. All of us begin to enunciate this basic question early in life. It is the root question of meaning for the human condition and the foundation for both philosophy and theology. *Are?* The verb of being cuts to the core of human life. We exist, but we will not exist forever, and so begins the foundational question of being. What does it mean "to be"? and, somewhat insidiously, to "not be," as Shakespeare's Prince Hamlet would have us reflect. "To be, or not to be? That is the question!" *You?* This question is of subjective identity. It is my "you" and not your "you" that is in question here. To what does this "you" refer? Is there an enduring "I" or only an ephemeral passing presence of neurotransmitters that camouflages the absence of self by providing a continuity of experience that appears to have permanence and identity? Who are we really? *Here?* Where is here as opposed to there? How do we define time and space, especially in a relativistic, expanding universe? Can you only be at one here at a time, or are there multiple "heres" (the multiverse) that we inhabit simultaneously, only one of which we are conscious of? This one little question in many ways encapsulates the profound questions of human life and provides the context for this book.

A. Mystery of Existence

The above question is one of the most profound questions that the human being can ask. As we mature, the thought finally occurs to us that there is no immediately evident reason that we should exist. We encounter the mystery of our life and its radical contingency. We need not be, and yet we are, and we realize this is true of everything that we encounter, from stars to butterflies. All existence is contingent, which leads us to ask whether there is something beyond the contingency. We have a profound awareness of something beyond ourselves upon which we and all that exists depend. Many cultures and individuals name this the Holy or the sacred. Rudolf Otto, in his classic, early-twentieth-century work *The Idea of the Holy*, called this the *mysterium tremendum et fascinans*, the tremendous (awe inspiring, trembling) mystery that is also fascinating. Elizabeth Johnson observes, "*Mysterium* refers to the hidden character of the Holy, beyond imagination not just because of our intellectual limits but because of the very nature of the subject. Far from being a pessimistic experience, however, encounter with the Holy as mystery is laced with the promise of plenitude: more fullness exists than we can grasp."[1] This is what we mean by the spiritual dimension of life, of human experience. It is to embrace or be embraced by the Holy experienced in wonder and mystery. This is a transcendent fullness that goes beyond our ability to fully comprehend and as such stands over against us, reminding us of our finitude and mortality. It can make us tremble with both fear and awe as we become aware that we do not possess it but that it possesses us. We are humbled in the presence of the great mystery of all existence, whether seen through the electron microscope, the Hubble telescope, or the beauty of a sunset. We are driven to wonder, and wonder, as we have seen, is the root of all religion and of all faith. Wonder also drives us to fascination. We are fascinated in the presence of this mystery for which no name, no theory, no model, and no religion will ever be complete or all inclusive. The Holy defies our ability to demarcate at the same time that it draws us to itself with the power of fascination and wonder.

What is it we are a part of but do not see? Loren Eiseley talks in similar terms in his book *The Star Thrower*, particularly in a chapter titled "The Hidden Teacher."[2] A paleontologist searching for fossils, he was walking up an arroyo in the American Southwest one summer's day when he ventured upon a yellow and black orb spider. She was spinning her web right at eye level, over a crack in the face of the gulch. More out of curiosity than malevolence, Eiseley took a pencil out of his pocket and gently touched the spider's gossamer web. The thin threads started to vibrate until they were a blur of motion. The spider sat at the center of the web fingering away at the filaments of the universe that she had created from the interior of her own being. Finally, the vibration slowed until it came to a stop, and she sat there motionless, no longer interested. As Eiseley put the pencil back into his pocket, he realized that his pencil was an intrusion from the outside of this spider's universe for which she had no precedent. Spider universe was circumscribed by spider ideas. It was sensitive to a raindrop or a moth's flutter, but a pencil point was an intrusion for which she did not, and could not, have comprehension. In the spider universe, he did not exist.

---

1. Elizabeth Johnson, *Quest for the Living God: Mapping Frontiers in the Theology of God* (New York: Continuum, 2008), 8–9.

2. Loren Eiseley, *The Star Thrower* (New York: Harcourt Brace Jovanovich, 1978), ch. 11, "The Hidden Teacher," 116–28.

As Eiseley wandered away, he mused, How different were humans from the spider? Here we sit at the center of our self-created webs of sensory extension, radio telescopes, microscopes, satellite telemetry, fingering away at that which we try to understand. What in our world constitutes an intrusion for which we have no comprehension? That is where the mystery of the Holy comes in. The Holy is that beyond in the midst of life for which we have no categories of thought or experience. It will not fit into our schemas, and yet we sense it is there and that it draws us to itself as the mysterious source from which all else has come. There is a spiritual yearning deep within the human person that the material world alone cannot satisfy, a yearning that seeks for the beyond in the midst of life. The Holy has the power to entice as well as to open our hearts and make us aware of the very longing for meaning, for purpose, and for the ultimate that is at the heart of our own being. As Augustine once said in his book *Confessions*, "Our hearts are restless, O Lord, until they rest in You."[3]

B. SEARCH FOR THE ULTIMATE

Abraham Maslow was a humanistic psychologist. As such, he did not see himself as religious in any traditional sense of the term, and yet, as he reflected on the very nature of human need in formulating his famous "hierarchy of needs," he was driven to place self-transcendence at the top as necessary for self-actualization. This decision was based on his research of "peak experiences," which are transpersonal, ecstatic, interconnecting, even euphoric types of human experiences.[4] In the context of the present discussion, they would be considered examples of experiences of the transcendent mystery of existence, of the Ultimate, and open to anyone regardless of religious perspective.

Elizabeth Johnson observes three factors that root this fundamental, age-old quest for the Holy, for the living God, in life. First, the very nature of what is being sought is incomprehensible, limitless, unfathomable, and beyond description. Second, the human heart is insatiable and is driven by an immense longing in all human fields of creative endeavor but especially in matters of religion, where a brief taste drives us to a hunger for more. Third, it is the ongoing quest for the experience of God, which is always mediated through the changing history of human cultures. She concludes, "Putting all three factors together leads to an interesting realization: the profound incomprehensibility of God coupled with the hunger of the human heart in changing historical

---

3. Augustine, *Confessions* 1.1. Albert Outler, ed, *Augustine: Confessions and Enchiridion*, Library of Christian Classics (Philadelphia: Westminster, 1955), 38.

4. Abraham Maslow, *Religions, Values, and Peak-Experiences* (New York: Penguin, 1994).

cultures actually *requires* that there be an ongoing history of the quest for the living God that can never be concluded."[5] Throughout human history, human beings in all times and places have been driven to try and understand the ultimate, which has been given many names and characterizations, but all will fall short, even our most cherished images. If we treat them as absolute, then they become idolatrous, for we are absolutizing something of human origin and construction. We are treating as infinite something that is finite, something as divine that is not divine. That is why the quest for the Holy must involve faith, for only in faith does one reach beyond human understanding or conceptualization to catch a glimmer of that which is beyond human origin. It is faith as trust that gives rise to a dynamic human capacity.

2. FAITH AS A VERB

A. FORMS OF FAITH

At least since the Middle Ages, the Christian tradition has commonly distinguished the content of faith (the object of devotion, that believed in, *fides quae creditur*) from the process of having faith (the process of expressing devotion, the faith by which we believe, *fides qua creditur*). I find it helpful to think of this distinction not simply as a content/form distinction but as a grammatical one as well. Faith can be both a noun (the object of faith) and a verb (the process of engaging in faith commitment, "faithing"). For this reason, faith must also be distinguished from "belief" as well as from "religion." James Fowler observes that belief in more recent thought has come to be equated with intellectual assent to propositional statements, particularly those that codify the doctrines or ideological claims of a particular tradition or group. Belief may be a part of a person's or group's faith, but it is only a part. Likewise, religion refers to the cumulative tradition composed of beliefs and practices that express and form the faith of persons in the past or present.[6] Religion can include everything from art and architecture to symbols, rituals, narrative, myth, scriptures, doctrines, ethical teachings, music, and much more. If you will, religion can be viewed as the cultural embodiment of faith but is not identical to it. We turn, then, to a more generic and functional analysis of faith that focuses on process rather than on content, on faith as a verb.

The sixteenth-century Reformer Martin Luther was well aware of this distinction; indeed, in late medieval theology, faith had four aspects: *notitia*

---

5. Johnson, *Quest*, 13 (italics in original).

6. James W. Fowler, *Faithful Change* (Nashville: Abingdon, 1996), 55–56.

("knowledge"), *assensus* ("assent"), *voluntas* ("action of the will"), and *fiducia* ("trust"). Luther was a practical and realistic thinker, and as he struggled with his own faith life, he came to realize that ultimately trust (*fiducia*) encompassed all of the forms of faith. Without trust in God's justifying grace, none of the other expressions of faith were effective or meaningful. Luther's favorite definition of faith was Heb. 11:1: "Now faith is the assurance of things hoped for, the conviction of things not seen." By employing this text, he defined faith fundamentally as trust, trust placed in the justifying grace of God. *Faith is trust in that to which one gives ultimate devotion or loyalty.*

Luther understood well the subjective dynamics of faith and realized that our fundamental temptation was precisely to trust something other than God (idolatry). We will have faith. We are meaning-seeking creatures and will create an object for our devotion if there is not one visible (for example, the story of the golden calf in Exodus 32). Commenting on this condition in regard to the First Commandment, Luther observed in the *Large Catechism*, "As I have often said, the trust and faith of the heart alone make both God and an idol. . . . That to which your heart clings and entrusts itself is, I say, really your God."[7] The issue, then, is, What does one trust with one's life? Whatever one trusts and devotes one's time and energy, affection and attention to, *functions* as "god" for that person, regardless of what that object is or what it is called. It can be anything from money and success to rock stars and the natural world. When we come to see faith as a verb, as a process and function of the human, we realize that all people place their trust in something, by means of which their actions and life take on meaning. The focus at this point is on the process of devotion, not on the worthiness of the object of devotion. This process of trust is open to both the theist and nontheist alike.

The great twentieth-century theologian Paul Tillich developed Luther's understanding further for our time. He said that faith is "ultimate concern,"[8] that which concerns you ultimately, that one concern on which you center your life. Tillich observed that "faith is a centered act of the whole human person" such that "in faith reason reaches ecstatically beyond itself."[9] Which is to say that this process of faith involves all the capacities of the human; it is a fully committed trust and devotion, which while not contradicting reason, fulfills the ultimate yearnings of reason by going beyond which reason alone can support

7. Martin Luther, "The Large Catechism," in *The Book of Concord*, ed. Theodore Tappert (St. Louis: Concordia, 1958), 365.

8. Paul Tillich. *The Dynamics of Faith* (New York: Harper Torchbooks, 1958), 1–2, 5.

9. Ibid., 8–9.

and defend. It is the completion of the yearnings of both the human heart and mind and will also necessarily involve doubt.

B. FORMS OF DOUBT

For Tillich, there are three forms of doubt, only one of which relates to faith.[10] First, there is "methodological" doubt, which arises from a method of scholarly study such as in the natural sciences. This doubt is programmatic in that it is built into the course of investigation and will be resolved if the study is successful. This is not the doubt of faith. Second, there is "skeptical" doubt, that which questions everything at least for a brief time. René Descartes is one of the greatest representatives of skeptical doubt in the West. In his "Meditations," he sought to question everything until he got back to an unquestioning foundation for belief. His famous conclusion "I think, therefore, I am" (*cogito ergo sum*) has been a paradigm for skeptical doubting ever since the seventeenth century. Descartes, however, did conclude that he could not question everything, and upon the basis of acknowledging his own thinking (To question that would be to question that he was questioning, which would be to cease questioning!), he then moved back to affirm much else in human life.[11] This also is not the doubt of faith.

For Tillich, the doubt intrinsic to faith—indeed, a structural feature of it—is "existential" doubt, the uncertainty and anxiety based on our very finitude. Existential doubt arises precisely when the finite attempts to commit itself to the infinite. As limited human creatures, we can never know with certainty that our object of devotion is fully worthy of such trust. We can never infinitely know, feel, or experience in this life, so there will always be an element of this doubt in every human expression of faith. It may not be on the surface and does not have to be present constantly, but it is there, and for this reason Tillich sees faith as requiring courage. Faith is the courage *to be* in the face of our *nonbeing*, our mortality. It is not only the pain and loss of a friend or family member that makes the pathos of a funeral so intense but also our knowledge that at some other time, and thank God we do not know when, it will not be someone else in that casket, but us. And what then? Where will we be? Whose will we be? Will we be?

Human beings live their lives in the dash, the dash inscribed on the grave marker between the date of birth and the date of death. Existential thinkers such

10. Ibid., 20.

11. This process contributes to the philosophical position known as "foundationalisms," which many postmodern thinkers, such a Richard Rorty, now seriously challenge and reject.

as Tillich invite us to contemplate our dash and how and why we live it. Do we rush through it? Do we "dash" through the dash? I find it interesting that such a terse and cryptic symbol comes to represent all the hopes and dreams, successes and failures, joys and sorrows of a human life. Perhaps it's very brevity bespeaks the nature of our time, but we must not let life pass us by. Theologians like Luther and Tillich invite us to pause and contemplate our lives and what we are committed to, for it affects all that we do. When we view faith as a verb, we begin to see that faith is not optional for humans but is of the quintessence of the human. While our feet are of the clay, our eyes and minds scan the stars. Humans exist juxtaposed between time and eternity, the finite and the infinite, in what I call the "mesocosmic," the cosmic middle between the microcosmic and macrocosmic forces of existence. We find our place between quarks and quasars in such a fashion as to contemplate both. We are an example of the universe become self-conscious, and we are able to reflect on time before our own beginnings and after our own demise.

C. STAGES OF FAITH

Human beings are always beings on the way (*Homo viator*).[12] Developmental change and growth are intrinsic to our very lives. Human beings are becoming beings. Indeed, our being is in our becoming. The entangled relationship between the becoming of individuals and of God is the focus here and throughout this text. Over the last several decades, a number of cognitive and developmental theories have been formulated that have opened up this fascinating human process. It is not my purpose here to survey them all but to highlight a few of the ideas that can be helpful in understanding the emerging field of faith-development studies. James W. Fowler is the founder of the discipline of faith-development research, although many others, including William James, in his *Varieties of Religious Experience*, have investigated the psychological dynamics of faith. Fowler, however, was the first to intentionally develop a new discipline, drawing on many developmental theories to investigate faith dynamics. His intention is descriptive, not prescriptive. It must also be said that this is not the only way of understanding faith development, and there are some criticisms of Fowler's approach, particularly as he attempts to merge a structuralist model (Piaget) with a psychosocial one (Erikson).[13] It

---

12. Much of this section comes from my earlier work, *Lutheran Higher Education: An Introduction* (Minneapolis: Fortress Press, 1998), ch. 5, sec. 2.

13. For critical review, see such works as Craig Dykstra and Sharon, eds., *Faith Development and Fowler* (Birmingham: Religious Education Press, 1986); Jeff Astley and Leslie Francis, eds., *Christian Perspectives on Faith Development* (Grand Rapids: Eerdmans, 1992); and articles such as Marlene M. Jardine and

is not our purpose to get into this internal debate but rather to simply indicate that one can talk about faith development in a clear and descriptive way that is approachable through clinical research and analysis. Undoubtedly, further revisions of the approach will be made, but it is still a helpful starting point for understanding the diverse positions and needs concerning faith.

Fowler has seven stages of faith development. In his words, "*The stages aim to describe patterned operations of knowing and valuing that underlie our consciousness.* The varying stages of faith can be differentiated in relation to the degrees of complexity, of comprehensiveness, of internal differentiation, and of flexibility that their operations of knowing and valuing manifest. In continuity with constructive developmental tradition faith stages are held to be *invariant, sequential,* and *hierarchical.* I do not claim for these stages *universality.*"[14] The seven stages are as follows.

1. Primal faith (infancy)
2. Intuitive–projective faith (early childhood)
3. Mythic–literal faith (middle childhood and beyond)
4. Synthetic–conventional faith (adolescence and beyond)
5. Individuative–reflective faith (young adulthood and beyond)
6. Conjunctive faith (early midlife and beyond)
7. Universalizing faith (midlife and beyond)

Fowler makes the point that faith development includes a number of factors: biological maturation, emotional and cognitive development, psychosocial experience, and religio–cultural influences. He concludes, "Because development in faith involves aspects of all these sectors of human growth and change, movement from one stage to another is not automatic or assured. Persons may reach chronological and biological adulthood while remaining defined by structural stages of faith that would most commonly be associated with early or middle childhood or adolescence."[15] He also goes on to indicate that a transition from one stage to another does not necessarily mean a change in the content or the direction of one's faith but rather in the way one holds, understands, and takes responsibility for one's faith.[16]

Henning G. Viljoen, "Fowler's Theory of Faith Development: An Evaluative Discussion," *Religious Education* 87, no. 1 (winter, 1992): 74–85; and William O. Avery, "A Lutheran Examines James W. Fowler," *Religious Education,* 85, no. 1 (Winter, 1990): 69–83.

14. Fowler, *Faithful Change,* 57 (italics in original).

15. Ibid. For the overview of the stages, see ch. 2 and his earlier work, *Stages of Faith: The Psychology of Human Development and the Quest for Meaning* (San Francisco: Harper & Row, 1981).

16. Ibid., 68.

Primal faith is prelinguistic and is grounded in the care given to the infant, to offset the anxiety that results from separations that occur during infant development. If their needs are met they will develop a trust towards adults and the world. Dependability confirms them as being "at home" in their life spaces, but if significant deficits occur, they can give rise to a foundational mistrust of self, others, and the larger environment.[17]

Intuitive-projective faith begins with the use of language and the use of symbols, stories, dreams, and the imagination. Not yet controlled by logical thinking, this stage combines perception and feeling to create long-lasting images that represent both the protective and threatening powers surrounding one's life. At this stage, a child cannot distinguish fantasy from fact, but there is in this stage the possibility for aligning powerful religious symbols and images with deep feelings of terror and guilt or of love and companionship. It is in this stage that the child develops their first representations of God.

With *mythic-literal* faith, we enter the first stage that, while beginning in middle childhood, can persist into adulthood. Individuals in this stage engage effectively in narrative, although they do not place themselves in the flow of the narrative itself. The use of symbols remains largely concrete and literal, and the transition to the next stage begins when these persons, whether children, adolescents, or adults, experience that "bad things happen to good people" and that evil persons do not necessarily suffer for their transgressions. It becomes impossible to maintain the concept of a God built along the lines of simple moral retribution. This may lead to a temporary or permanent giving up of belief in God.

With the *synthetic-conventional* stage of faith, one also enters into the full-blown physiological impact of adolescence. The emergence of early formal operational thinking (Piaget) enables young people to appreciate abstract concepts, and they begin to think about thinking and to name and synthesize meanings. While this developmental stage does involve "synthesis," it is still heavily tied to the thoughts and feelings of others and feels the pressure of the "conventional." It is with the next stage that truly individual reflection develops.

Fowler observes that for *individuative-reflective* faith to emerge two very important movements must occur. First the previous stage's tacit system of beliefs, values, and commitments must be critically examined; and second, one must define the personal identity one has developed independently of earlier conditioning relationships. The person becomes reflective about both their worldview and their personal relationships as they begin to assert their

17. Ibid., 58.

own personal identity and take over personal authority for themselves, a role previously conducted by others. This perspective permits a transcendental view of self-other relations and a standpoint from which to adjudicate conflicting expectations as one's own inner authority develops. One is then capable of codifying frames of meaning that are conscious of their own boundaries and inner connections, so that persons at this stage can "demythologize" symbols, rituals, and myths, translating their meaning into conceptual formulations. Clearly at this stage one has entered the phase of critical awareness and thinking.

Conjunctive faith in many respects requires the dismantling of some of the clearly defined boundaries produced in the earlier stage. In this stage, the "coincidence of opposites" (from Nicolas of Cusa, 1401–1464 CE) are found to be present in our apprehension of truth. One becomes aware that truth may be approached from a number of different perspectives and that one's own identity is heavily dependent on unconscious as well as conscious forces. Persons in this stage display what Paul Ricoeur has called the "second" or "willed" naïveté where, having passed through critical analysis of their faith, they are ready to enter the rich meanings of true symbols, myths, and ritual in a clear move beyond the demythologizing strategy of the earlier stage. As a correlate, this stage also exhibits a principled openness to the truths of other religious and faith traditions.[18] Clearly, this is a mature and rich stage of faith development, and one that many of us would be fortunate to achieve. Fowler does, however, open up the possibility of one last stage.

Universalizing faith is possible but rare. Gradually, the circle of those who count in faith, meaning-making, and justice expands to the point where one reaches a pervading inclusiveness. There is a degree of saintliness associated with such people because the self in this stage has moved beyond the usual forms of defensiveness and exhibits an openness grounded in the being, love, and regard of God.

The purpose of this overview has been to give us a sense of the types of stages and movements that may be found in faith-development analysis. But it must also be said that development in faith is not simply linear. It is more of a spiral,[19] a cycle that may return to questions and issues time and again as one reappropriates, revises, and perhaps even rejects the faith content of one's tradition. It is to reflection on this wider communal (not individual) expression of faith that forms tradition that we now turn as we consider the broader nature

18. Ibid., 65.

19. Fowler, *Stages*, especially "Structural Stages and the Contents of Faith," 274–81, and the spiral diagram on 275.

of religion itself. Like our discussion of faith, it is important to consider the functions of religion prior to focusing on specific content.

3. FUNCTIONS OF RELIGION

The word *religion* comes from the Latin word *religare* and means "to connect," literally "to bind" together. Historically it means to connect the human and the divine, and has to do with humanity's relationship to the transcendent. Religion usually includes patterns of belief (creeds, doctrines) and practice (rituals, liturgies) that are intended to help connect the individual person with what is embraced as holy or sacred. For this reason, all of the great world religions have some form of community at their base, a monastery, church, temple, mosque, synagogue, or tent. For this reason, religions usually involve some form of institutional expression, including religious leadership and communal structure. The religious individual thus usually exists in religious community. One provides support and resources, while the other provides oversight, guidance, and care. Religions usually serve three primary functions for the practitioner:[20] a frame of orientation, an object of devotion, and a source of transformation.

A. FRAME OF ORIENTATION/WORLDVIEW

We seek to make sense of our lives and of the world around us. We seek coherence so that we can function within that world. To provide such an orienting worldview[21] or frame of orientation is one of the main functions of religion not only for the individual but for the whole community of faith. A worldview usually communicates the fundamental beliefs and commitments of a culture, what is real and valuable, as well as how to achieve and sustain those commitments. A worldview simply communicates the "way things are" to its practitioners. It grounds a vision of reality. In the West, the "Christian worldview" has dominated for almost two thousand years. In this worldview, the origin of life and existence was understood to be the product of a beneficent creator God who then enters into this creation through Christ and is sustained in existence by the ongoing activity of the Holy Spirit. As we will get into in the fourth chapter, this threefold involvement of God with the creation gave rise to the doctrine of the Trinity. At this point, however, it is important to note

---

20. See Richard Creel, *Religion and Doubt: Toward a Faith of Your Own*, 2nd ed. (New York: Prentice Hall, 1990).

21. See Ninian Smart, *Worldviews: Cross Cultural Explorations of Human Beliefs*, 3rd ed. (New York: Prentice Hall, 1999), especially ch. 1, "Exploring Religion and Analyzing Worldviews."

that the Christian worldview itself replaced an earlier, polytheistic worldview embraced by ancient Greece and Rome. Today some would argue that the Christian worldview is in the process of being replaced by the "scientific worldview." It is one of the main purposes of this book to challenge that argument and to demonstrate how the Christian worldview can be reconciled, perhaps even harmonized, with the understanding of the world given in contemporary science. It is also important to note that the East has also had multiple worldviews for millennia, from the East Indian worldview of the karmic cycle and the ultimate existence of Brahman to the practical social worldview of Confucius in China. Worldviews are essential to coherent, organized cultures and their religious expressions. Paul Tillich observes that "religion is the substance of culture, culture the form of religion."[22] Religion tells the community or culture what is important and valuable, the second function of religion.

B. OBJECT OF DEVOTION

Every person and culture values something as ultimate, embracing it as "holy" or "sacred" and centering their life on it. This something may be recognized religiously as a "god" or "gods," but it need not—for example, "success," or "wealth." The power of a functional analysis of religion, precisely, raises our awareness of how something can function in this capacity in a person or society, whether it is formally recognized as such or not. Nationalism has often functioned in such a role and still does today in many countries. When a bumper sticker can read, "My Country Right or Wrong!" the country is functioning as an object of devotion, as holy or sacred, as something ultimate, and is treated as such, even though it would never be referred to as a "god." One of the primary purposes, then, of the object of devotion, the Holy or sacred, is to ground or center the worldview of a religion. What is most important in life is that on which we center our lives and to which we makes sacrifices of time, energy, and possessions. The emphasis on consumerism in contemporary American culture is a case in point. When a person sees the main purpose of work as providing income for them to buy things and to acquire their heart's desire, then consumerism functions as a religion. Religions change people and direct their actions, and that is the third function of religion.

---

22. Paul Tillich, *Theology of Culture* (New York: Oxford University Press, 1964), ch. 1.

C. SOURCE OF TRANSFORMATION

In addition to providing an orienting worldview and an object of devotion, religions also function as change agents. In the Abrahamic faiths (Judaism, Christianity, Islam), one hears the term *conversion* when one becomes a member of a particular faith tradition. That process assumes some foundational change in understanding and in action. "I was blind but now I see," as composer John Newton put it in his hymn "Amazing Grace," describing his shift in worldview and commitment from slave trader to English clergyman. Change is not only possible but often desired and necessary in life. Religions provide such change. They can also propel social transformations as well, as witnessed by the eventual dominance of Christianity in the Roman Empire or the forced dominance of Maoism in China, more recently.

Religions thus orient in life, provide a basis for devotion, and direct change both personally and socially. Perhaps two brief examples of these functions in what would be considered nonreligious realms of thought and experience will demonstrate that it is really not a matter of whether one is religious but of what one is religious about.

The first example is Marxism. In its classical expression in *Das Capital*, Marxism, despite being avowedly atheistic, contains all the functions of religion. The frame of orientation is "dialectical materialism," where everything is understood in terms of the socioeconomic value it possesses. Individuals are units of production, and the worker is the fundamental social unit, *homo economicus*, economic humanity if you will. Workers are defined by what they produce. You are what you make. This frame of orientation, then, centers on the ultimate goal for Marx, that of the classless society, the final overcoming of capitalism as an exploitive and oppressive economic and social system. The change agent that brings this about is the proletariat (worker) revolution, in which the workers will take the means of production into their own hands and use it for mutual benefit, as the *Communist Manifesto* says. This was captured in Marx's phrase, "From each according to his ability, To each according to his needs."[23] Thus classical Marxism contains all three functions of a religion and indeed functions as such for ardent Marxists, who have been and are willing to die for their "faith." One need not believe in God to express religious devotion.

The second example, and more germane to the purpose of this text, is scientism. Scientism sees natural science, particularly the physical and life

---

23. Karl Marx, "Critique of the Gotha Programme," in *Marx/Engels Selected Works* (1875; Moscow: Progress Publishers, 1970), 3:13–30, accessed at http://www.marxists.org/archive/marx/works/1875/gotha/.

sciences, as the sole arbiter of truth and meaning for our time. It takes science as a method of investigation and elevates it to a worldview. It is assumed in such a worldview that only material existence is real, there is no spiritual or transcendent realm, and only scientifically demonstrable knowledge is worth knowing. Truth is that which can be discovered by one or another expression of the scientific method, that is, that which can be observed, measured (quantified), and repeated by others in a systematic way. So scientism's frame of orientation is scientific materialism, the object of devotion is scientific truth, and the sources of transformation are the various scientific methods of study and investigation, which leads to new truth and understanding of the material world. While this may strike the reader as a fairly narrow definition and source for truth, it is being widely encouraged by the so called "new atheist" movement led by Richard Dawkins. In his book *The God Delusion*, Dawkins makes explicit claims for the role of science in defining all truth and meaning worth knowing.

Science itself, of course, cannot demonstrate scientifically the acceptance of science as the sole arbiter of truth. That is not a scientific but a philosophical claim, though Dawkins's working assumption is that it is scientific. Science, specifically evolutionary biology, functions like a religion for Dawkins and those like him.

It is helpful, then, to understand the functions of both faith and religion if we are to truly begin to understand the role of religion in personal and social life. This then raises the question of knowing, of epistemology. How can we know anything about the world, much less about the divine or that which is embraced as holy or sacred? While religion provides the framework and object of commitment, one must also consider how it is possible to know what these objects and frameworks are. That is, how do we go about the knowing process? While a great deal has been written on this from both a philosophical and scientific perspective, I will attempt in the next chapter to give a simplified overview of the process and to demonstrate that all human processes of knowing involve something like what I refer to as the "House of Knowing."

KEY TERMS

Abrahamic Faiths
Belief
Forms of Doubt
Forms of Faith
Functional Definition of Faith

Functions of Religion
Holy
Mystery of Existence
Orienting Worldview
Religion
Scientism
Spiritual
Stages of Faith
Ultimate Concern

DISCUSSION QUESTIONS

1. Note the definition of the *spiritual*. What is the relationship between the spiritual and Holy mystery? How does this differ from your understanding of religiosity? How is it similar?

2. Consider the question, Why are you here? Which of the words/concepts in this sentence do you find most valuable?

3. In what ways do humans seek the sacred or the Holy? What functions as religious to people of traditionally religious and secular backgrounds?

4. What is surprising or controversial about Fowler's seven stages of faith development? Does society speak to the betterment of one stage over another?

5. The topic of doubt is addressed on its own and in the context of faith development. In what ways does doubt alter, deter, or strengthen "religious" (not in the traditional sense) worldviews?

2

Knowledge

Credo ut intelligam.
"I believe in order that I might understand."
—ANSELM OF CANTERBURY,
PROSLOGIUM

Intelligo ut credam.
"I understand in order to believe."
—ABELARD OF PARIS, *SIC ET NON*

The human question of why always hangs suspended between the finite and the infinite. Juxtaposed between time and eternity, humans seek meaning before our own beginnings and after our demise. Human beings are meaning-seeking creatures. It is quintessentially human to ask the question why? Why, for example, is there any correlation between the human mind and external reality? The great mathematician Eugene Wigner pondered this many years ago in an article titled "The Unreasonable Effectiveness of Mathematics."[1] Why should something as abstract as mathematics have any relationship to the external world beyond the human mind? This wonder at the regularity with which the physical world can be understood, and reverence toward its possible source, gave inspiration to both religion and science. It also opens up transcendence and spirituality within the realms of knowledge.

We are a form of incarnation. The spiritual is made manifest in the material precisely in the transcending of self-interest.[2] Spirituality consists in opening up

1. Eugene Wigner, "The Unreasonable Effectiveness of Mathematics," *Communication on Pure and Applied Mathematics* 13 (1960): 1–14.

to the needs of the other, to transcendence of the self, and to the possibilities of meaning beyond materialistic consumption alone. Nicholas Berdyaev once observed, "To eat bread is a material act, to break and share it is a spiritual one."[3] The spiritual need not, indeed must not, be separated from the physical, for it is in the use given to the physical that the spiritual becomes manifest. So to ask questions, have doubts, and most importantly to seek understanding is a spiritual endeavor. Faith and reason need not be opposed but can complement one another in the quest for human understanding. I will attempt in this chapter to give a simplified overview of this process and to demonstrate that all human processes of knowing involve something like what I refer to as the "House of Knowing."

1. House of Knowing

A. Experience and Abstract Reflection

How do we "know" what we know? It sounds like a really simple question until we begin to break it down. Then we realize that what we really "know" is in our minds, and these concepts, ideas, theories, and so on are at some distance removed from our direct senses. Drawing on some understandings in linguistic philosophy, cognitive psychology, and the social-construction-of-reality theorists in sociology, we can visualize this process in a very simplified way as what I call the "House of Knowing."[4] Several centuries ago, in what some call the birth of modern philosophy or a Copernican revolution in epistemology (study of knowing), Immanuel Kant argued that the mind is active in the knowing process but that we can only know the object as it is presented to us (phenomena) and not the thing in itself (noumena, the *Ding an sich*). The mind is active in organizing sense perceptions and does not simply passively receive them, as British empiricist (sensory-based) philosophers such as Hume and Locke had thought. There is a foundational distinction between what something is in itself and what we can know about it. Our knowing is always *our* knowing, so when we try to know or understand anything, it always involves the human process of reflection, which includes abstraction, mainly through language, from the specific sense experience. Think about this

2. See John B. Cobb Jr., *The Structure of Christian Existence* (Philadelphia: Westminster, 1967), esp. ch. 10.

3. Quoted in Langdon Gilkey, *Shantung Compound* (New York: Harper & Row, 1966), 229.

4. This concept is a further development of an idea originally found in Richard Creel, *Religion and Doubt: Toward a Faith of Your Own*, 2nd ed. (New York: Prentice Hall, 1990), ch. 1.

for a moment. This abstraction from sense perception to language characterizes the whole of human reflection, even when you desperately want to know or communicate something to another human being. When you look into the eyes of your beloved and get all mushy inside and coo, "I love you!," you immediately know it is insufficient. You feel so much more than you can communicate with words. So you say it with flowers, poetry, candy, or whatever. That is the plight of human finitude. We will *always* experience more than we can ever communicate to another human being, no matter how much we desire to do so. Now, if this is true of simple things like daisies and trees or lakes and mountains or more complex experiences like love or science, how much more must it be true of something as complex as God? This is why we must always resort to metaphor and analogy to communicate anything about our experience or understanding to another human being. We can never communicate the thing in itself. This is where my little "House of Knowing" comes in.

B. HYPOTHETICO-DEDUCTIVE METHOD OF REASONING

Imagine, if you will, a three-storied house with the first floor the ground of immediate empirical (sensory) experience. We walk into the house and onto the first floor through the Door of Perception, which is to say that everything we know in terms of discursive thought (I am leaving out of this discussion mystical or artistic awareness) enters into our minds through one of our five senses. This is the raw data of experience. Say you have a red apple on the table in front of you. What I am saying is that you do not see "apple" but rather a red form of some kind in your visual field of perception. "Apple" as a linguistic and cognitive concept exists up on the third floor, where reflection takes place. What happens, in simplified fashion, is that light from a lamp or from the sun through the window strikes the apple, and certain wavelengths are absorbed and others are reflected, in this case toward the red end of the visual spectrum. These "wavicles" (light is simultaneously a wave and a particle, a photon) pass through the space in the room and enter the lens of your eye, where they are focused and inverted and then hit the rods and cones at the back of your eye, where they are converted into electrochemical energy. They then pass along the optic nerve to the brain, specifically the visual cortex, in the back of your head. Now, the point of going through all of this is to indicate that what physically arrives in your brain where you really "see" has no physical resemblance whatsoever to the object on the table. The neuro-synaptic firings in the brain convey the sense of the visual perception, but other parts of the brain need to be engaged to really make sense out of what you are seeing. This involves memory such as taste, having seen a similar object before, and also linguistic memory, where the name "apple" enters into our conscious mind. In another culture, it could be "apfel." So we reflect on the third floor of the house, two floors removed from the floor of direct sensory experience. In trying to understand or "make sense" of our observation, we then need to employ what David Tracy refers to as the analogical imagination,[5] which draws on analogy from human experience and employs the ability to image. Imagination here means the ability to create abstracted, linguistic images, not simply fantasy. This is why language is so crucial. *Thought is internalized speech.* The more precision we have in our speech, the more precision we can have in our thought. Language is one of the most fundamental ways in which a culture communicates its values and perspective, ethics, and worldview to the next generation. Ideas are the most powerful possessions of the human individual or community.

All of what I have just been describing I try to communicate in the little drawing in figure 1. In addition, I have added basic logical processes. When one moves from the particular to the general going up the staircase (from seeing an apple to the idea of "apple"), one is engaged in induction. Induction is the attempt to formulate more generalized principles or ideas from specific observations, measurements, experiences, and so on. This is how we get to the third floor; we employ the analogical imagination to abstract from the particularity of immediate experience in order to be able to think about it. When we go the other direction, down the stairs, we move from the general to the particular. This is known in logic as deduction. We try out our ideas, principles, theories, models, paradigms in the world of observation and experience to see if they apply again in a new situation. (Is this fruit an "apple"?)

What I have been describing in simplified terms is what is known as the "hypothetico–deductive method of reasoning." In a general way, this is the type of reasoning most often employed in the physical and life sciences as well as in the humanities.[6] Where these fields of study differ is the area of empirical experience they focus on. One may choose, for example, to carve out biology or physics or history or sociology from all the possibilities on the first floor for more precise and focused study. Theology is no different in this regard, except that theology chooses to focus on what is named as "sacred" or "holy" in the

---

5. David Tracy, *The Analogical Imagination: Christian Theology and the Culture of Pluralism* (New York: Crossroad, 1998).

6. See Ian G. Barbour, "Models and Paradigms," in *Religion and Science: Historical and Contemporary Issues* (San Francisco: HarperSanFrancisco, 1997), 107.

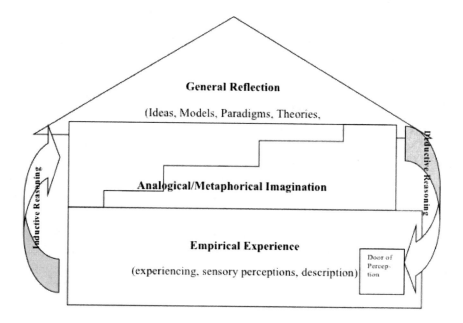

Figure 1. House of Knowing

realm of experience. Theology is a human endeavor like any other. All areas of human reflection, theology included, draw on human experience and thought to try to understand something about the world presented to it but that can never be known in itself. This is why symbol, analogy, and metaphor are so important in theological reflection. It is to these critical tools of thought that we now turn.

2. SYMBOL, ANALOGY, AND METAPHOR

A. SYMBOL VS. SIGN

Paul Ricoeur, the great French philosopher and biblical interpreter, once said that "the symbol gives rise to thought."[7] Symbolic reference is at the heart of the knowing process, the transformation of experience into reflection by means of linguistic expression. Paul Tillich very helpfully makes a further distinction between sign and symbol.[8] He indicates that both point to a reality beyond

---

7. Paul Ricoeur, *The Symbolism of Evil* (New York: Beacon, 1969), 347.

8. Paul Tillich, *The Dynamics of Faith* (New York: Harper Torchbooks, 1958), 47.

themselves, but while signs are constructed, symbols participate in the reality to which they point. There is nothing intrinsic about octagonality that means "stop," or triangularity that means "yield." In the United States, for recognition purposes, these shapes have been selected to be used to indicate that one must bring their car to a stop or give right of way. Symbols, however, participate in the reality they point to, so the cross as a symbol for Christianity represents something significant about the reality of Christianity, as does the Star of David for Judaism or the crescent moon for Islam. Symbols allow the mind and heart to soar beyond the immediate circumstances as well as to disclose something about reality that might not be immediately available for display. It is when symbols are connected with other forms of imagination that theological reflection can truly begin. While symbols point beyond themselves, there is always an intrinsic sense of limitation or contrast involved. They are not the same as the reality. Cultivation of this distinction opens up the two most important forms of human reflection, analogy and metaphor. Both analogy and metaphor involve a tension or a negation in what they attempt to communicate, and it is precisely in this tension that the power of these methods of reflection is found.

B. THREE MOVES OF ANALOGY

Analogy draws on experience and yet also affirms that that to which it refers is not identical to itself. There is both a similarity, hence the analogy is useful; but also a dissimilarity, otherwise the analogy would simply be redundant. Elizabeth Johnson points out that analogy as a method of reflection involves a three-step process: affirmation, negation, and the negation of the negation, which is again a form of affirmation. First, the statement. For example, "God is good." But we immediately know that the goodness of God cannot be the same as human goodness, so the analogy is negated, "God's goodness is not the same as human goodness." But then the negation is negated, which results in an affirmation, "Even though God's goodness is not the same as human goodness, God is still good in a divine way."[9] Analogy thus assumes some type of parallel between the base reference of the analogy and that to which the analogy refers.

The analogical imagination employs such a process of negation and affirmation in its reflection. Drawing on the important work of Thomas Aquinas in this area, Roman Catholic thinkers employ analogy as their main form of reflection. A second expression of the imagination, by contrast, is the

---

9. Elizabeth Johnson, *Quest for the Living God* (New York: Continuum, 2008), 18.

method preferred by Protestant theologians, that of metaphor, which employs the dialectical imagination.[10]

C. METAPHORICAL TENSION

Metaphor is the concept of understanding one thing in terms of another. The word comes from the Greek term *metapherō*, which literally means "to carry over."[11] Metaphors carry an image from one area of experience or understanding, usually familiar, over to an area less familiar and thus increase the understanding in that less familiar area. Metaphors thus have built into them a basic tension of "is" and "is not." Indeed, it is this tension that allows metaphors to work. For example, in act 2, scene 7 of Shakespeare's play *As You Like It* occurs the famous phrase "All the world's a stage, and all the men and women merely players; they have their exits and their entrances." Now we know that the world is not really a stage, but by transferring this theatrical image over to describe the world, Shakespeare indicates not only the performative nature of life but also its transitoriness. It expresses something about the subject we are trying to understand that we did not know before. It is this added understanding that makes metaphors so powerful.

This simultaneous affirmation and negation is at the core of the dialectical movement of the imagination when employing metaphor. The dialectical imagination seeks to affirm something from our familiar experience and then "carry over" this image to the unfamiliar in such a way that a tension is created which illuminates the unfamiliar. Dialectical imagination does not back away from paradox, though it does not actively seek it out either. Later on, as we move into both quantum and Trinitarian theory, we will encounter paradox and the dialectical imagination. It is this dialectical, simultaneous tension that distinguishes metaphor from analogy. Analogy employs a negation movement leading to an affirmation, while metaphor remains within the tension, both affirming and negating at the same time. Discerning levels of explanation can help clarify this.

D. LEVELS OF EXPLANATION AND EMERGENCE

The theologian John Haught observes that "if a hammer is your only tool, then everything looks like a nail; if objectification is your only cognitional instrument, then everything looks like an object."[12] He is criticizing the objective reductionism present in scientific materialism and made popular by

10. Ibid., 19.

11. *Wikipedia*, s.v. "Metaphor," last modified October 7, 2013, http://en.wikipedia.org/wiki/Metaphor.

writers such as Richard Dawkins in *The God Delusion*.[13] His point is that if you allow only one level of analysis, then everything has to be defined in the terms of that level. It is not that objective reductionism is wrong but rather that it cannot tell the whole story. It must be supplemented by synthetic holism. To make the claim that it can tell us all the truth fit to know is an exercise in cognitive hubris (pride). Since this will be an important part of understanding the relation between theology and science, let us look into these distinctions in a bit more detail.

Reductionism, as the name implies, is the procedure of "reducing" a whole to its parts. The most well-known form of reductionism is dissection, where a whole animal is broken down into its constituent organs, muscles, nerves, and so on. When we break a whole down to its parts, we learn a great deal about what constitutes the whole. You may recall dissecting a frog in high school biology class. You learn a lot about a dead frog and, fortunately, most of that also applies to a living frog. But something is missing. Reductionism tells only part of the story, as came to be realized through such emerging sciences as ecology. We must also treat wholes as wholes and not just as the sum of their parts. Analytic reductionism, analyzing a whole by breaking it down into its constituent parts, must be complemented by synthetic holism, looking at the whole as an interconnected and interrelated unity. Reductive analysis tells only part of the story.

Synthetic holism integrates, "synthesizes," the parts together in such a way that some new trait, capacity, structure becomes possible, emerges out of the constituent parts. Emergence is key to increased complexity in structure, such as we have in biology. While dissection tells us a lot about a dead frog, we do not learn what a frog does in its native habitat or what it does to mate, eat, move, and so on. Indeed, what Kermit means when he sings, "It ain't easy bein' green." The parts make mobility, sound, habitat adaptation, and so on possible, but in themselves cannot explain the whole. Another simple example of the emergence of new properties is the "wetness" of water. Hydrogen and oxygen molecules do not have little bits of "wetness" within them that form the wetness of water when the atoms are put together to form a water molecule. Wetness is an emergent property and must be understood on its own level (molecular) rather than the constituent elements alone (atomic). It is also important to remember that the lower levels of structure do put constraints on the upper levels, while not fully explaining them. Water requires hydrogen and oxygen, not sulfur

12. John Haught, *God and the New Atheism: A Critical Response to Dawkins, Harris and Hitchens* (Louisville: Westminster John Knox, 2008), 83.

13. Richard Dawkins, *The God Delusion* (New York: Houghton Mifflin, 2006).

and carbon, for example. The existence of emergence thus requires levels of explanation if we are to approach the understanding of complex phenomena.

In his book *God and the New Atheism*, Haught uses an effective analogy in explaining the concept of levels of explanation. As one looks at the words on a page, several levels of explanation are necessary to understand what is happening. Haught observes, "For example, one explanation of the page you are reading is that a printing press has stamped ink onto white paper. Another is that the author intends to put certain ideas across. Still another explanation is that a publisher asked the author to write a critical response to the new atheism. Notice that these three layers all explain the page you are reading, but they are not competing or contradicting one another. . . . The distinct levels are noncompetitive and mutually compatible."[14] To borrow a distinction from philosophy, while the analysis of the chemical properties of ink, for example, tells us something *necessary* to know if we are to understand the process of printing, which makes reading possible, it is not *sufficient* for full understanding. We will need additional levels of explanation to sufficiently understand the process. To say that chemistry is the only level of explanation necessary is to deny the very cognitive content of the statement that says it is all that it is necessary. We need emergent, interrelated levels of explanation to explain complex phenomena, not simply as parts but as wholes. It is this process of incorporating various levels of explanation that assists us in understanding one of the most profound questions we can ask. What is the nature of being? Are physics, biology, and chemistry all that is necessary to explain life? Or does the human experience of "existing," of experiencing one's own "being," require more? Indeed, to even ask that question requires a higher level of explanation. The interaction of these levels can be illustrated by the dramatic revolution brought about by physics. Through the revised understanding of the physical world that twentieth-century physics brought (relativity and quantum theories), we now understand physical and thus human existence in a new way. It is a change from understanding being as grounded in enduring substance to discovering that it exists in dynamic relationships. It is a change in ontology, the very study of what it means "to be." This necessarily leads to reflection on what it means to exist and the nature of being itself.

3. SUBSTANTIVE VS. RELATIONAL ONTOLOGY

What does it mean to be, to exist? This question has driven philosophical and theological reflection in both East and West for millennia, in particular,

14. Haught, *God and the New Atheism*, 84–85.

reflection on the relation between permanence and change. It is also a question that often trickles down the back of our spines in the wee hours of the morning when the uncertainty, indeed the un-necessity, of our life creeps in on us. Is there something at the root of life, of existence, that is permanent and unchanging on which the flux of life, like clothes on a clothes line, is hung? Or is the flux, the change, itself fundamental, and we have only the appearance of permanence because of the regularity of change? The ancient Greeks thought the former, and contemporary science tells us the latter. The transition between these two perspectives on the nature of existence is one of the great intellectual transformations of the twentieth century, the demise of substance.

A. THE RISE OF SUBSTANCE

The classical Greek quest, especially embodied in Socrates and Plato, was to find that which is permanent in an impermanent world. Only that was worth knowing which did not change under the vicissitudes of history and human life. The only knowledge worth pursuing and possessing was unchanging, eternal knowledge, and they both found this knowledge to reside in the transcendent realm of ideas (*ideon*), which lies beyond this immanent world of change (see Plato's *Timaeus*). In one of the most famous allegories in all of classical literature, Plato in the "allegory of the cave" (book 7 of the *Republic*) describes life in this world as if one were tied to a chair in a cave and forced to view only the passing shadows reflected on the cave wall by objects passed between one's back and a fire burning further back. One would take this realm of passing shadows to be reality, unless someone (Socrates) freed the person and took them out of the cave to show them the real fire (the sun) and real objects like birds, trees, and rocks to contrast with their artificial representations in the cave. Reason could bring the soul to recall this eternal realm of truth and free oneself from the delusion of taking this impermanent, shadowy existence for reality. Indeed, Socrates was so convinced of the existence of such an eternal realm, from which the immortal soul had come and by which through rational recollection it could recall, that he was willing to die peacefully in the knowledge that while his body was perishable his soul was eternal (see Plato's "death of Socrates," the *Phaedo*). Hence the classical dualisms between soul and body as well as between the transcendently real and the immanently perishable were introduced into Western culture and eventually came to influence Christian theology.

Plato's student Aristotle had a different perspective, one that helped him become in many ways one of the fathers of empirical science in the West. Aristotle said yes, ideas are indeed the subject of knowledge, but they do not exist in some transcendent realm but rather reside in the objects of our knowledge in this world. Ideas are abstract generalizations from the particular perceptions of life. While the mind does discern these ideas, they must have some connection to physical reality in order to be discernable in the world. To ground the permanence of existence and form the basis for later perceptions, Aristotle proposed the existence of prime matter, substance (*substantia* in Latin, *ousia* in Greek) that was permanent and unchanging beneath the passing realm of changing perceptions that we experience on a daily basis, which constituted the accidents of life. Substance, as Descartes was to define it centuries later, is the unchanging subject of change, which needs nothing but itself in order to exist. It lies beneath the passing realm of changing forms that our senses perceive.

Aristotle then proposed a fourfold causal analysis by means of which to trace the movement of any physical existent from potentiality to actuality. They are

- **formal**: what something is—its "form," for example, a chair;
- **material**: what something is made of—its "matter," for example, wood, fabric, steel;
- **efficient**: how something is made—its "maker," for example, Lay-Z-Boy; and
- **final**: why something exists—its "end" or "purpose," for example, to sit or recline.

Aristotle's own example of this analysis lies in comprehending the transition of an acorn into an oak tree. An acorn is a "potential" oak tree, and by knowing its purpose, its *telos* or end, you understand what it is intended to be in existence, in its being. All the temporary forms through which it passes on the way to becoming the oak tree are its accidents, its temporary external appearances. What allows it to endure through these changes, these becomings, is the permanence of substance that underlies it. This ontological (study of being) understanding was to endure in the West for over two thousand years and greatly influence the Christian tradition's understanding of God, especially during the Middle Ages. In the twentieth century, we saw the demise of this concept of substance through various scientific discoveries, especially in physics.

B. THE DEMISE OF SUBSTANCE

Building on the discoveries of Isaac Newton in the seventeenth century, scientists in the eighteenth century (1700s), sometimes referred to as the "Age of Reason," saw physical existence as ultimately fully explainable in natural, scientific terms. Indeed, the paradigm for nature was the "machine," which, like human-made machines, did have a designer but then was fully capable of functioning on its own. (It is this philosophical perspective that gave rise to deism, which will be discussed in the next chapter.) As scientific knowledge progressed through the nineteenth century, with the discoveries of evolution, the wave nature of light, and electromagnetic radiation, for example, there was tremendous optimism that nature, the physical world, was predictable and fully knowable. It was simply a matter of cranking out all the implications of Newton's laws, and science would have a complete picture of the natural world. Physicists' work, in particular, would be done.

It is hard to imagine such a progressive confidence in the power of reason over a century later, but our hindsight includes two world wars—indeed, the "War to End All Wars" (World War I)—as well as the negative effects on nature and ourselves from the misuse (abuse?) of scientific knowledge. All of that lay ahead in the late nineteenth and early twentieth centuries, but that unbridled optimism was to come crashing down in the trenches of World War I, as the military applications of scientific knowledge brought destruction on a scale unprecedented in human history. From the tank, airplane, and submarine to machine gun and mustard gas, science had made killing on a mass scale possible. World War I taught the world that reason, as well as its scientific offspring, was not unequivocally good. Reason can serve more than one mistress, and knowledge can be turned to destructive purposes as easily as constructive ones. It was in the wake of such global destruction that scientists were also to discover that substance was not permanent, indeed did not even exist.

It is impossible to overstate the transformational impact of the discoveries in physics of the early twentieth century. Those discoveries changed not only science but an entire worldview. The very rocks beneath our feet were placed in motion. Beginning with Einstein's discovery of special relativity in 1905, leading on through his development of general relativity ten years later, to the discoveries of the quantum nature of the subatomic world by Bohr, Schrödinger, and Dirac as well as the indeterminate nature of that realm by Heisenberg, the fundamental nature of the physical world was redefined. Newton's laws, of course, still hold true for much of our daily life, but these discoveries demonstrated that when one moves to the very small or the very fast, his laws break down. It began in earnest when Einstein, in the special theory of relativity, put in doubt Newton's concept of absolute space and time. Einstein then went on to question the fundamental notion of gravity as a force, arguing that instead it is the warping of space-time by matter. Quantum theory (which will be discussed in much greater detail in chapter 7) demonstrated that there was not an unchanging subject of change at the base of physical existence but rather discrete units (quanta) of energy that were in a constant state of flux or motion. These discoveries demonstrated a seemingly contradictory nature to elementary particles. They appeared to simultaneously, and somewhat paradoxically, embody quite distinct paradigms. The famous wave/particle duality of light is the classic example. When one is measuring for waves, light appears to be a wave, but when measuring for particles, it is found to be in discrete units called photons. Paul Dirac was later to resolve this seeming paradox somewhat with the creation of quantum field theory, which understands a particle as simply the momentary collapse of a wave. But the damage to the concept of substance had been done. There was no turning back.

The very nature of the "real" and what it meant "to be" had changed. Aristotle's prime matter was found not to exist, and therefore the very nature of permanent physical existence was called into question. All the metaphors, theories, and understanding (including theology) that had been based upon foundational permanence on the ground floor (remember the House of Knowing) were also called into question. Since all thought is derived from human experience, especially of the physical world, when that understanding changes everything built upon it also changed. "Critical" realism was born. Conceptual theories, to have relevance in everyday life, must be connected to what is understood to be the "real" world. A foundational change in the understanding of that "real" world brings about profound changes in the conceptual world as well. The basic vision of reality shifted from giving priority to permanence to that of change. Substantive ontology was dead, and relational ontology was born.

C. RELATIONAL ONTOLOGY

These revolutions in physics tell us that there is nothing permanent at the base of physical existence. All is in process; all of existence is a product of constant change at the most elemental levels. What this means is that becoming is foundational to being, not the other way around. We have a becoming of continuity, not a continuity of becoming, to borrow from Alfred North Whitehead. This becoming is also intrinsically relational. Relationships constitute existence as becoming. Think of how you might introduce yourself to someone you do not know. You will tell them your name, where you are from, what you do or study, what you like or dislike. They also perceive what you look like, hair and skin color, height, gender, clothing, and so on. What are all of these descriptions? They are types of relationships, which come, collectively, to define and express who you are. They are linguistic (name, spoken language), geographical (hometown, country), intellectual (academic field), physiological (hair and skin color, height, etc.), sociological (clothing, appearance), and psychological (likes and dislikes). We are constituted by our relationships. To be is to become, and to become is to be relational. There is still continuity, identity, and uniqueness, for no two weavings of relationships are the same, but our self is emergent out of the collective diversity of relationships that constitute our existence.

But there is one critical relationship left to address. That is the relationship to God. This becoming self is related to the divine and emerges within the divine community of existence. This is what the multirelatedness of the Trinity expresses. We are related to God in multiple ways; indeed, we are in God and God is in us. It is this relationship that gives us life and, ultimately, life everlasting. We cannot do this by our own fleeting becoming, but God can through the eternal divine becoming that is more than this temporal existence. To unpack this understanding, we will need to take a closer look at what constitutes theology and, in particular, panentheism as a model for the God-world relationship. This will be introduced in the next chapter and explicated more fully in chapter 8. While we are composed of stardust and the world is moving beneath our feet, we also rest in the loving presence of God, which transcends our flux and can sustain us beyond this life of perpetual change. What reason ultimately seeks is beyond its grasp. For it seeks a completeness and hope beyond rational explanation alone. Finite reason yearns for but cannot fully grasp the infinite. Faith, while not contradicting reason, reaches ecstatically beyond it to affirm a hope and peace that passes human understanding. This is what Anselm has in mind when he says, "I believe in order that I might understand."

KEY TERMS

Analogy
Deduction
Emergence
Enlightenment
Epistemology
House of Knowing
Hypothetico-Deductive Method
Induction
Metaphor
Ontological

Reductionism
Relational Ontology
Substance
Symbol

Discussion Questions

1. Community is essential in reaching shared values and goals. In what ways do Christian (or traditionally religious) communities contribute to "consumption," "concern for others," and other important issues that face humanity today?

2. Regarding the "House of Knowing," what process takes us from the first to third floor? How is the process utilized in theology?

3. When discussing analogy and metaphor, Simmons states, "Both analogy and metaphor involve a tension or a negation in what they are attempting to communicate." How are tension and negation important when using theological metaphors?

4. How does reductionism teach us about the parts of a whole? In what ways does reductionism fall short of encompassing or describing the whole?

5. How did the "demise of substance" alter a worldview about humanity? In what ways did this worldview fall short of its expectations?

3

Theology

Si comprehendis, non est Deus
"If you have understood, it is not God."
—AUGUSTINE (SERMON 117.5)[1]

From the beginning of the Enlightenment (c. 1648), with its emphasis on reason alone, through the middle of the twentieth century, it became common to speak of a separation between fact and value, science and religion, nature and history. Nature, as object, had no intrinsic development but was rather to be understood through scientific analysis in a value-free inquiry, where both human and religious purposes were considered to be irrelevant.[2] History, however, was the realm of human purpose and religious value in which civilizations rose and fell, charting their course in dominating an impersonal world. While there are many scholars today who still affirm such a separation, I have come to understand it as a false duality, and I invite you to reflect with me on this observation.

1. CONTEMPORARY SPIRITUAL CRISIS

A. SEPARATION OF FACT FROM VALUE

Our time is one of systemic change, in which old explanations and certainties have given way to questions and uncertainty. How we come to know and

---

1. QUOTED IN Elizabeth A. Johnson, *QUEST FOR THE LIVING GOD* (New York: Continuum, 2008), 13. ALSO CITED IN Douglas John Hall, "Against Religion," *THE CHRISTIAN CENTURY*, January 11, 2011, 31.

2. See the discussion of Richard Rorty on "foundationalism" and Parker Palmer on "objectivism" in Mark Schwehn, *Exiles from Eden* (New York: Oxford University Press, 1993), ch. 2; and also works by Reuther, McFague and Gilkey in the bibliography.

understand something as well as the way this knowledge should be used cry out to be reconnected. Parker Palmer observes that epistemologies (ways of knowing) have moral trajectories; ways of knowing are not morally neutral but morally directive.[3] Ways of knowing necessarily include ways of valuing, so a complete separation of fact and value is not possible. The challenge is to retain the achievements of objective reflection without perpetuating its limitations. This also relates to levels of explanation (discussed earlier) and the process of interpretation. *All facts are value laden.* Facts are contextual truths that arise from the processing of raw data through paradigms and models of interpretation.[4] There is an interpretive (hermeneutical) arc between data and fact that transforms meaningless data into meaningful fact.

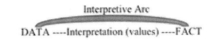

Interpretive Arc

DATA ----Interpretation (values) ----FACT

Figure 2.

This process of interpretation contains values, commitments, definitions, and purposes that become laden in the data as they are transformed into fact. *There is no such thing as an uninterpreted fact.* Interpretation creates facts in the first place. Totally value-free inquiry is not possible. The task, then, is to be self-consciously aware of the values implicit in one's interpretive process and not pretend they are absent. This is one of the biggest moves from a modern to a postmodern understanding of meaning and knowledge.

While all knowledge is perspectival, not all perspective is knowledge. We can adjudicate truth claims at the same time that we acknowledge their contextual character.[5] Religion requires a view of the world for its expression, and science requires values for the consideration of its applications. History would not exist without nature, and nature itself has a history. Humanity has always connected history to nature through technology and its impact on the surrounding environment. Many civilizations have fallen because of the environmental destruction they reeked on their supporting nature.[6]

3. Referred to in Schwehn, *Exiles*, 25.

4. See Ian Barbour, *Myths, Models and Paradigms: A Comparative Study in Science and Religion* (New York: Harper & Row, 1974); as well as Barbour, "Models and Paradigms," ch. 5 in *Religion and Science: Historical and Contemporary Issues* (San Francisco: HarperSanFrancisco, 1997), 106–136.

5. See Gregg Muilenberg, "An Aristotelian Twist to Faith and Reason," *Intersections* (Summer, 1997): 8.

Technology is a prime example of the intentional connecting of fact and value. The values intrinsic in scientific research are given embodied expression through technological application.[7] Today we see this with a clarity that is unprecedented in human reflection, and with it comes an increased responsibility to properly steward such a relation, in effect, to reconnect fact and value.

B. SPIRITUAL STRUGGLE

In such a context, it is important to point out that a growing number of scholars from various fields consider the present social and ecological crises of Western culture to be fundamentally a spiritual and not a material struggle. In our time, the question of God has been transmuted into the question of meaning, and the search for meaning is a spiritual one. The present quest for spiritual direction is real, with nothing less than human cultural survival at stake. Books ranging from Robert Bellah's *Habits of the Heart*[8] and Cornel West's *Race Matters*[9] to former Vice President Al Gore's, *Earth in the Balance* and *An Inconvenient Truth*[10] all affirm the spiritual and moral character of our contemporary crises. Former Vice President Gore observes, "The more deeply I search for the roots of the global environmental crisis, the more I am convinced that it is an outer manifestation of an inner crisis that is, for lack of a better word, spiritual. . . . But what other word describes the collection of values and assumptions that determine our basic understanding of how we fit into the universe?"[11] In other words, how do we formulate a new worldview that assists us in addressing the common global problems of our age?

In their coauthored book, *The New Universe and the Human Future: How a Shared Cosmology Could Transform the World*, Nancy Abrams and Joel Primack point out the absence of a common worldview. They observe, "We're divided on the most fundamental question of any society: what universe are we living in? With no consensus on this question and no way even to think constructively

6. See Albert Gore, "Climate and Civilization: A Short History," ch. 3 in *Earth in the Balance: Ecology and the Human Spirit* (New York: Houghton Mifflin, 1992), 56–80. Also Albert Gore, *An Inconvenient Truth* (New York: Rodale, 2006).

7. See Frederick Ferre, *Hellfire and Lightening Rods: Liberating Science, Technology and Religion* (Maryknoll, NY: Orbis, 1994).

8. Robert Bellah et al. *Habits of the Heart: Individualism and Commitment in American Life* (Berkeley: University of California Press, 1985).

9. Cornel West, *Race Matters* (Boston: Beacon, 1993).

10. Gore, *Earth in the Balance*.

11. Ibid., 12.

about how we humans might fit into the big picture, we have no big picture. Without a big picture we are very small people."[12] They further state, "Our goal is to show how our society might begin to conquer seemingly intractable global problems by filling the gaping hole in our thinking, applying these new ideas, and eventually becoming a new global society with a common origin story."[13] What they hope is that the current scientific cosmological view can come to form a new metanarrative for our time that can transcend national, racial, and religious divides so that we can work together to form a global society capable of addressing our common global crises. It is a laudable goal, and they recognize the spiritual character such a metanarrative must have if it is to be effective. They also affirm the value of religious expression if it can become scientifically informed. They state, "If religions hold tightly to literal understandings of scriptures, they cannot serve the cause of world peace or the spiritual needs of an emerging global civilization. But if enlightened religions are willing and able to expand to encompass new knowledge, then there is a tremendous role for them, and they can be an irreplaceable part of the long-term solution."[14] In other words, the world's religions and religious faith can be part of the problem or part of the solution to our common global problems. In part 3 of this text we will turn to the construction of a scientifically informed theology of the Trinity. For now, however, let us turn to investigate the nature and methods of theology.

2. DEFINITION AND SOURCES OF THEOLOGY

If faith is about what concerns us ultimately and there is also a need to engage the world around us, which there inevitably is, then we must also reflect on that faith within us. We must "give reasons for the hope within us" as the Bible enjoins (1 Pet. 3:15), and that reflection on faith is what we call theology.

A. DEFINITION

The word *theology* refers to communication and reflection about God. To move to a bit more fully developed definition of theology, one could say, following Joseph Sittler, that "theology is the proposing of relations between the testimony of a community of faith and the life of that community in nature and history."[15] This definition shows that theology is a dynamic, indeed

---

12. Nancy Ellen Abrams and Joel R. Primack, *The New Universe and the Human Future: How a Shared Cosmology Could Transform the World* (New Haven: Yale University Press, 2011), xii.

13. Ibid., xv.

14. Ibid., 206.

dialectical, enterprise moving between the twin commitments of faith and life. If theology is doing its job properly, it should help to connect the faith witness (testimony) of a community with the wider context in which that community resides (life). *Testimony* in this definition is understood to include not only sacred Scripture but also creeds and confessions that might arise within the community of faith. I particularly like the fact that life is understood to include not only nature (what happens to the community by acts other than human cause, e.g., earthquakes, floods) but also history, which includes human action from Crusades to the founding of hospitals and denominations. Theology works in service to a community of faith and seeks to explicate the faith of the community in a coherent and intelligible way in light of the community's context. This understanding of theology would be true of all communities of faith that are theistic. So this broader definition applies not only to Christianity but also to the "Abrahamic faiths" of Judaism and Islam, as well as theistic Hinduism, for example.

Theology is thus always contextual. It draws on the ideas and understandings of a particular period in human history just as it responds to the events of that period. In the early church, for example, Greek philosophical categories were some of the most sophisticated explanations available at that time. Early Christianity was heavily influenced by Greek understandings of truth, being, perfection, and deity. It was also limited by them, as we shall detail later in this chapter. So theology is dynamic and contextual; it also has multiple sources and occurs in different forms relative to those sources.

B. SOURCES

Since this is a book on the Christian understanding of the Trinity, I will primarily focus on Christian sources and forms. As Bradley Hanson summarizes in his book *Introduction to Christian Theology*, there are basically five sources to Christian theology: revelation, Scripture, tradition, reason, and experience.[16]

Revelation: This is the disclosure of God in either the natural world of creation, which is general revelation, or in specific acts in history such as the exodus or the incarnation, which constitute what is called special revelation.

Scripture: Revelation coming from God and recorded in written form constitutes special revelation in the form of Scripture, which, while divinely

---

15. Joseph Sittler, *Essays on Nature and Grace* (Minneapolis: Fortress Press, 1972), 5.

16. Bradley Hanson, "Faith and Theology," ch. 1 in *Introduction to Christian Theology* (Minneapolis: Fortress Press, 1997), 1–18.

inspired, is itself the record of that revelation as it is recorded and preserved within the community of faith. Careful reflection on Scripture gives rise to *biblical theology*.

Tradition: Tradition is the history of the experience of a community of faith as it attempts to reflect and faithfully witness to the formative revelation of its community. Tradition includes creeds, doctrines, confessions of faith, and regular rituals and practice. Reflection on history and doctrine give rise to *historical theology* and *doctrinal theology* respectively.

Reason: It is understood that the capacity of human reason is a gift from God and is to be fully employed in reflection on the faith. Some have even argued that it is the image of God (*imago Dei*) within the human, the reflection of the Creator in the creation. It must also be affirmed that while reason is employed in theology, God can never be fully encapsulated in any human structure, even those of thought. That is the point of Augustine's comment at the beginning of this chapter. All theology must be undertaken with a great deal of humility and awareness of the impossibility of ever fully capturing the reality of God. The mystery of God always transcends human conceptualization. This will become especially apparent as we move to the emergence of the doctrine of the Trinity in the next chapter. Careful use of reason and the meaning of concepts gives rise to *philosophical theology*.

Experience: This includes the wider sociohistorical context within which theological reflection is conducted, as well as the relevance of theological concepts to the reality of lived human life. Theology should connect with the life of the individual and the community and should be of help in expressing the faith through its connection to their experience. If there is no connection, there is no relevance. Reflection on human experience in light of faith leads to the need for new understandings and formulations, and this gives rise to *constructive theology*. Most of the material in part 3 of this book is an exercise in constructive theology.

3. Ground Rules for Theology

These sources then lead to several ground rules for doing theology, which will inform the nature of theological method and need to be kept in mind whenever one is engaging in reflection on the divine. Elizabeth Johnson helpfully indicates three ground rules for theology.

A. INEFFABLE MYSTERY

God is ultimately beyond human experience and reflection, and this must always be kept in mind. Johnson observes, "The first and most basic prescript is this: the reality of the living God is an ineffable mystery beyond all telling. The infinitely creating, redeeming, and indwelling Holy One is so far beyond the world and so deeply within the world as to be literally incomprehensible."[17] This should not be seen as a source for despair but rather as a source for inspiration and hope. God is greater than our constructions of God, and only because of this can God truly be God. Johnson recounts the story of Augustine, bishop of Hippo in North Africa (d. 430 CE), who was one of the first major formulators of the doctrine of the Trinity in the West. One day, as he was walking along the Mediterranean shore contemplating the mystery of the Trinity, he saw a small child running back and forth with a bucket and dumping sea water into a hole in the sand. He naturally asked, "What are you doing?," to which the child replied that he was "trying to put the sea into my hole." Naturally the adult response was, "You can't do that; it won't fit." Johnson continues, "The child, who turned out to be an angel in disguise, replied, 'Neither can you put the mystery of the Trinity into your mind; it won't fit.' Thus was passed on the wisdom of the ages to one of the keenest minds in the Christian tradition."[18] As we venture further into reflection on the Trinity, we must keep this story in mind. God is always more than we can conceive, and even more than we can't even conceive.

B. NO LITERAL EXPRESSION

Because of this ineffability, no finite expression or formulation is ever going to be adequate, much less literally descriptive. Here the role of symbols, analogy, and metaphor, discussed in the previous chapter, becomes important. Employing the image of the House of Knowing, our discussion of God, including God's attributes and actions, are always going to be subject to the limitation of human experience. It is, if you will, the finite trying to describe the infinite, so there will always be an impenetrable gap in description and understanding. The danger comes when we forget this and begin to treat our formulations as if they were truly accurate. What we are doing, in effect, is creating linguistic or conceptual idols, which are as destructive to faith as any physical representation that might be made. True, there are disclosures of the divine in revelation that are beyond human construction, but they are always

17. Johnson, *Quest*, 17.
18. Ibid.

received and embodied by a finite human vessel. Whenever we begin to trust our own constructions too fully, idolatry always lies close at hand. Something can be true and meaningful without literally being a fact.

C. Necessity of Many Names

The inability of language to refer directly to God leads finally to the insight that humans, in the rich diversity of human history, culture, and experience, have given God many names, no one of which is exhaustive. We have, of course, the Hebrew Tetragrammaton (meaning four letters), YHWH, "I AM WHO I AM," revealed to Moses from the burning bush (Exod. 3:14) as well as of course the person "Jesus" from the incarnation in the New Testament. We also have rich female images of power such as those that come from the Wisdom/Sophia tradition as well as, one might add, Allah. The names of God speak with power and clarity at specific times in human history, but there are many names that no longer speak with that same power, for example, Zeus, Apollo, Athena. One thing we will have to keep in mind in doing theological reflection is that names come and go, as well as particular conceptual expressions. When we realize that this has and continues to happen, we also begin to realize the constructed nature of the names and that, as with the other two ground rules, we must never take them too literally in relation to the ineffable mystery of the divine.

4. Theological Method

With these ground rules in mind, we can now return to the definition of theology given earlier in this chapter and reflect briefly on what constitutes theological method, especially the method employed in this text.

A. Natural vs. Revealed Theology

As was mentioned in the description of revelation, there are two basic types, each of which can ground a form of theology. General revelation, which is the disclosure of God in creation, gives rise to rational reflection on the disclosure of God in nature, which is called *natural theology*. Thomas Aquinas, in the Middle Ages (c. 1250 CE) is perhaps the most famous theologian to employ natural theology in his reflection on nature and the so-called arguments for the existence of God. Natural theology, perhaps, can say something about the existence of God—for example, that God exists—but it cannot say anything about who God is, much less God's disposition toward the world or the sinner within it.

Reflection on the other source of revelation, special or specific revelation in history, produces what is called *revealed theology*, which does address the disposition of God and to some extent the self-disclosed character of the divine. The main sources for revealed theology are Scripture and tradition, not nature. A further distinction must also be made between natural theology and a theology of nature. Natural theology is the attempt to *reason* to the existence of God through reflection on nature, while a theology of nature is the attempt to understand the presence or activity of God *within* nature. In this text, I will draw on a theology of nature but not attempt to do natural theology. Also, in Christian theology, the doctrine of the Trinity is drawn from Scripture and tradition, not from reasoned reflection on nature, so the argument of this text is a form of constructive, revealed theology, which attempts to understand the nature of the Trinity in relation to the current understanding of the natural world given in the natural sciences. This approach, then, leads to a specific form of theological method.

B. METHOD OF CORRELATION

In his *Systematic Theology*, Paul Tillich employs what he calls a "method of correlation."[19] He was particularly concerned that theology respond to the real questions people were asking, not just running off on their own merry, disconnected (and irrelevant) way. He focused, therefore, on the problems of human existence, particularly the issues of finitude and mortality, expressed in what is known as existential theology. He also thought philosophy expressed the most careful reflection on human existence and so believed philosophy must raise the questions for theology to address. The "method of correlation," then involved, correlating philosophical questions and theological answers in what he called the theological circle. It is really more of an ellipse, for two mutually interacting foci generate an ellipse and not a circle in geometry. So I will refer to the theological ellipse in my reflections.

In the sixty years since Tillich first proposed this method, many new schools of theology have developed that address significant centers of human suffering or need as well as the desire for coherent connection to the wider world. It is the coherent connection of faith to the wider world understood by the natural sciences that is the main focus of this book. A modified form of the method of correlation will be employed in this text, where the primary dialectic is between theology and science in creative mutual interaction.[20] The method of correlation will be used to generate a constructive theological formulation

19. Paul Tillich, *Systematic Theology* (Chicago: University of Chicago Press, 1973), 1:61.

of the relationship between the doctrine of the Trinity and concepts in contemporary quantum theory in physics. Theology is dynamic and dialectical (relational), as well as being an exercise in the use of the analogical/metaphorical imagination. As an exercise of the imagination, constructive theology is a form of theory construction similar to other forms of human knowing. Theology will never be complete, for divine reality always transcends human knowing and will remain hidden from its grasp. That is why theology is an exercise in faith reflection (*fides quaerens intellectum*, "faith seeking understanding," see chapter 2) undertaken with humility and in service to a community of faith.

5. Ways of Relating God and the World

Since this text involves correlation between theology and science, which involves some understanding of the relation of God and the world, it will be helpful to briefly address the major ways this relationship has been articulated in the West. Since the days of Aristotle's *Logic*, it has been argued that two objects, concepts, or realities can have three possible relationships: that of *identity*, *difference*, or some *combination* of the two.

A. Identity: Pantheism

In a relationship of identity, *a* equals *b*; that is to say, the two are the same, and what can be said about one can be said about the other. They are indistinguishable. In regard to the God–world relationship, the identity relation results in *pantheism*, which means all (pan) is God (theism). This theological expression is found particularly in East Indian thought, where God, in one of many millions of expressions, is believed to fully dwell in the natural world. This position stresses *immanence*, which refers to the nearness or closeness of God. It does not, however, emphasize *transcendence*, the beyondness of God. That is the hallmark of the second form of relationship.

B. Difference: Theism/Deism

The opposite of identity is difference, and this is indicated in certain expressions of *theism*, particularly *Deism*. A relation of difference stresses the otherness of the divine, its beyondness, and as such emphasizes transcendence. *A* does not equal *b*, indeed, has no connection with *b*. Deism, the complete separation

20. See ch. 7, and Robert John Russell, "Eschatology and Physical Cosmology: A Preliminary Reflection," in *The Far-Future Universe: Eschatology from a Cosmic Perspective*, ed. George F. R. Ellis (Philadelphia: Templeton Foundation Press, 2002), 266–315.

of God and the world, emerged during the Enlightenment of the eighteenth century, where, with a strong emphasis on rational observation and explanation, as found in the emerging natural sciences, it was believed that God was totally absent from the world. Perhaps God started the process of nature off with an originating creation—natural laws do seem to indicate a natural Lawgiver—but from then on let the world go on alone. Hence the image of the divine watchmaker, according to which God put the pieces together with purpose in mind but then let the watch/world run on its own. No supernatural intervention was to be allowed to mess up the natural processes. One was to conduct one's life and analysis of the world *etsi Deus, non daretur*, "as if God did not exist." This position stresses transcendence to the point of irrelevance. Modern theism, which will be critiqued in the next section, does not go as far as deism, but it too produces a model of God that is of little use in the contemporary worldview.

C. COMBINATION: PANENTHEISM

The final option for relationship is that of combination, where *a* includes but is greater than *b*. This position is known as *panentheism*, which means that God is in the world (immanent) but more than the world (transcendent). One could also say that the world exists in God (immanence), so God is always in the world but goes beyond the world (transcendence). It is not pantheism precisely because it stresses that God is more than can be found in the natural world, no matter how inclusive one makes that understanding. This position allows for both the intimate presence of God in the world while at the same time acknowledging that God is more than the world in the ultimate unknowable mystery of the divine referred to earlier. Because it holds the most significant promise for understanding the presence and transcendence of the divine in relation to the Trinity as well as to the natural sciences, it is this position that will be argued for in the present text. Such a position allows for divine presence without supernatural intervention in the natural world. God works in, with, and under the material forms of nature in a sacramental presence that providentially guides but does not intervene in natural processes. This position, known as noninterventionist objective divine action (NIODA), will be explained later, in chapter 8. In the meantime, however, we turn to a critique of what is probably the most prevalent and yet unsatisfactory model of God present in contemporary American society, modern theism.

6. Critique of Modern Theism

In his book *The God Delusion*, Richard Dawkins, despite his intentions, has perhaps done contemporary theology a great service. Dawkins critiques the understanding of an all-powerful, transcendent God who miraculously intervenes in the natural world and is despotically and somewhat obsessively concerned with adoration and obedience. This model is of a monarch at the pinnacle of power and being often depicted as the great, old, white man with a beard up in the sky, typified by Michelangelo's depiction of God on the ceiling of the Sistine Chapel. This is the God created by the modern world, not the biblical world, and is indeed the God who is "dead" in postmodern society. What does this mean?

Elizabeth Johnson concisely summarizes the problems with modern theism and provides a helpful, shorthand critique, which will be drawn on here.[21] She observes that this concept of God is a construction of the seventeenth-eighteenth-century Enlightenment, which emphasized reason and the powers of inference as found in the emerging natural sciences. Instead of drawing on Scripture, sacramental worship, and the theological tradition as in the past, theologians were drawn into this rationalistic process. She observes,

> Now, however, to counter the Enlightenment's criticisms, they [theologians] switched to the same playing field as their opponent. Leaving behind Christian sources and adopting philosophical methods of thinking that sought objective knowledge about the universe on a rational basis, they set out to shape "clear and distinct ideas" about the divine. Starting with the natural world, they reasoned to the existence of God using a process of inference, thereby constructing a theology where God appears as the highest component in an intellectual system. This all but assured that while God is a powerful individual above other powers in the world, he remains a member of the larger household of reality. His attributes are deduced by a reasoning process that contrasts what is infinite with the limitations of the finite. . . . In a fascinating way it compromises both the transcendence and immanence of God as honed in classical Christian theology.[22]

God then becomes a part of the intellectual system rather than remaining over and above it. This eventually leads to God being further and further removed

---

21. Johnson, *Quest*, 14–17.
22. Ibid., 15.

from relationship with the world, to the point where God is no longer engaged in the world but despotically manages it on high. Certainly, there are parts of Scripture that might be used to portray such a deity (Dawkins goes to great pains to ferret them all out!), but this is not the dominant representation of God in Scripture and must be supplemented by the many other images in both text and tradition. *If God is only a part of the system, even the biggest part, God cannot be the savior of the system nor the ground for hope beyond it.* It is, however, this drive for rational, scientific understanding of the world based on objective, reductive analysis that came to form the basis for what has been called the modern Western worldview. Overemphasis on this method of understanding, to the denial of other levels of explanation, has resulted in the separation of fact from value and set the stage for our contemporary spiritual crisis.

By contrast, the scholarly discussion of the relationship between religion and science has been pursuing a scientifically informed theological expression for more than fifty years. The present work is intended as a further contribution to that endeavor, as it attempts to address one of the most central, if often misunderstood, doctrines of the Christian tradition, the Trinity. The Trinity attempts to affirm the mystery of God on the one hand while simultaneously affirming the accessibility and relatedness of God to humanity and the creation on the other. These dual affirmations can be more cogently maintained in light of the understanding of the physical world and its entangled nature coming out of contemporary quantum physics. In other words, this book is an attempt to allow contemporary scientific thinking to inform theological reflection in such a way that a more accessible global society might become possible. We all have a responsible role to play in addressing our contemporary global crises, and hopefully the present reflection will contribute something to that endeavor.

Before we turn to the metaphorical appropriation of several key concepts in quantum physics for reflection on the Trinity in part 3, we must address the development of the doctrine itself in part 2 in order to see what this can teach us about the historical and constructive theological formulation of Christian experience.

KEY TERMS

Biblical Theology
Constructive Theology
Deism
Hermeneutics
Historical Theology

Immanence
Interpretive Arc
Method of Correlation
Modern Theism
Philosophical Theology
Natural Theology
Pantheism
Panentheism
Polytheism
Revealed Theology
Theism
Transcendence

DISCUSSION QUESTIONS

1. Summarize the five sources and forms of theology. Do some seem to carry more significance in the Christian tradition than others? Why or why not?

2. In what way is pantheism different from panentheism? How does the Christian Trinity represent a panentheistic understanding of God?

3. Consider analogies and metaphors used to describe God. In what ways are they helpful in the Christian tradition, and in what ways might they risk misinterpretation or literalism?

4. How does the separation of fact and value lead to a spiritual crisis? Do you think this is a significant issue? Why or why not?

5. Why is the "search for meaning" a spiritual one? How is this search important on a global scale?

PART II

Trinitarian Development

4

Bible to Nicaea

The grace of our Lord Jesus Christ, the
love of God, and the fellowship of the Holy
Spirit be with you all.

—St. Paul (2 Cor. 13:13)

The doctrine of the Trinity uniquely expresses God's accessibility to all of creation, humanity in particular. Encountering Jesus as the Messiah, the anointed one of God, early Christians also experienced the creative and sustaining activity of God. Reflection on the Trinity moved from three to one, the early Christian community giving priority to the diversity of their spiritual experience. Over centuries of reflection, as theologians attempted to coherently place this threefold Christian experience of the divine somewhere between the pluralistic polytheism of the Greco-Roman world and the singular monotheism of the Jewish tradition, this diversity crystallized into the doctrine of the Trinity. Early Christians developed a paradoxical language that allowed them to speak of the divine as both transcendent and immanent at the same time. In effect, early Christians experienced *pluralistic monotheism*, multiple relatedness to the singular God. Elizabeth Johnson states,

> In shorthand, we might say that they [New Testament Christians] experienced the saving God in a threefold way as beyond them, with them, and within them, that is, as utterly transcendent, as present historically in the person of Jesus, and as present in the Spirit within their community. These were all encounters with only one God. Accordingly, they began to talk about God in this threefold

pattern: "the grace of our Lord Jesus Christ, the love of God, and the fellowship of the Holy Spirit be with you all."[1]

The experience of the divine in the biblical witness connects both the beyond and the intimate.[2] The early community of faith embraced a complex idea of the transcendence of God, the "beyond"; the immanence of Christ, and the abiding presence of the Spirit, the "intimate." The Christian encounter with God thus began in threeness and moved toward oneness. The Trinity was neither a logical puzzle nor a philosophical assertion but rather a dynamic engagement with the living God in all aspects of life.

Understanding God as an intrinsically differentiated union, early believers started with multiple intimate vantage points of observation as they gazed toward the far-off infinity of the divine. The Trinity gave them perspective on the mystery of God and highlighted the ultimate inadequacy of all human thought to contain it. William Placher observes,

> Traditional trinitarian terminology does not embody some appropriate theory of how the Trinity fits together; rather, the terms were developed to preserve the mystery of a God we cannot understand. So why try to talk about the Trinity at all? It is hard to answer that question if we begin with one God and ask why we should think of that God as three. But that is not the logic of trinitarian thought. Rather, Christians begin with three, and the doctrine of the Trinity is the explanation of their oneness.[3]

The concept of the "Trinity" was an expression of heartfelt faith.

As the early Christian community sought to articulate its experience of God, it eventually developed a scriptural canon that it believed was true to the witness of such a God in history. As time went on, Christians employed this canon in their reflection on the Trinity. As Ted Peters observes in *God as Trinity*, "The task of Trinitarian theology is to explicate the biblical symbols in such a way as to gain an increasingly adequate set of ideas for conceiving

1. Elizabeth Johnson, *The Quest for the Living God* (New York: Continuum, 2008), 204.

2. Ted Peters, *God as Trinity: Relationality and Temporality in Divine Life* (Louisville: Westminster John Knox, 1993), 18–20. This text provides an excellent overview of the issues in the resurgence of theological interest in the Trinity as well as a brief overview of a number of major contributors to the discussion.

3. William Placher, "Believing in the Triune God," *Christian Century*, April 17, 2007, 30, excerpted from his book *The Triune God: An Essay in Postliberal Theology* (Louisville: Westminster John Knox, 2007), 136.

of God's creative and redemptive work. . . . . The notion of one being in three persons is simply a conceptual device for trying to understand the drama of salvation that is taking place in Jesus Christ."[4] As a result, the roots of the idea of God as Trinity most profoundly developed out of biblical witness. It is the purpose of this chapter to explore that biblical witness and the early developments following from it. Later chapters in part 2 will selectively follow this development into our own time.

1. ROOTS OF TRINITARIAN THOUGHT: BIBLICAL WITNESS

A. HEBREW SCRIPTURES (OLD TESTAMENT)

In his book *The Tripersonal God*, Gerald O' Collins indicates that there are three images for God in the Hebrew Scriptures (Old Testament) that are germane to the discussion of the Trinity: God as Father, divine Wisdom and Word, and the Spirit of God.[5] However, before we can turn to these images, we must first examine the image of the name of God given to Moses out of the burning bush (Exod. 3:14, 6:6–8: YHWH—a verb meaning "I am what I am." Or "I will be what I will be").

Yahweh: This four-letter personal name YHWH (Yahweh, distinguished in English Bibles as "Lord") occurs 6,800 times in the Old Testament.[6] Known as the Tetragrammaton (meaning four letters),[7] this name, which is the name of the God of Israel, is considered by many Jews to be so holy that it should not be uttered out loud. Some believe the reason for this has to do with caution surrounding the commandment, "You shall not take the name of the LORD in vain" (Exod. 20:7 NRSV). Various other terms such as *El Shaddai* ("God," "the one of the mountains," "Almighty God" in some translations), *Elohim* ("divine God"), and *Adonai* (*Kyrios* in Greek, "Lord" in English) were spoken instead. Indeed, in some of the Dead Sea Scrolls, YHWH was considered to be too holy to even be written and was replaced with four dots (. . . .). So at the beginning of our discussion of the biblical sources for the Trinity, we see first of all that God is revealed through a holy personal name.[8] All other names or images of God

4. Peters, *God as Trinity*, 70.

5. Gerald O'Collins, *The Tripersonal God: Understanding and Interpreting the Trinity* (Mahwah, NJ: Paulist, 1999), 12.

6. Ibid., 13.

7. See *Wikipedia*, s.v. "Tetragrammaton," last modified October 11, 2013, http://en.wikipedia.org/wiki/Tetragrammaton, for more details and history.

8. O'Collins, *Tripersonal*, ch. 1, "The Scriptural Roots," 11–84.

reflect on the divine squarely with human experience and in human history while at the same time stressing divine mystery. Hebrew witness of grappling with the name of the divine such as in Exodus 3 forms the foundation for all later biblical reflection. The tension between the "beyond and the intimate" is thus foundational in all reflection on God in both Judaism and Christianity.

This tension between the beyond and the intimate is why metaphor and symbol become so important in theological expression. As mentioned in chapter 2, metaphor has an "is, is not" character to it that illuminates at the same time that it makes us aware of the incompleteness of the illumination. The dialectical tension built into the very nature of metaphor helps keep us mindful of the limitation of human language as well as humble in the presence of the divine we seek to understand. When we turn to the other biblical images for the Trinity, we must acknowledge both their status as metaphors and that they capture something true and resonate within religious experience.[9] This is certainly true of the heavily used metaphor of "Father."

Father: God is addressed as "Father" a little more than twenty times in the Old Testament.[10] Within this image are many nuanced meanings of the word. The people of Israel were reminded who their true parent was when they were tempted to stray to other deities (Deut. 32:6). Also the royal psalms conveyed Davidic kingship as a divine choice and legitimation (Ps. 2:7). Gerald O'Collins notes, "The Davidic king will address God as *Father*, the God whose strong fidelity to his covenanted love allows God to be also named as *Rock of salvation*"[11] (Ps. 89:26-29). This imagery will, of course, be continued in the New Testament, where Jesus is portrayed as being from the "house and lineage of David." This image of personal relationship leads to other divine images that are central in the Hebrew Scriptures, that of Wisdom, Word, and Spirit. Each of these becomes a personified expression of divine activity. They are not to be seen as independent personifications but rather more as personal characteristics of the divine. This is especially true for the personification of Divine Wisdom.

Wisdom: Hokmah (*Sophia* in Greek) occurs 318 times in the Old Testament in one form or another (noun, verb, or adjective), especially in what is referred

---

9. See ch. 2 in this volume as well as Johnson, *Quest*, ch. 1, "Ancient Story: New Chapter," 7–24; and Sallie McFague, *Metaphorical Theology: Models of God in Religious Language* (Minneapolis: Fortress Press, 1982), ch. 2, "Metaphor, Parable and Scripture," 31–66.

10. O'Collins, *Tripersonal*, 14. O'Collins works through each of the biblical images in a very thorough and careful way, so there is no need to do that in the present text, see ch. 1, "Scriptural Roots," 11–84.

11. Ibid., 17 (italics original).

to as the "Wisdom literature" (Job, Proverbs, Ecclesiastes, Sirach, and Wisdom). Characteristics or attributes of the divine, especially Wisdom, are often personified, indicating how or in what manner the Wisdom of God finds expression in the world. Wisdom will come to be seen as divine gift that works in mysterious, inaccessible ways. O'Collins states, "Personified Wisdom or Sophia becomes increasingly related to the divine work of creation, providence, and salvation and grows in dignity and power along with OT sapiential thinking. Within a monotheistic faith, Wisdom takes on functions and attributes of YHWH, and within a strongly patriarchal religion, Wisdom emerges in a feminine way."[12] These last two points are especially important for our later reflection on the Trinity. Not only do they specify several of the ways in which the activity of God finds expression in the experience of the community of faith, but the concept of Wisdom/Sophia also enfranchises the feminine dimension of human life as a legitimate expression of divine activity. The book of Wisdom clarifies this point in a classic passage, which reads, "She [Sophia] is a breath of the power of God and a pure emanation of the glory of the Almighty: therefore nothing defiled gains entrance into her. For she is a reflection of eternal light, a spotless mirror of the working God, and an image of his goodness" (Wis. 25–26). Divine Sophia is active in the life of creation, liberation, and the life of faith. She is a major expression of divine presence in reflection on biblical sources for the Trinity. Wisdom also prepares the way for reflection on the Word and the Spirit.

Word: While many are familiar with the understanding of the use of *Logos* ("Word") in the New Testament from the Gospel of John, there is an active sense of the Word in the Hebrew tradition as well. Like Wisdom, the Word is with God from the beginning and is active in creation, "and God said, 'let there be . . .'" (Gen. 1:1—2:4). O'Collins observes, "At times, the OT scriptures set *word* in parallelism with *spirit* or *breath* as instruments of creation: 'The Word of the Lord created the heavens; all the host of heaven was formed by the Breath of his mouth.' (Ps. 33:6)."[13] He concludes, "In brief, *word* matches *wisdom* as a way of expressing God's creative, revelatory, and salvific activity."[14] Spirit also matches wisdom in the process of creation.

Spirit: The Spirit (*ruach* in Hebrew, *pneuma* in Greek) is often associated with wind and breath. Indeed, the English "spirit" comes from the Latin *spiritus*,

---

12. Ibid., 24.
13. Ibid., 31 (italics original).
14. Ibid. (italics original).

which means breath. The word implies an animating power that moves and enlivens but that is not visible and is only detectable by its effects. In the Hebrew tradition, *ruach* is that which moves over the face of the waters in creation (Gen. 1:2) and enlivens prophets, enabling them to speak God's word (Isa. 61:1; Ezek. 2:1-2). The Spirit moves "where it wills" and is associated with the expression of God's will and activity in the world. The Spirit is the ongoing presence of God in the creation. As such, *ruach* is frequently associated with Wisdom and Word as almost equivalent expressions for God's creative, redeeming, and revealing activity in the world. The Jewish Scriptures bear witness to the activity of God in the world and grounded the faith tradition of the earliest Christians. To the extent that they are denigrated, one also denigrates the faith of the historical Jesus and the roots of the Christian faith. It is out of the Jewish faith tradition that Christianity was born, and without its witness to God's activity in the world and its messianic expectation, the Christian faith would not have arisen. It is precisely to this emergence we now turn, as we address the scriptural bases for the understanding of the Trinity found in the New Testament.

B. CHRISTIAN SCRIPTURES (NEW TESTAMENT)

Where in the New Testament does the idea of the Trinity come from? Or where did the early church writers look in the New Testament for inspiration in developing the idea of the Trinity? The goal in this section is not to be exhaustive of all treatments but rather illustrative of the types of experiences and witness that provide a basis from which to reflect on the Triune activity of God. The development of the Trinity comes out of new experiences over time, so historically speaking, each age adapts the image for its needs, building on the experiences of those who have gone before. Two things are at stake. One is a steady element of the tradition, and the second is the unique development of that tradition over time and in particular places. These are not "proof texts" but rather illuminating passages from the life of the early community of faith in their encounter with the living God.

In a very helpful summary, William Placher concisely lists several of the major Trinitarian references in the New Testament. He observes,

New Testament writers sometimes seemingly went out of their way to employ language that at least included three elements. The most explicit passages are the following:

1. The baptismal formula at the end of Matthew: "Go therefore and make disciples of all nations, baptizing them in the name of the Father and of the Son and of the Holy Spirit" (Matt. 28:19).

2. Paul's benediction at the end of 2 Corinthians: "The grace of the Lord Jesus Christ, the love of God, and the communion of the Holy Spirit be with all of you" (2 Cor. 13:13).

3. Paul's contrast of variety and oneness in 1 Corinthians: "Now there are varieties of gifts, but the same Spirit; and there are varieties of services, but the same Lord; and there are varieties of activities, but it is the same God who activates all of them in everyone" (1 Cor. 12:4-6).[15]

One can sense the beginning attempt to make connections between the differing activities of God in the community of faith and yet also the tension with the understanding of unity in God that came from the Hebrew faith expressed in such statements as the Shema, "Hear, O Israel: the Lord is our God, the Lord is One" (Deut. 6:4), which is the foundation of the inherited faith of Israel. Placher goes on to note, "None of these texts states the doctrine of the Trinity as it developed in subsequent centuries, but they do provide triune starting points that, in turn, led Christians to ask, 'What has to be true, if it makes sense for us to say things like this?'"[16] This question is really critical for understanding the development of Trinitarian doctrine in later centuries.

As the early church wrestled with reconciling the God of creation with faith in the concrete enfleshment of the Messiah and the enlivening activity of the Spirit at Pentecost, this was the foremost question. If this is how we experience God acting in our lives and in creation, what then must be true of God beyond these experiences that will help us understand and witness to them? The community struggled not only to make cohesive sense of its dynamic and diverse experiences of God but also to retain and enrich its inherited monotheism. It is this tension, derived from experience, that gives rise to the development of the Trinity as a way of holding these two dynamic commitments together, the expression of *pluralistic monotheism*. We find the seeds of this early reflection buried within the texts of the New Testament, beginning with Jesus himself. It was remembered that Jesus referred to God as "Father" and that this was at the heart of his prayer life, such as in Gethsemane,

---

15. Placher, "Believing in the Triune God," 30, excerpted from *The Triune God*, 136–37.
16. Ibid.

"Father, if you are willing, take this cup from me; yet not my will, but yours be done" (Luke 22:42), and even on the cross, "Father forgive them, for they know not what they do" (Luke 23:34). This "Fatherhood" was continued in the Lord's Prayer, which, perhaps through the influence of the *Didache* (an early Christian treatise and teaching text), was encouraged twice daily in personal or corporate worship. What we learn from such texts is that reflection was taking place within the context of worship very early on in the church and that these threefold affirmations of God's activity were being affirmed in ritual and practice long before they found expression in systematic theological formulation. At this point in the faith life of the early church, it is not a formula that is important but rather the encounter with Jesus as the Christ, as truly human and truly divine. Added to the mix was the communal experience of the animating and comforting presence of the Spirit within the community. This too had to be affirmed.

So what we find in the New Testament is not doctrine but retention of early Christian communal experience and witness, which the later church will ultimately hold up as Scripture authoritative in matters of faith and life. It would take several centuries for the number and nature of New Testament Scriptures to be determined and the canon finalized, but within it lies the kernels of early threefold communal witness. Placher concludes,

> The language to say what the church came to feel needed to be said evolved only over several centuries. Yet, as J. N. D. Kelly has remarked, a threefoldness in thinking about God "was embedded deeply in Christian thinking from the start . . . all the more striking because more often than not there is nothing in the context to necessitate it." Long before the church worked out technical trinitarian terminology, New Testament writers sometimes seemingly went out of their way to employ language that at least included three elements."[17]

The early witness, while affirming monotheism, felt obliged to acknowledge multiplicity in its encounter with the divine. The biblical texts bear witness to God's transcendence as Creator through Wisdom and the Word as well as personal and intimate, through names such as Father, through the incarnation, and through the activity of the Spirit. There is, then, a threefold witness to be found in the biblical material. How to relate these elements was to occupy

17. Ibid.

the thought of some of the greatest minds of the church for the next several centuries.

2. EARLY DEVELOPMENT

As the Christian faith began to spread throughout the Roman Empire, thanks to the missionary work of St. Paul, the "missionary to the gentiles," among others, Christians in Roman Judea and throughout the empire were increasingly forced to engage with the wider Greek and Roman world of thought and religious practice. Already dialoguing with its parent faith of the Hebrew tradition, early Christian thinkers were to draw on the thought of the day to present, explain, and defend the faith (known as apologetics) against an ever-increasing array of alternative beliefs and practices. How was the Christian faith to distinguish itself not only from Judaism but also from Epicureanism, Stoicism, Greco-Roman religions such as Mithraism, Caesarian imperial or Isis worship from ancient Egypt, or any number of other Greek and Roman philosophies? The pattern of encounter for future leaders was modeled by Paul himself when he stood in front of the Areopagus in Athens and referred the Athenians to their statue "to an unknown God" and remarked that he knew of this God, who "made the world and everything in it," and that he, Paul, had come to proclaim him (Acts 17:23-24). It is also important to note that the period we are considering occurred during the time of the formation of what was to become the New Testament and that these thinkers contributed to that process as well as to clarification of doctrine.

A. APOSTOLIC FATHERS

The "Apostolic Fathers" (ca. 50–150 CE) were the first generation of Christians after the disciples. Some of them were believed to have studied and been brought to the faith by the apostles or those "who had seen the Lord." Polycarp, some traditions say, was taught by the disciple John, for example. According to legend at least, there was a direct link between the early apostles and the Apostolic Fathers. We know most about this period from extant letters written by these earlier leaders, bishops of the emerging church, such as Polycarp of Smyrna (Turkey), Ignatius of Antioch (Syria), Clement of Rome (Italy), and others from various other parts of the empire.[18] This period, while punctuated by frequent persecution and martyrdom, saw rapid expansion of the Christian

---

18. See, for example, Henry Chadwick, *The Early Church* (New York: Penguin, 1993), and William H.C. Frend, *The Early Church* (Minneapolis: Fortress Press, 1982). For an early account of this period, also see the classical work by Eusebius, *The Church History*, trans. Paul Maier (Grand Rapids: Kregel

faith as it traveled the trade routes of the ancient Roman Empire and entered Roman homes mainly through the back door, the servants' entrance. It was especially among the disenfranchised, the slave and servant classes of the empire, that Christianity found its most welcome listeners. This was in part due to the willingness of early Christians to embrace the needs of the poor, as we see in Acts 4. Given the dominance of several philosophies of resignation (for example, Epicureanism and Stoicism), where one was told that there was no way out of their status in society, no hope of change, one simply had to accept their lot in life. If you were born a slave, you would die a slave, so "Just accept it!" This was a time of struggle for the faith as well as a period of great witness, as the early Christians showed tremendous courage and faith in going to their deaths under Roman persecution. They sought to meet the needs of others, especially the poor. They sought to embody in word and deed the Christian injunction to love one's neighbor as oneself. It may be said that it was more the Christian witness of love of neighbor than any sophisticated teaching that helped bring many new believers into the faith.[19]

While there were some reflections, primarily for worship use and introductory catechesis, such as the *Didache*, it was not a period characterized by systematic formulation of Christian understanding. Reflection on the Trinity was limited to the continuation of the New Testament witness through liturgical practice such as in baptismal formulas and prayers. It is from these proto-creeds that the later creedal statements of the faith were to develop. That phase was really to begin with the third generation of Christian thinkers, in the period known as the early church. In this period, Christian thought was refined and reformulated to address new issues before they became codified in creedal and doctrinal formulation. It is to this period of creative ferment and challenge that we now turn, with the formative thinkers Justin Martyr (d. c. 165), Irenaeus of Lyons (d. c. 202), and Tertullian (d. c. 220), as well as their opponents.

B. Justin Martyr

Justin Martyr is considered the first Christian Apologist. By this is meant that he is the first of whom we still have written records of his attempt to explain the Christian faith to its cultural and religious challengers, in this case the Roman authorities as well as perhaps those of the Jewish tradition. Christians were challenged by the Romans to move to a more polytheistic

Academic, 2007). For original writings of the Apostolic Fathers in English, see *The Apostolic Fathers*, vols. 1–2, trans. Bart D. Ehrman, Loeb Classical Library (Cambridge, MA: Harvard University Press, 2003).

19. Ibid.

stance or, by Jewish interlocutors, to reject the divinity of Christ to more clearly affirm monotheism. The early Apologists had to chart their course between polytheism and monotheism. In his *Second Apology*, Justin is mainly focused on affirming the divinity of Christ, arguing on the one hand for the divinity of Christ and on the other for the unity of God. Could acceptance of Christ as divine be reconciled with belief in one God? He argues that the Son is the "Word who is with God" (following John 1:1). After arguing that the Father is "unbegotten" and unoriginated, he writes, "His Son (who alone is properly called Son, the Word [*Logos*] who is with God and begotten before all creation, when in the beginning God created and ordered all things through him) is called Christ because he was anointed" (*Second Apology* 5).[20] Using the high titles of "Son" and "Word," Justin was then driven to explain the relationship of the Son to the Father. It is here that we see one of the first great steps in Trinitarian formulation, as he begins by identifying Jesus with the divine Wisdom of Proverbs (8:22), the first postapostolic thinker to do so. This will then allow him in his later writings such as *Dialogue with Trypho* to connect the divine Wisdom with the divine being, or *ousia*, in order to suggest that the divine remained undivided.

In explaining the generation of the Word, Justin used the image of the Sun sending forth its rays, and his language of "light from light" would eventually make it into the Nicene Creed over a century later.[21] While this does imply a type of subordination of the Son to the Father, at this early stage in development, the point was that the Christ was also divine, and this eternal begetting did not split or diminish the divine Father/Creator as its source. We are not dealing here with two Gods, which is one of the main charges that Trypho "the Jew" makes against Christianity in the dialogue. At this stage of Christian thought, Justin was mainly concerned with the relationship between the Father and the Son, as this was the main charge against Christians at the time. He does briefly refer to the Spirit as the "Spirit of prophecy" and being in the "third place" (*First Apology* 13),[22] affirming the role of the Spirit, but he was preoccupied with affirming the divinity of Christ without moving to polytheism. With Justin, then, we find a first-rate philosophical mind grappling with some of the most basic issues in Trinitarian thought and a person whose firm belief eventually resulted in his being beheaded in Rome during the reign of Marcus Aurelius, thus fully deserving the appellation "martyr," meaning

20. Quoted in O'Collins, *Tripersonal*, 88.

21. Ibid., 89.

22. Ibid., 91.

"witness." Gerald Bray concludes, "It was in the writings of the second-century Christians that the main lines of the Christian intellectual assault on paganism were laid down, to remain largely unchanged until paganism itself was suppressed."[23]

C. IRENAEUS

While Justin debated the divinity of Christ, Irenaeus, the first systematic theologian in the Christian tradition, argued for his humanity, in order to counterbalance the claims of Gnostics who emphasized the deity of Christ. Most likely born in Smyrna in modern-day Izmir in western Turkey during the first half of the second century (c. 125–140 CE), Irenaeus heard the preaching of Polycarp and was possibly his student. Consequently, Irenaeus may possibly stand in a direct line back to the apostle John. Sources indicate that he became a priest and bishop in the city of Lyons following the martyrdom of the preceding bishop. After this persecution ended, around 180 CE, during the reign of Marcus Aurelius, Irenaeus was able to direct his attention to two of the great challenges to the faith, that of the Gnostic (from *gnōsis* in Greek, meaning "wisdom") teacher Valentinus and that of Marcion, who claimed that the God of the Old Testament and the God of the New were two different gods. Valentinus had his own school in Rome and aspired to become bishop.

Valentinus claimed to have received a new revelation that supplemented the biblical witness, arguing that material life was evil and beyond redemption. He borrowed ideas from Middle Platonism and emphasized that the faithful strive for a purity of the spirit. Those who were truly spiritual (pneumatics) were already saved; those who were living souls (psychics) could be saved; however, those who were people of matter (hylics) were incapable of being delivered from matter and were therefore beyond redemption.[24] Giving a dualistic spin to John's Gospel, Valentinian Gnostics also sharply differentiated between Christ, the only-begotten (*monogenēs*), supernatural aeon or *Nous* (mind) on the one hand, and the historical figure of Jesus the man on the other.[25] There were many layers of existence beyond this life, and the goal was to release oneself fully from any material bondage. Valentinian Gnosticism thus taught a clear matter-spirit dualism, with matter being evil and spirit being good. In this scheme, the last thing that could be affirmed was that the divine had entered into matter in the form of human flesh.

---

23. Gerald Bray, "Explaining Christianity to Pagans; The Second Century Apologist," in *The Trinity in a Pluralistic Age*, ed. Kevin J. Vanhoozer (Grand Rapids: Eerdmans, 1997), 10–11.

24. O'Collins, *Tripersonal*, 97.

25. Ibid., 100.

This is exactly what Irenaeus affirms in his classic work *Adversus Haereses* ("against heresies"), written to refute both Valentinus and Marcion. In it, he argues that human beings are made "spiritual" not by abolishing the flesh but by sharing in the Spirit of God. Salvation is mediated through the flesh, beginning with the Word of creation, which is then embodied in the creation itself in the incarnation. Christ, in the incarnation, "recapitulates" (repeats the principle stages of) human creation as God had originally intended it to be. Christ is the true Adam, who restores the creation to what God had intended before the arising of sin. The sin of Adam and Eve for Irenaeus was immaturity or ignorance, not willful disobedience, as later Latin tradition in the West would at times argue. Far from a dualism that splits matter and spirit, Irenaeus observes, Christ "became what we are, that He might bring us to be even what He is Himself."[26] This process came to be known as divinization (*theōsis*), which has been preserved primarily in the Eastern Orthodox tradition.

Marcion was expelled from the Roman Christian community in 144 CE for teaching that the Creator God (demiurge) of the Hebrew Scriptures (Old Testament) differed almost to the point of cruelty from the loving Father of Jesus. The God of the Old Testament was a different God from that of the New and should be rejected. By his separation of the two testaments, Marcion also set in motion the formation of the New Testament canon (*kanon* in Greek, for "measure") that we have today. Regarding this rejection, O'Collins observes, "Marcion rejected all the Jewish scriptures and reduced the Christian scriptures to a truncated version of Luke and 10 (emended) letters by Paul."[27] "Marcion," Irenaeus comments, "divides God into two and calls one God good and the other just. In so doing he destroys the divinity of both" (*Adversus Haereses* 3.25.2). By affirming the Jewish Scriptures as the Scriptures of Jesus, Irenaeus set the stage for later reflection on the Trinity by affirming the intimate connection between creation and redemption as well as the active relation between the Father and the Son. In this way, Irenaeus responded to the challenge of Marcion. Anders Nygren observes in this regard:

> As Irenaeus allows no distinction between God the Creator and God the Redeemer, so he allows none between God of the Old and of the New Covenant, the God of the Law and of the Gospel. There are not, as Marcion thought, two separate Gods, but one and the same. Irenaeus is, of course, fully conscious that there is a fundamental

---

26. Irenaeus, *Adversus Haeresus*, in *The Ante-Nicene Fathers*, vol. 1, ed. Alexander Roberts and James Donaldson (1885–1887), www.ccel.org

27. O'Collins, *Tripersonal*, 96–97.

difference between fellowship with God in the form it took before and after the coming of Christ, and he insists most strongly that everything has become new because the Word has become flesh. But that is not to say that we now have a new God. Christ has taught us to worship God *in a new way, but not to worship a new God.*[28]

Irenaeus was able to preserve the unity of God as well as that of creation and by so doing opened up a coherent way to understand the specific creation of humanity. Marcion's idea had been that God cannot be experienced in matter, only spirit. Irenaeus, by claiming that God can be experienced in the incarnation, is making a Trinitarian claim.

Irenaeus's most famous Trinitarian formulation is his "two hands" metaphor. Building on Justin's interpretation of Gen. 1:26 (the "Let us" in the creation of humanity) and seeking to safeguard the transcendence of the Father, Irenaeus argues for the two hands of God in creation, Word and Wisdom, Son and Spirit, and clearly points to a Trinitarian formulation. He comments,

> In carrying out his intended work of creation, God did not need any help from angels, as if he did not have his own hands. For he has always at his side this Word and Wisdom, the Son and the Spirit. Through them and in them he created all things of his own free will. And to them he says, "Let us make human beings in our image and likeness." (*Adversus Haereses* 4.20.1)[29]

While there is some implied subordinationism (Son or Spirit being below the Father) here, it is clear that Irenaeus is thinking with a threefold understanding of God's activity as experienced by the early Christian community. This includes the act of creation and the involvement of God in the material world through the incarnation and the ongoing activity of the Spirit. Matter is not evil but is the result of the goodness of God in creation, and the Spirit is not to be divorced from matter but is to be seen as being sanctified by God's entering into it. Irenaeus thus affirms both the Hebrew Scriptures' understanding of creation as good and the continued identification of the Spirit with the Wisdom tradition. Irenaeus's "two hands" metaphor moves the formulation of the Trinity along as it simultaneously resists dualisms both of matter and spirit and of divinity. There is a certain refreshing gentleness and sarcastic humor in

---

28. Anders Nygren, *Agape and Eros* (Evanston, IL: Harper & Row, 1969), 397 (italics original). See also Irenaeus, *Adversus Haereses* 3.10.2.

29. Quoted in O'Collins, *Tripersonal*, 99.

Irenaeus's writings. As one of the last theologians in the West to use Greek, the language of the New Testament, Irenaeus represents Christian reflection before its Latinization. As we move further into Christian history, our next thinker is clearly on the Latin side, being trained as a Roman lawyer as well as writing all his treatises in Latin. He is the father of the most well-known language regarding the Trinity, that of "person."

D. TERTULLIAN

Tertullian (160–220 CE) was probably born in Carthage in North Africa during the second century of the Roman Empire. A younger contemporary of Irenaeus, Tertullian also was responding to challenges on several different fronts and provides the oldest extant record of the use of the word Trinity (*trinitas*) in Christian history. He rejected polytheism and Gnostic divisions of divinity on the one hand and modalist monarchianism (one being), which denied the Trinity, on the other. He too faced the challenge of affirming the tension of multiplicity with unity. Modalistic monarchianism argued that the distinctions between Father, Son, and Holy Spirit are no more than transient manifestations and not permanent presentations of the divine being. They are three self-manifestations of the one God, three different relationships (what they called "modes") that the one God assumed successively in creating, redeeming, and sanctifying.[30] They are not simultaneous but successive, with one replacing the other. We will focus on this challenge, as it has the most to do with the further refinement of the doctrine of the Trinity.

Fighting against polytheism on the one hand and modalist monarchianism on the other, Tertullian was forced to think about the question of whether affirmation of the divinity of the Son and the Holy Spirit was really compatible with monotheism. In writing against a modalist named Praxeas, Tertullian, drawing on the threefold experience of God's activity, observed that Praxeas had "driven away the Paraclete and crucified the Father" (*Adversus Praxean* 1). In responding to him, Tertullian was to lay the foundation for much of later trinitarian thinking, for he distinguished between God's one "substance" and God's three distinct but undivided "persons" (*Adversus Praxean* 2, 12). He is the first to use both Latin terms in describing the relationship between the Father, the Son, and the Spirit. O'Collins reflects, "In writing of one divine substance (*substantia*) in three persons, Tertullian was the first Christian writer to exploit the term *person* in theology, the first to apply *Trinity* (*Trinitas*) to God (*De pudicitia* 21.16, *Adversus Praxean*, 8) and the first to develop the formula of

---

30. Ibid., 104.

one substance in three persons." He continues, "Hence where the Greeks wrote of *ousia*, Tertullian used *substantia*, a term already applied to God by Seneca (d. 65 CE). Where *substance* stood for the common fundamental reality shared by the Father, Son and Holy Spirit, Tertullian understood *person* as the principle of operative individuality."[31] Today, of course, the term *person* has taken on a quite different meaning than in Tertullian's time, which contributes to confusion over the Trinity.

While today *person* may connote an independently existing individual who is self-contained, at that time the Greek *prosōpon* (Latin *persona*) was used to refer to a "mask" worn by an actor in the theater. Tertullian, however, did not have this usage simply in mind, for his use of *persona* does not endorse some form of modalism but rather a true expression of divinity, which expresses not a phase of divine action but an ongoing presence of divine relatedness. This would connect back to the person the actor is manifesting. The Trinity is *neither* the mathematical problem of reconciling "three" independently existing entities in "one" entity, *nor* seeing them as transitory and successive masks of the one entity. Tertullian marks out a position between these two extremes by arguing that the substance to be found in each expression of the divine is *the same substance* as it develops in fully continuous steps. Here he is being faithful to the biblical witness and to his own community of faith. The challenge is to be faithful to Christian experience, not simply to solve a theoretical problem. Employing vivid analogies, Tertullian explains,

> The Spirit makes the third from God [the Father] and the Son, as the fruit from the shoot is the third from the tree, the canal from the river the third from the source, the point of focus of a ray third from the sun. But none of these is divorced from the origin from which it derives its own properties. Thus the Trinity derives from the Father by continuous and connected steps. (*Adversus Praxean* 8)[32]

By this formulation, Tertullian is able to reject both the idea of multiple gods to explain the different divine functions and the idea of modalism by affirming that it is the same divine being at work in each of the separate expressions of divine activity. There is no succession in the activity, but simultaneity. The concrete nature of these analogies also indicates that we are dealing with experience and not purely abstract concepts.

31. Ibid., 105 (italics original).
32. Quoted in ibid., 106.

We have now reached the point at which the first great ecumenical council of the church was convened, that of Nicaea, where these reflections, among others, assumed the status of creedal formulations.

E. ARIUS/ATHANASIUS: NICAEA

The Council of Nicaea (325 CE) has a very complex history, involving theology, politics, and church authority. The first ecumenical (church-wide) council of the church, it was convened by the Roman emperor Constantine (d. 337 CE). The fact that the emperor himself called the council signals a significant change in the status of Christianity within the empire. He was interested in clarifying certain theological issues as Christianity was on its way to becoming the official religion. We do not have space to go into such a great council in major depth. Many excellent treatments are available.[33] We are only interested in its relevance for Trinitarian thinking, and for that we return to one of the basic issues that the early church had already been wrestling with for several centuries, that of the divinity of Christ. Christ had been experienced as divine but also as human. What, then, does this say about the nature of God and how are we to relate the joint experiences of humanity and divinity? As before, theologians were trying to refine the Christian tradition in ways they thought were true to their experience of God and what they read in the authoritative biblical witness, but they were divergent among themselves. The councils were called to decide among alternative interpretations and meanings, and by so doing, orthodoxy (*ortho*, "correct," and *doxa*, "opinion," in Greek) was formulated. There would be winners and losers in conciliar decisions, and the losers were referred to as "heretics" because their thinking was determined to be "other" (*heteros* in Greek) or "heterodox" and not "orthodox." These thinkers are often some of the most interesting characters in church history, and Arius, the theologian who precipitated the council, is no exception. His arguments and position drove the Roman emperor to convene the first ecumenical council of the church, which tells you immediately that more was at stake here than theological discernment.

Constantine, on the eve of the Battle of the Milvian Bridge in 312 CE, a battle that would contribute to the reunification of the empire in the West, is said to have seen in a vision or a dream the sign of the Chi-Rho, the image of the Greek letters X and a P superimposed on one another. These are

---

33. See among other sources J. N. D. Kelly, "The Nicene Crisis," ch. 9 in *Early Christian Doctrines* (London: Longman, 1978); J. N. D. Kelly, "The Creed of Nicaea," ch. 7 in *Early Christian Creeds* (London: Longman,1972); William Rusch, ed., *The Trinitarian Controversy*, Sources of Christian Thought (Minneapolis: Fortress Press, 1986).

the first two letters in the Greek name for Christ (*Christos*). This image was accompanied by the statement, "In this sign, [you shall] conquer" (Greek, *En touto nika*; Latin, *in hoc signo vinces*).[34] Constantine is said to have then had the image drawn on his banners and shields and was victorious in the battle. This was a turning point in Christian history, because soon after in 313 CE the Edict of Milan was declared, which brought an end to the persecution of Christians and allowed open practice of the faith. This declaration, agreed upon with the leader of the Balkans, Licinius, followed closely upon the Edict of Toleration declared by the emperor Galerius posted in Nicomedia in 311.[35] Christianity was on its way to becoming the established religion of the Roman Empire, and Constantine needed to know which expression of Christianity to affirm and which to suppress (read persecute). At this point in Western history, Christianity ceased being persecuted and in a few years became, under the auspices of the empire, the persecutor. With the establishment of Christianity, its fate became tied to that of the empire, and the political needs of the empire often usurped and dictated the needs of the church. As one of the first examples of this shift, we turn to the debate leading up to the first ecumenical council at Nicaea, and more specifically to Arius and his opponent Athanasius.

Arius (d. ca. 336 CE), from Alexandria, Egypt, sought, like so many theologians, to clarify and explicate his faith. Arius reasoned that if the Father and the Son were of the same type of substance, then they were coequal and were thus two gods.[36] Arius wanted to protect monotheism. Following this motivation, he argued that the Son, the Logos, while having been created before all the rest of creation, was nevertheless a created being and not equal to the eternal Father. His famous jingle was, "There was a time when he [the Son] was not."[37] The technical term in Greek that Arius used was *homoiousios*, of similar or like substance/being (*homoi*, "similar"; *ousia*, "being"). For Arius, the Logos was created first, and through the Logos everything else was created; nevertheless, the Logos was created and not coeternal with God. From Justin Martyr on, the developing tradition had argued, as we have seen, that the Son

---

34. Eusebius, *Life of Constantine* (*Vita Constantini*) 1.27–29, quoted in Charles Matson Odahl, *Constantine and the Christian Empire* (New York: Routledge, 2004), 105, and Timothy D. Barnes, *Constantine and Eusebius* (Cambridge, MA: Harvard University Press, 1981), 43.

35. "Edict of Milan," Oxford Dictionary of the Christian Church, 1974.

36. Catherine LaCugna, *God For Us: The Trinity and Christian Life* (San Francisco: HarperCollins, 1993), 32.

37. O'Collins, *Tripersonal*, 112. For a more complete treatment of Arius, see Rowan Williams, *Arius: Heresy and Tradition*, 2nd ed. (Grand Rapids: Eerdmans, 2002), as well as for the whole trinitarian discussion. See also Rusch, *Trinitarian Controversy*.

was coeternal with the Father, and the term that was developed to describe this was *homoousios*, of the same substance/being (*homo*, "same"; *ousia*, "being," in Greek). Once again, then, the issue revolved around how to understand the divinity of Christ without violating the principle of monotheism. The Council of Nicaea was convened to resolve this controversy, and Arius's chief opponents were the *homoousians*, including Alexander bishop of Alexandria and his secretary Athanasius..

Athanasius (d. 373 CE), also from Alexandria, was the chief proponent of homoousian thought after Nicaea. Constantine, who called the council to determine which position would become the orthodox position, inclined toward the term.[38] "Fatherhood," Athanasius argued, belongs eternally to God and defines the being of God. The Son, in the expression of Nicaea, is "begotten, not made," which means that the Son is from the Father while not being the Father and is definitely not a creature, which would be "made." Athanasius, arguing strongly for the divinity of the Logos—"He [God] has made all things out of nothing through his own Logos, Jesus Christ our Lord"[39]—also reflected on the nature of the Holy Spirit, observing, "As the Arians in denying the Son deny also the Father, so also these men in speaking evil of the Holy Spirit speak evil also of the Son" (*Letter to Serapion* 1.1).[40] The Arians, according to Athanasius, had misunderstood the Spirit as an angelic creature and as creature had denied its divinity as well. Gerald O'Collins concludes, "In positive terms, this meant that a true doctrine of the Spirit stood or fell with a true doctrine of the Son, and vice versa. According to Athanasius, being truly divine, the Spirit 'proceeds' from the Father and is 'given' by the Son."[41] It would appear that the homoousians won the day, but the consensus at Nicaea was far from universal. Exiles and condemnations between the "Arians" and the "Athanasians" were to continue on for several decades. Athanasius himself, as bishop of Alexandria, was exiled no less than five times from Alexandria for periods from four months to seven and a half years. The Roman emperors often supported the Arian position and had him exiled. It was not until Theodosius I became emperor in 379 CE and convened the

---

38. LaCugna, *God for Us*, 36. see Kelly, *Early Christian Creeds*, 205–95; and R. P. C. Hanson, *The Search for the Christian Doctrine of God: The Arian Controversy, 318–381* (Edinburgh: T&T Clark, 1988), 152–54.

39. Athanasius, *On the Incarnation of the Logos* 17.1, quoted in Jaroslav Pelikan, *The Christian Tradition*, vol. 1, *The Emergence of the Catholic Tradition (100–600)* (Chicago: University of Chicago Press, 1971), 203–4.

40. O'Collins, *Tripersonal*, 128.

41. Ibid.

second ecumenical council at Constantinople in 381 that Arianism was finally suppressed. It was also at this council that the divinity of the Spirit was more fully addressed and was affirmed in the final Niceno–Constantinopolitan Creed, found in most hymnals today.

The formation of what was to become "orthodoxy" is not always an easy or a clear process. Catherine LaCugna observes that "theologians of the second, third and fourth centuries tried out many different syntheses of biblical revelation, philosophy, experience and faith before arriving at what we now call 'orthodoxy.'"[42] Clarity was to come in some areas of interpretation while new areas were raised. The journey from persecution to eventual establishment clarified the divinity of Christ and the community's experience of personal relationship with the divine. The nature of the Spirit and its relation to the Father and the Son then moved to the foreground. Between Nicaea and Constantinople, a group of theologians in western Turkey, in the region known as Cappadocia, made further refinements of the understanding of the relationship between the Father, Son, and Spirit. Known as the Cappadocian Fathers, these theologians employed a key term that significantly advanced Trinitarian reflection. While Nicaea had argued for the divinity of the Son, Constantinople was to argue for the divinity of the Spirit and place all three in a dynamic interrelationality known as *perichōrēsis* ("mutual indwelling"). The road to Nicaea led to Constantinople, where these questions were addressed. Such is the formation of tradition as councils attempt to be faithful to spiritual experience and contemporary understanding. They seek to express the dynamic faith of the living, not archaic formulas of the dead. As the Christian tradition developed, it sought to remain true to its experiential roots and biblical witness while also addressing new issues and questions. The early Christian community's threefold experience of the divine was sustained through ongoing centuries, but the multiplicity of *pluralistic monotheism* still demanded further clarification.

Key Terms

Apologetics
Demiurge
Homoousios
Nicea
Ousia

42. LaCugna, *God for Us*, 31.

Persona
Ruach
Substantia
Wisdom/Sophia
Subordinationists
Yahweh

Discussion Questions

1. What were the most surprising elements of early Christian experiences of God with regard to the Trinity? Do you think the threefold understanding of the Trinity is warranted from this experience? Which experience resonates the most with you?

2. How is the issue of the divinity of Christ connected to the understanding of the Trinity? Why did it have to be answered first in doctrinal development?

3. Which thinker in the early church do you find the most interesting and why?

4. Why is confessional unity important to a community of faith? Should it be?

5. Do you find any parallels between the experiences of God in the early church and different religious convictions found in contemporary life and thought?

5

Constantinople to the Reformation

> *"But the formula 'three persons' has been coined, not in order to give a complete explanation by means of it, but in order that we might not be obliged to remain silent."*
>
> —AUGUSTINE, *DE TRINITATE*

The Council of Nicaea did not settle the early church's issues of the experience of God as Trinity. Indeed, debates carried on and alternative positions continued to be promoted. Constantine even reversed himself on the status of Arius and exiled Athanasius for a period of time. Theodosius I, emperor in 380 CE, seeking to clarify Nicene Christianity regarding the nature of Christ, convened the second ecumenical (church-wide) council of the church, held at Constantinople in 381 CE. This council produced what is commonly called the Nicene Creed but is technically called the Niceno-Constantinopolitan Creed. There also remained the need to settle the question of the divinity of the Spirit and its place in the Trinity. As before, the direction is from three to one, with priority given to the early Christian community's diverse spiritual experience of God as *pluralistic monotheism*, multiple relatedness to the singular God.

1. PERICHORESIS: THE CAPPADOCIANS AND JOHN OF DAMASCUS

A. CAPPADOCIAN FATHERS

In response to these needs there arose a trio of theologians who would not only defend the Nicene Creed but also provide terminology for the understanding of the Trinity that is still in use today. Basil the Great (d. 379 CE), bishop of Caesarea, is the oldest of the three, with his brother Gregory (d. 395 CE), bishop of Nyssa, and his friend Gregory of Nazianzus (d. 389 CE), patriarch of Constantinople, constituting the group of theologians collectively known as the "Cappadocian Fathers," for they all lived in the Roman province of Cappadocia, what is now central Turkey. Each is a unique thinker in his own right and deserves extended treatment. But in reference to the Trinity, they are basically of one mind and can, for the sake of space, be treated to together. Each refines the thought of the other and makes major contributions to the formation of the doctrine of the Trinity affirmed at the Council of Constantinople in 381 CE. Gerald O'Collins observes how the Cappadocians build on but go beyond Athanasius. He states, "Where they clearly went beyond Athanasius was in developing their language of three coequal and coeternal *hypostaseis* or persons/subjects sharing the one divine *ousia* or essence/being/substance."[1] The Cappadocians also added the concept of interpersonal communion, or *koinōnia*, at the heart of God, with communion as the function of the three divine persons and not simply of the Holy Spirit.[2] He concludes, "For this interpersonal model of the Trinity, God's inner being is relational, with each of the three persons totally related to the other two in 'reciprocal delight.'"[3] This understanding of divine communion advanced Trinitarian reflection by allowing for a dynamism within the *ousia* which is expressed through the *hypostaseis*. This dynamic movement of the *ousia* became known as *perichōrēsis* ("mutual indwelling"), which we will return to in more detail in chapter 8. O'Collins concludes, "Even if the term and the full deployment of the associated theology came later with St. John Damascene (d. ca. 749 CE), we find in the Cappadocian theology an early intimation of the *perichoresis* or 'cyclical movement,' the being-in-one-another of the Trinity. In a unique 'coinherence' or mutual interpenetration, each of the trinitarian persons is transparent to and permeated by the other two."[4] In other words, the Cappadocians set the divine being in relational motion.

B. JOHN OF DAMASCUS

John of Damascus (also known as John Damascene) later on, in the early 700s, further refined the concept of *perichōrēsis* and employed it to understand how the divine persons "make room for" (*chōrein*) one another. While having been

---

1. Gerald O'Collins, *The Tripersonal God: Understanding and Interpreting the Trinity* (Mahwah, NJ: Paulist, 1999), 131–32.

2. Ibid.

3. Ibid.

4. Ibid.

used earlier to describe the two natures of Christ, John of Damascus gave this term its first significant use in relation to the Trinity.[5] It was said that the three "mutually indwell" with one another, and while distinct in function are inseparable in being. Karl Barth who, along with Karl Rahner, is most responsible for the renewal of Trinitarian reflection in the twentieth century, described it this way: "The divine modes of being mutually condition and permeate one another so completely that one is always in the other two and the other two in the one."[6] This concept will be central to our later constructive efforts in relation to the concept of quantum entanglement. (See chapters 8 and 9.) Here I merely want to place it in the context of historical development and give it pride of place in the clarification of the doctrine of the Trinity. Its use began in the Greek East but was also adopted in the Latin West to describe this dynamic relational *ousia* ("being") that the Cappadocians had developed.

The Cappadocians' providing the Greek *ousia/hypostaseis* formulation to be affirmed by the wider church at the Council of Constantinople allowed for the affirmation of the divinity and coequality of the Spirit. *Ousia*, however, is not some abstract essence, as it is sometimes interpreted in the West. LaCugna corrects: "In Cappadocian theology, however, *ousia* expresses concrete existence. Each divine person *is* the *ousia*; the divine *ousia* exists hypostatically, and there is no *ousia* apart from the hypostases. To exist as God is to be the Father who begets the Son and breathes forth the Spirit."[7] Thus, for the Cappadocians, the divine existence *is* in the dynamic relationships, which cannot be separated from one another. The *ousia* only exists hypostatically, so that each person *is* the divine nature. LaCugna concludes, "The heart of the doctrine of the Trinity lies here. The definition of divine person as relation means that to be a person is to be defined by where a person comes from; *what a person is in itself or by itself cannot be determined.*"[8] In this way, the language of *hypostasis*/person does not mean an independently existing being separate from the other two. This conceptuality avoids a plurality of Gods, or "tritheism," and preserves monotheism, for there is only one common *ousia*.

All this technical language can be a bit deceiving. By using this language, the Cappadocians did not understand themselves as explaining the divine nature

---

5. John of Damascus, *Orthodox Faith* 1.8 "Concerning the Holy Trinity."

6. Karl Barth, *Church Dogmatics* I/1:370, quoted in William Placher, *The Triune God: An Essay in Postliberal Theology* (Louisville: Westminster John Knox, 2007) 155.

7. Catherine LaCugna, *God For Us: The Trinity and Christian Life* (San Francisco: HarperSanFrancisco, 1993), 69.

8. Ibid. (italics original).

but rather as preserving its mystery. William Placher notes, "The purpose of terms like *ousia* and *hypostasis* was to preserve the mystery, not get rid of it."[9] The Cappadocians, as with most Greek theology, strongly affirmed the *apophatic* (to deny) tradition in theology, which emphasizes divine mystery and the ultimate unknowability of the infinite divine by any finite mind. This contrasts with the *kataphatic* (to affirm) tradition, which speaks positively of divine attributes. Each mutually corrects the other in theological formulation. Drawing on the thought of Gregory of Nyssa's work *Against Eunomius*, Placher continues, "Gregory is not here defining *ousia* or *hypostasis*, nor is he even insisting that they are the terms that must be used in Trinitarian discussion. He is, rather, identifying a *rule* for the use of *whatever* terms we use to point to that beyond what any of our language can express: whatever term we use should be used equally of Father, Son, and Holy Spirit."[10] Our "naming" of God is always limited, and all analogies will break down, as they are tied to finite experience. This language then tells us where the limits are and functions as a form of theological limiting concept, which points us to the mystery but does not specify what the mystery is, for to do so goes beyond human conception. (Think of an asymptotic curve on a graph as it moves from the vertical to the horizontal axis, drawing ever closer but never reaching the axis itself.) In one of the most insightful comments ever made about this language of three *hypostaseis*, Augustine, one of the greatest authors in the Latin West, in his *De Trinitate* ("On the Trinity") observed, "But when it is asked 'Three what?' then the great poverty from which our language suffers becomes apparent. But the formula 'three persons' has been coined, not in order to give a complete explanation by means of it, but in order that we might not be obliged to remain silent."[11] It is to this great thinker and the later Western development that we now turn.

2. ANALOGY: MIDDLE AGES AND REFORMATION

A. AUGUSTINE

The most extended treatment of the Trinity in Christian theology prior to the fall of Rome was written by Augustine (d. 430 CE). As bishop of Hippo Regius in North Africa, Augustine lived during tumultuous times as the classical world in the West was coming to an end and the medieval world was about

9. Placher, *Triune God*, 126.

10. Ibid.

11. Augustine, *De Trinitate* 5.10, quoted in O'Collins, *Tripersonal*, 141.

to begin, witnessing the death of one and providing direction for the other. His great work *The City of God* (*De civitate Dei*), which first describes Christian life as a pilgrimage through this world, sets out the contrast between the city of humanity, with its material instability and temporal flux, and the city of God, with its permanence and eternal timelessness. This dual conception of the two cities was to provide the intellectual model for much of the medieval worldview. Christians are pilgrims in this world, for their ultimate citizenship, thanks to Christ, is in the eternal city of God. This was both a comfort and an inspiration during a time of extreme instability in the Roman Empire when the unthinkable had happened: eternal Rome had been sacked by Alaric the Visigoth in 410 CE. The barbarians were no longer at the gates; they had breached them and had entered the city. The invasion and sacking would continue until the ultimate fall of Rome in 476 CE. Amazingly, through all of this tumultuous time, Augustine was able to write and think, producing one of the first introspective reflections of Western literature in his *Confessions*, as well as numerous treatises on everything from Christian doctrine to free will and, for our purposes, the Trinity. As Augustine lay dying in August of 430 CE, the Vandals were literally laying siege to his community. (Today we still employ the name of this east-Germanic tribe of invaders by using the word *vandalize* to indicate wanton, unwarranted destruction.) It is impossible to overstate the impact his life and thought have had on later Christian history. There are many excellent works that summarize the life of this great theologian and bishop as well as the influence of his thought.[12] That will not be our task here but rather to simply summarize his understanding of the Trinity and how his use of two human analogies became influential in forming later Christian doctrine.

Augustine was one of the primary thinkers to employ the concept of "relation" in his Trinitarian thinking, and this certainly begins with multiplicity. In the West, there had developed a problem when the Greek terms were translated into Latin. It seemed that both *ousia* and *hypostasis* could be translated as "substance" and used to describe the essence of divine being. These terms were undergoing significant development during the third and fourth centuries, as is illustrated by Athanasius first using *hypostasis* as equivalent to the three *prosōpa* ("persons") (362 ce) and then later used it again for *ousia* (369 CE).[13] The Cappadocians had sought to sort this out by using *hypostasis* exclusively for the three. John Zizioulas contends, "Augustine is known for

---

12. See among others Peter Brown, *Augustine of Hippo: A Biography*, 2nd ed. (Berkeley: University of California Press, 2000), for a very readable life narration and excellent bibliography.

13. Placher, *Triune God*, p. 124.

his extensive use of the concept of relation in his Trinitarian theology. . . . The three are neither substances nor accidents but relations which have real subsistence—an idea already taught by Plotinus and Porphyry."[14] It is the concept of relations that drives the two most important analogies to the divine that Augustine employs, that of the *social* (love): the relation of lover, beloved, and the love between them; and the *psychological* (mind): memory, understanding, and will.

Drawing on the biblical understanding of humanity created in the image of God (Gen. 1:26), Augustine among other theologians talked about *vestigia trinitatis*, vestiges of the Trinity to be found imprinted on the human soul.[15] These vestiges are conveyed through relations and get expressed by Augustine in some of his more famous analogies of relationship. In book 8 of *De Trinitate* (8.8.12), he employs the triad of the lover, the beloved, and the bond of love.[16] This, of course, is not a perfect analogy because only the first two elements (lover and beloved) are distinct individuals, while the love they share is not, seeming to reduce the Spirit to less than a fully participating individual in the relationship. Also, this analogy of human love must be purified of its carnal desires before it can be an adequate expression of divine love. In the first epistle of John, when the text reads "God is love" (1 John 4:8, 16), the word for "love" in the Greek text is not *eros* but rather *agape*, the love of self-giving. It is such self-giving that characterizes the love of God. Nevertheless, one begins to see the method and power of analogies to help understand the relationship of the divine persons. All three are required if the understanding of the love they share is to be comprehended. The three are intrinsically interconnected, even if there is differentiation.

In book 10 (10.10.14–16), Augustine employs an even more famous triad, that of mind, which he originated. The human mind, so the analogy goes, finds expression in three ways, through memory, understanding, and will. The key here is that these activities are not something the mind happens to engage in but rather that the mind exists precisely in the doing of these activities. They are intrinsic to the understanding and expression of mind. LaCugna observes, "The triad of memory, understanding and will is consistent with what Augustine had

14. John Zizioulas, "Relational Ontology: Insights from Patristic Thought," in *The Trinity and an Entangled World*, ed. John Polkinghorne (Grand Rapids: Eerdmans, 2010), 147; Augustine *De trinitate* 5–7.

15. See LaCugna, *God for Us*, 93–96.

16. This analogy is not unique to Augustine but was employed commonly in the East and in the West by, among others, Richard of St. Victor in the twelfth century and Bonaventure in the thirteenth. Placher, "Believing in the Triune God," *Christian Century*, April 17, 2007, 28.

earlier developed in the theory of relations. Together, memory, understanding and will are not three substances but one substance. And each faculty exhibits the characteristics both of substance and of relation."[17]

The employment of relations in such an intrinsic way is one of Augustine's great contributions to reflection on the Trinity, and it is one that will be even more fully developed in the twentieth century with the move from a substance ontology to a relational ontology. If everything is constituted by relations, then it is no surprise that this imagery, limited though it is, can be helpful in understanding the relationship of God and the world as well as the interrelatedness of the divine life. There are some limitations with the analogies, of course, which Placher summarizes: "The social analogy gives us too much threeness, while the psychological analogy does not give us enough."[18] These problems, which are intrinsic to any human analogy, nevertheless do move reflection on the Trinity forward a great deal and influenced many later Christian thinkers. The use of relations found in human experience, these vestigial trinities, both ties Trinitarian reflection directly to human experience, from which it has emerged, and enlivens not only reflection on human experience but also, by analogy, connects it to the divine. In the thirteenth century, Thomas Aquinas will also employ these analogies, developing a sophisticated philosophical method that makes use of the way of negation (*via negativa*) in order to introduce important distinctions in how to understand analogies.

B. AQUINAS

Significant change took place in the over eight hundred years of European history that elapsed between the death of Augustine and that of Thomas Aquinas (d. 1274). The Western half of the Roman Empire fell into chaos after the fall of Rome, and out of that emerged the feudal system of regional fiefdoms and local governance by dukes and princes. With the collapse of centralized political authority, the Roman Catholic Church became the largest and most influential power in Europe for the next one thousand years. The Eastern half of the empire, Byzantium, survived uninterrupted until its capital, Constantinople (now Istanbul), fell to the Ottoman Turks in 1453. Theologically, the Council of Chalcedon in 451 CE had defined the nature and person of Christ to resolve debates that had been going on for over four hundred years. The council affirmed that Christ was indeed one person but with two natures, one divine

17. LaCugna, *God for Us*, 95.
18. Placher, *Triune God*, 29.

and one human. Arianism was finally put to rest. In the West, as witnessed to by the Council of Toledo in 589 CE among others, the word *filioque* ("and the Son") was added to the Nicene Creed, affirming that the Holy Spirit proceeded from both the Father and the Son. The Eastern church objected to this addition, arguing that it subordinated the Holy Spirit within the Trinity and implied two principal sources within the Godhead. The resulting dispute, coupled with resistance to Rome's claim to be the central authority in Christendom, contributed to the Great Schism of 1054, in which each church mutually anathematized (rejected) the other and the Christian church was split in two. Attempts to heal this breach were to involve a good part of Thomas Aquinas's intellectual career.

One of the oddities of the fall of Rome was that, for all intents and purposes, the thought of the philosopher Aristotle had been lost to the West. A student of Plato, Aristotle had also been the tutor of Alexander the Great (d. 323 BCE), the king of Macedon. Alexander, one of the greatest military and intellectual strategists of ancient Greece, conquered most of the known world by the time he was thirty-two and consequently was responsible for sowing Greek culture throughout the Mediterranean. He built libraries, theaters, arenas, temples and other expressions of Greek culture, all of which contributed to the distribution of the thought of Aristotle his teacher. So when libraries were lost in Europe after the fall of Rome, the thought of Aristotle, among many others, was preserved in the libraries Alexander had spread around the Mediterranean, such as in Alexandria in northern Egypt, which he founded and named after himself. With the Muslim invasion, the thought of Aristotle was reintroduced into Europe. Muslim armies having been turned back at the Battle of Tours in 732 CE, Islamic scholars settled in Spain and began to engage in dialogue with Christian scholars throughout Europe. In this odd manner, the thought of a native European thinker was reintroduced to Europe and was used to raise serious challenges to Christian thought, which through the work of Augustine, Origen, and others had become intimately connected with the "noble philosopher" Plato. In effect, Thomas Aquinas was charged with the task of reconciling the Platonized Christian faith with Aristotelian philosophy, a philosophy he found very exciting.

Aquinas did not see faith and reason as at all in opposition but rather complementary, and he sought to synthesize the two. Helping to forge what came to be known as the "scholastic synthesis," Aquinas argued that our knowledge of God comes from two books, the book of faith (Scripture) and the book of nature (creation). These two books cannot contradict one another because they have the same author, God, who bestows on each the appropriate form of revelation. In creation, God's action is found through general (universal) revelation as the source of order in creation; and in Scripture, God is disclosed through the special (particular) revelation of the Prophets, the Law, and of course the incarnation. Each revelation had its appropriate human capacity, with reason being employed with the book of nature and faith with the book of Scripture. This also gave rise to two forms of theology, natural theology, reasoning from creation, and revealed theology, through faith from Scripture (see chapter 3). These two theologies were understood to complement each other. For Aquinas, creation can tell us that God exists but cannot tell us who God is, much less God's disposition toward humanity. For that the particular revelation found in Scripture is needed. Drawing on fundamental distinctions in types of causation that he found in Aristotle (see chapter 2), Aquinas developed his arguments (not proofs!) for the existence of God, the classic task of natural theology. He argued, regarding natural knowledge, that "what is in the mind was first in the senses," stressing the empirical (sensory) base of all knowledge. Knowledge of the Trinity for him, however, arises primarily in the realm of special revelation, although Aquinas does affirm the "vestiges of the Trinity" (*vestigia trinitatis*) within humanity.

Influenced by the thought of Aristotle, Aquinas begins his great theological work *Summa Theologiae* with a discussion of the unity of God's essence and so creates a division between the two: on the one God (*De Deo Uno*) and on the Triune God (*De Deo Trino*). By doing so, he reverses the process of the previous thousand-plus years, which began reflection on the Trinity with the economy (work) of God in salvation and human experience in creation. This is a critical shift. LaCugna observes,

> In general Thomas followed the order of Peter Lombard's *Sentences* [the main theological text for teaching theology in the medieval period]; however, Thomas reorganized the contents of the *Summa* according to the Dionysian cycle of emanation and return. In the *Sentences* Peter had treated the subject of God (*De Deo*) in the first section called the *de mysterio Trinitatis* ["on the mystery of the Trinity"]. Thomas went beyond Peter by dividing De Deo into two parts: *De Deo Uno* and *De Deo Trino*. . . . The much more significant structural feature of the Summa is its starting point with the divine essence, explored apart from existence in triune personhood. The way for this had been prepared by Augustine, but Thomas' innovation was to use the metaphysics of Aristotle as the basis for his

theology. The move toward Aristotle is reflected in what Thomas explicitly sets out as the focus of the *Summa*; God in himself.[19]

Despite Thomas's intention to affirm the unity of God, this distinction was to create a division in reflection on God that was to endure for another eight hundred years, until the modern period.

Also following Aristotle, Thomas focuses on the essence of God, which is wholly simple. God does not have a body or parts, is not in space–time, has no potential, and is immutable and necessary.[20] As such, God is pure act; there is no movement from potential to actual within God. Hence God is perfect, which means that God cannot change and is self-sufficient. God needs nothing else in order to exist, and indeed God necessarily exists. For Thomas, while we cannot know God directly because the finite cannot contain the infinite, reason can come to know something about God by taking the characteristics of this world and negating them. If God is other than the world as pure act and if we take the attributes of the world and negate them, taking their opposite, we can indirectly comprehend something about God. This approach of via negativa (way of negation) allowed Thomas to say something about the One God. LaCugna notes, "God's goodness subsists and is complete independently of things; they add no fulfillment to God, and there is no absolute need for God to will them. Absolute goodness and absolute perfection amount to absolute self-sufficiency, for Thomas."[21] This makes it difficult for Thomas to talk of God's relationship to the creation in any way that might constitute expressions of the Trinity. LaCugna concludes,

> In the end, Thomas is scrupulous to avoid any hint that the identity of the divine persons is constituted by or caused by their relation to creation. . . . This means that the creative activity of God is somehow beyond the trinitarian life of God. "Person" is disjoined from "nature." The net effect is that Thomas posits an intradivine self-communication that is really distinct, if not totally separate from, whatever self-communication may take place in creation. Thomas' separation of God-Creator and God-Trinity works to the detriment of his insight that creation is a relation.[22]

---

19. Ibid., 147
20. Peter Vardy and Julie Arliss, *The Thinker's Guide to God* (Alresford, UK: John Hunt, 2003), 26.
21. LaCugna, *God for Us*, 162.
22. Ibid., 166–67.

This leads to the conclusion that, "the 'immanent' Trinity, *theologia,* is severed—for the sake of upholding the absolute freedom of God—from the 'economic' Trinity, *oikonomia.*"[23] Later in neoscholasticism and in formal Roman Catholic manuals of theology, this division was made rigid. LaCugna observes,

> *De Deo Uno* became a philosophical treatise on the divine nature and
> attributes. This enterprise, known as natural theology, was presented
> as that which reason alone, apart from revelation, could determine
> about God. The treatise on the Trinity then assumed not just second
> place but became of quite diminished importance except as a formal
> treatment of processions, persons, relations.[24]

This severing of the two and of the Trinity from creation contributed to the later marginalization of the doctrine of the Trinity.[25] Consistent preoccupation with God in unity in succeeding centuries contributed directly to the Trinity's becoming the "forgotten doctrine" of the Christian tradition, embarrassingly trucked out once a year on Trinity Sunday and clouded over in obfuscating rhetoric about mystery and divinity. This is a far cry from the experiential dynamism of God's presence in creation, which gave rise to the doctrine from the biblical witness.

C. BONAVENTURE

In contrast to Thomas, Bonaventure, who died in 1274 CE, the same year as Aquinas, started from a different metaphysical position, understanding divine goodness to necessarily overflow into creation, being the nature of such absolute goodness. LaCugna again:

> God creates because God the Father—this particular person, not
> God in general—is by nature self-diffusive Good. Creation, while
> absolutely free, is a "natural" egress from the self-diffusive Good.
> Thus, in Bonaventure's thought, Good is not identified with self-
> sufficiency but with plenitude (fullness) overflowing. Bonaventure's

---

23. Ibid., 167.

24. Ibid.

25. Ibid. LaCugna remarks, "But it must be acknowledged that one of the fruits of Thomas' theology was the marginalization of the doctrine of the Trinity, something Thomas himself assuredly would have protested vigorously as contrary to his intention and to his own religious experience."

reason is simple: If God were not self-communicating, God would not be the highest Good. The most perfect is the most diffusive.[26]

Being from the same historical period, we can see that one theological method alone need not dominate and that the concept of essence need not be interpreted as purely self-contained but instead is the source of all existence, the expression of divine Goodness. The overflowing plenitude of God's love will be very important in later chapters as we address the relationship of God to creation and how plenitude relates to entanglement.

Bonaventure, a Franciscan, started not with Aristotle but with the life of Francis himself and his affirmation of the beauty of creation and Christ's love for all creatures. Peter Vardy and Julie Arliss contend,

> Bonaventure and the Franciscan tradition were not afraid of picturing God as a lover who lures human beings to love God and to love each other. The presence of beauty in the world was seen as a central part of the message—just as beauty is present everywhere so God is present throughout God's creation and God uses beauty as a way to open the minds of human beings to God. The God of the Franciscan tradition, portrayed through philosophers like Duns Scotus and William of Ockham, was a temporal God—a God in time.[27]

It makes a considerable theological difference, then, whether one begins the discussion of God and the Trinity, from the perspective of divine unity or divine economy, from God in God's self or God in creation. This distinction will play a major role in the Protestant Reformation, as the Reformers turn primarily to focus on Christ and salvation as found in Scripture and reject the medieval scholastic reliance on philosophy, particularly that of Aristotle.

D. LUTHER

Just as Augustine lived at the transition between the classical and the medieval world, Martin Luther (d. 1546 CE) lived at the transition between the medieval and what was to eventually, after the Enlightenment, become the modern world. Born in 1483, Luther was but a young boy when Columbus encountered the Western hemisphere, and he grew up during the flourishing of the Italian Renaissance. Michelangelo, Raphael, Machiavelli, Copernicus, and

---

26. Ibid., 165.
27. Vardy and Arliss, *Thinker's Guide*, 29.

the Medici were his contemporaries. An Augustinian monk, Luther sought to find a forgiving God and in so doing challenged the received understanding of God's righteousness and grace. Luther returned theological reflection to the economy of salvation by focusing on the cross of Christ, and he approached the Trinity through a theology of the cross planted in the soil of creation. For him, the Word (*logos*) incarnate was also the Word of creation itself, and the dynamic, creative Spirit (*Spiritus Creator*), which sustained Christian community, was also an expression of the divine Word in its Trinitarian manifestations of grace. Christine Helmer observes, "Luther's conviction regarding the divine status of the word emerges as a deterministic factor in his trinitarian understanding. The word is conjugated across the three persons in order to identify each person as a subject of speech. The identification of a person with the word is part and parcel of a trinitarian hermeneutic that Luther sees rooted in Scripture and in the history of its interpretation."[28] Luther affirmed the received doctrine of the Trinity and wrote his catechetical work (the *Small Catechism* from 1529)[29] along those lines, focusing on the three articles of the Apostles' Creed. In the *Large Catechism*, Luther observed, "In the Creed you have the entire essence, will, and work of God exquisitely depicted in very brief but rich words," for "in all three articles God himself has revealed and opened to us the most profound depths of his fatherly heart and his pure unutterable love."[30] As an Augustinian monk and scholar, Luther was deeply influenced by Augustine's understanding of the Trinity. But the Trinity was not at issue in the Reformation; the concepts of grace, Scripture, Papal authority, and the sacraments were flash points, not the Trinity. Still, his experience of the divine Trinity led Luther to see grace, for example, in a very Augustinian way, and this challenged other views of his day. He particularly connected grace to the dialectical tension between law and gospel and with this moved theology into metaphorical use.

Luther was concerned to avoid discussing God where God does not reveal God's self—the hidden God (*Deus Absconditus*)—and chose to focus instead on where God has revealed God's self in Christ and on the cross—the revealed God (*Deus Revelatus*). In other words, Luther focused on the Trinitarian history of God through the action of God in the world, not God within God's self. With Luther, we have a theology of the cross rooted in the Trinitarian experience of

28. Christine Helmer, *The Trinity and Martin Luther: A Study on the Relationship Between Genre, Language and the Trinity in Luther's Works (1523°1546)* (Mainz: Verlag Philip Von Zabern, 1999), 268.

29. Martin Luther, "Small Catechism," in *The Book of Concord*, ed. Robert Kolb and Timothy Wengert, 2nd ed. (Minneapolis: Fortress Press, 2001), 345–77.

30. Martin Luther, "The Large Catechism," in *The Book of Concord*, 439.

God in the world. The cross becomes the lens through which to approach and understand all of God's activity in the world. Luther places redemption at the center of God's work but does not relegate the other activities of God to the periphery; rather, he sees them as intimately connected to the acts of salvation. Luther returned reflection on the Trinity to its biblical roots (*sola Scriptura*, "Scripture alone") and to the foundational experiences of God's redemptive activity in the world (*solus Christus*, "Christ alone") as the beginning point for reflection on the activity of God. Luther rejected the scholastic approach of moving from the one God to the Triune God, preferring to seek the unity of God in and through the interrelated activity of God in Christ, the economic Trinity. It was Luther who first used the term the "crucified God." In the cross, God does not die but rather death enters into God, and it is there in God that we mortal creatures have hope of overcoming death. Luther's own suffering and struggles in faith (*Anfechtungen*) certainly led him to see a connection between the love of God and suffering, and this was most clearly embodied on the cross, which is the center of his theology. The cross alone is our theology (*Crux sola est nostra theologia*).

While Luther certainly focused on redemption, he did not neglect the activity of God in creation and sanctification. Commenting on an additional "confession," Luther added to his polemical writing against Ulrich Zwingli regarding the Eucharist, *Confession Concerning Christ's Supper* (1528), Niels Gregerson observes, "In this confession, at once a personal witness and a conscious attempt to speak on behalf of the common Christian faith, Luther shows his courage to take seriously the Trinitarian understanding of the unity of God."[31] Although Luther affirms the activity of all three persons of the Trinity in creation, "one rarely finds the expression of the view that also the Father, the source of all divine life (*fons deitatis*), gives Himself to creation."[32] Nonetheless, Luther specifically develops God's activity in creation in a Trinitarian manner. He confesses,

> These are the three persons and one God, who has given Himself to us all wholly and completely, with all that He is and has. The Father gives himself to us, with heaven and earth and all the creatures, in order that they may serve us and benefit us. But this gift has become obscured and useless through Adam's fall. Therefore the Son subsequently gave himself and bestowed on us all his works,

---

31. Niels Gregerson, "Grace in Nature and History: Luther's Doctrine of Creation Revisited." *Dialog* 44, no. 1 (Spring 2005): 22.

32. Ibid.

sufferings, wisdom, and righteousness, and reconciled us to the Father, in order that restored to life and righteousness, we might also know and have the Father and his gifts. But because this grace would benefit no one if it remained so profoundly hidden and could not come to us, the Holy Spirit comes and gives Himself to us also, wholly and completely. . . . We find here a particularly beautiful articulation of the threefold divine self-giving, of Father, Son, and Holy Spirit, to the world of creation.[33]

Luther immerses the Trinity in the creation and in so doing makes God's threefold activity accessible to the believer through the activity of God in creation. He once again harkens back to the threefold affirmation of divine accessibility to human experience found in the biblical witness. Luther rejects pursuit of God in God's self, for that attempts to know the hidden God. We can only know the economic Trinity, which is God for us (*pro me*), most profoundly revealed on the cross.

In the renaissance of Luther scholarship during the last century, the focus was on what was "new" in Luther's thought, and most considered his reflection on the Trinity traditional and therefore familiar and not the cutting-edge theology they wanted to emphasize. Christine Helmer observes, "The effort to locate the historical-theological intersection between 'new' and 'old' in the Reformation breakthroughs ends up distancing Luther from what precedes him."[34] The consequence of this was that little research or writing was done on Luther's understanding of the Trinity. The action in Luther's thought was perceived to be elsewhere. Paul Althaus in his classic work *The Theology of Martin Luther*, for example, devotes only two pages to the Trinity.[35] The dearth of scholarly reflection, however, does not mean that Luther himself ignored the doctrine. In his reform of the German Mass, Luther reintroduced the Aaronic blessing, which he saw as a direct expression of the Trinity, at the close of the service. It was his way of concluding Christian worship with a clear affirmation of the Trinity. The Aaronic blessing is: "The Lord bless you and keep you; the Lord make his face to shine upon you, and be gracious to you; the Lord lift

33. Martin Luther, "Confession Concerning Christ's Supper" (1528), in *Luther's Works*, vol. 37, *Word and Sacrament III*, ed. Robert H. Fischer (Minneapolis: Fortress Press, 1976), 366 (*D. Martin Luthers Werke* [Weimar Ausgabe] [Weimar: Böhlau, 1883–1993], 26:505–6), quoted in Gregerson, "Grace in Nature and History," 22.

34. Helmer, *Trinity and Martin Luther*, 9.

35. Paul Althaus, "The Trinity," ch. 16 in *The Theology of Martin Luther* (Minneapolis: Fortress Press, 1966), 199–201.

up his countenance upon you, and give you peace" (Num. 6:24-26). In 1532, Luther wrote an entire sermon in the vernacular to explain the reintroduction of this Israelite blessing into the worship service. Gregerson comments,

> Luther can therefore conclude that the Aaronitic blessing could simply be abbreviated as follows: "The Father, the Son, and the Holy Spirit bless you." For just as the work of creation is attributed to the Father, so is the work of redemption attributed to the Son, whereas the Holy Spirit is attributed the task of daily sanctification as well as the final accomplishment in resurrection. Thus Luther's sermon on the Aaronitic blessing at once points to the efficacy of divine action and to the full involvement or cooperation of the human person in the divine activity of preserving and renewing the world.[36]

It is abundantly clear that Luther affirmed the doctrine of the Trinity and reconnected it to the lived experience of the worshiping community, to creation, and above all to the activity of redemption. The years following Luther's death, however, were to see wars, bloodshed, and the rise of the scientific method to the point that the Trinity was to become the "forgotten doctrine," seen in the Age of Reason, which we have come to call the Enlightenment, as highly irrational. We will turn to those issues in the next chapter, but before doing so let us briefly summarize what has been covered in these chapters on the emergence and refinement of the doctrine of the Trinity.

In this historical overview, we have seen that, starting with the biblical witness, the understanding of the Trinity has emerged out of the lived experience of the Christian community. The Christian experience that somehow "God was in Christ reconciling the world to Himself" drove the early church to relate their redeeming experience in Christ to God. When this was connected with the enlivening power of the Spirit experienced within the community of faith and the preceding understanding of everything being created by God from the Jewish heritage, we have the experiential basis for the Trinity. The direction, then, is from experience to reflection, not the other way around. *Trinity is the uniquely Christian way of attempting to understand the experience of the dynamic and diverse activity of God in the world.*

Through succeeding centuries, this understanding was refined using the most technical and sophisticated concepts of the time, first in Greek and then in Latin. The unity of God was understood as a relational, dynamic becoming (*ousia*), which was expressed in three *hypostaseis* ("persons, subjects"), which

---

36. Gregerson, "Grace in Nature and History," 26. *Luthers Werke*, 30:III.583.

exist in dynamic, mutual indwelling (*perichōrēsis*). For this development to occur, both the divinity of Christ and the goodness of material existence in the creation had to be affirmed, as well as both the social character of the divine and the divine mystery beyond all description. During the Middle Ages, the distinction between the essence (immanent nature) of God (unity) and the activity (economic nature) of God (Trinity), became overemphasized, and this led to an emphasis on the unity of God that lasted for centuries. The Protestant Reformation returned reflection to the activity of God in the world (economy) through emphasizing the experience of redeeming grace in the context of the created world. During the Renaissance, which stressed a return to the sources (*ad fontes*) as well as the beauty of the human and the order of the natural world, Europe saw the emergence of scientific thinking, which emphasized reason and searched for truth independent of divine revelation. The great scholastic synthesis between faith and reason, general and special revelation, was broken apart and has yet to be reconnected. We are now in our story at the emergence of the modern world, and in that context the Trinity was to become the "forgotten doctrine."

KEY TERMS

Apophatic
Hypostases
Kataphatic
Koinōnia
Perichoresis
Vestigia Trinitatis
Via Negativa

DISCUSSION QUESTIONS

1. How would you describe the concept of perichoresis, and why do you think it was so important in developing the understanding of the Trinity?

2. Describe and evaluate Augustine's two analogies for the Trinity. Do you find one more persuasive than the other? Why or why not?

3. Compare and contrast Aquinas's and Bonaventure's approaches to the Trinity. Do you find one more helpful or meaningful in understanding the Trinity for contemporary life?

4. How does Luther relate a theology of the cross to the Trinity? Do you find this helpful?

5. What do you find most significant in this overview of the doctrine of the Trinity?

6

Contemporary Trinitarian Development

The "economic" Trinity is the "immanent"
Trinity and vice versa.

—RAHNER, *THE TRINITY*

The doctrine of the Trinity is nothing other
than the conceptual framework needed to
understand the story of Jesus as the story of
God.

—MOLTMANN, *THE CRUCIFIED GOD*

The motto of the Renaissance was *ad fontes*, "to the sources," and this signified a return to the original sources of Western thought in their original languages. It was a return to what we would refer to today as "primary" sources. This return opened up new avenues of thought and especially deepened understanding of all things human, including the powers of reason. Conflict was inevitable. With these new avenues of thought came conflict with established ways of thinking and with the established powers who benefited from such intellectual structures. We saw this in the Reformation, particularly as the church tried to control what it considered aberrant thought through coercive means first by ecclesiastical order and then imperial power and military force. Luther was worried that during his time a religious civil war would break out that would divide and destroy the Holy Roman Empire and the unity of the church. This did not happen during his lifetime, but it did afterward in the next century.

Known as the Thirty Years War, lasting from 1618–1648, this religious civil war laid waste to much of Europe and set family against family, sometimes even within individual families. Protestant and Roman Catholic armies marched around Europe burning rival churches and killing priests and pastors with impunity. It was mutual Christian slaughter, all done in the name of God. When it was all over and settled at the Peace of Westphalia in 1648, the position was affirmed that had first been proffered at the Peace of Augsburg in 1555, namely, that each prince would have the right to determine the religion of his region (*cuius regio, eius religio*), either Catholic, Lutheran, or Calvinist. With so much bloodshed and emotional pain as well as the growing success of the emerging natural sciences, an intellectual movement arose that took as its primary emphasis the role of reason over emotion and of toleration over oppression. It advocated for individual rights over against the divine right of rulers and through its advocates eventually developed the concept of a social contract theory of government. In the process of these struggles, the Trinity became the forgotten doctrine.

1. The Forgotten Doctrine

A. THE ENLIGHTENMENT

Beginning in the seventeenth century and flowering in the eighteenth, initially known as the Age of Reason, this movement became known as the Enlightenment. Intellectually, the American and French Revolutions, as well as the Declaration of Independence, were products of Enlightenment thinking, with Jefferson and Franklin being two of its strongest proponents in the "New World." The Enlightenment sough to bring all thought under the scrutiny of reason, including religious doctrine. The machine was the epitome of Newtonian science and enlightened reason at the time, such that even the concept of God was not immune. As mentioned in chapter 3, this resulted in a form of theology known as deism, where God was basically understood as a mechanical "watchmaker" who assembled the pieces, set it running, and from then on let it carry out its functions autonomously. The Enlightenment was obsessed with the machine and with the rational human ability to understand the fundamental physical processes to construct them. In such a machine paradigm, there was no room for mystery and thus certainly not for something as seemingly illogical as the Trinity, with its paradoxical three-in-oneness. There were very significant critiques of the so-called arguments for the existence of God such as found in David Hume's (d. 1776 CE) *Dialogues*

Concerning Natural Religion, as well as John Locke's (d. 1704 CE) earlier *The Reasonableness of Christianity*. The Enlightenment reached its pinnacle in the thought of Immanuel Kant (d. 1804 CE) with his *Religion within the Limits of Reason Alone* and his great *Critique of Pure Reason* as well as his *Critique of Practical Reason*.

Kant's predecessors had tried to argue, as most empiricists, including Thomas Aquinas, did, that what was in the mind was first encountered by the senses. The mind was a clean slate (*tabula rasa*) on which sense experience wrote its images, a passive receiver of information from outside itself. Kant was to change all that and in so doing give birth to modern philosophy. In what is known as Kant's "Copernican Revolution" in philosophy, he argued that the mind is not passive but an active organizer of sense experience such that it transforms experience into meaningful categories of thought through what he called the "transcendental unity of apperception." To borrow a British phrase, these categories are like "spectacles behind the eyes" that focus our thought, much like spectacles before the eyes, on the nose, focus our vision. This led, then, to a fundamental division in types of knowledge.

Because the mind is active in organizing sense experience and is dependent on it, the mind can only know what is given to it, what Kant called the phenomenal, that which is presented to us for perception. By contrast, the mind cannot know the thing in itself (*Ding an Sich*), which Kant referred to as the noumenal. We cannot get behind our own perception and our own thought to see the object of our perception in itself. So the end result is that the mind, and human thought with it, is ultimately closed off from ever knowing anything from the inside, so to speak, except for ourselves. We can never know God directly, nor can we know anything about God with any absolute precision. Thus removing theology from metaphysics and placing it under the control of rational critique, Kant then moved it to the realm of ethics, what he called practical reason, which influences behavior but not our ultimate understanding of the world. One can now begin to see how the Enlightenment helped to give birth to what became known as modernity. Since all that we can know is rationally derived phenomenal knowledge, reason, aided by empirical science, is the path to the only reliable knowledge and truth that we can have.

Enlightenment historian Peter Gay has argued that Enlightenment thinkers broke through what he refers to as "the sacred circle," the interdependent relationship between hereditary aristocracy, the leadership of the church, and the text of the Bible.[1] It challenged and eventually brought down the "divine right of kings," which had dominated European thought and life for over a thousand years. The Enlightenment argued for individual rights instead, which were, in the words of Thomas Jefferson, "inalienable" and endowed by their "Creator." In such a worldview, religion functioned to support ethics but did not provide any significant knowledge about the "way things are" in the natural world. At the time of his death, Jefferson (d. 1826 CE) was editing the New Testament, in the original Greek, to more accord with this understanding. Known as the Jefferson Bible, it excludes any passages that would appear to contradict reason, such as all the miracles and events like the resurrection. For Jefferson, who is very emblematic of the emerging modern world, the New Testament was a good source for ethics, such as in the Sermon on the Mount, but otherwise not of much use for understanding the world. For such empirical understanding, one turned to reason and its primary manifestation, the natural sciences. In such a milieu, with theological reflection generally put on the defensive by rational critique, reflection on and even use of the Trinity in Christian thought became quite problematic and was mostly avoided; hence the "forgotten doctrine."

B. MODERNISM

I already briefly critiqued modern theism back in chapter 3, so I will not repeat that here. Rather, I will focus on the impact of modernism, basically through the nineteenth to the mid-twentieth centuries, on Trinitarian thinking and why a renaissance in such thinking was necessary. Ted Peters summarizes, "Modern liberal theologians in the wake of Immanuel Kant found it presumptuous to think they could speak speculatively or metaphysically about the secret life of the immanent Trinity. The inner dynamics of the divine being belong to the noumenal realm, whereas human cognition is strikingly limited to the phenomenal realm. Kant opened the nineteenth century by diking off the flow of trinitarian speculation."[2] Reliance on Scripture or other sources of religious experience was perceived to be emotional if not irrational and so was not referred to, cutting off theological reflection from the very experiences that had led to the formulation of the doctrine of the Trinity in the first place.

Catherine LaCugna in her watershed work on the Trinity, *God For Us*, sees this as the culmination, in her words, of "the defeat of the Trinity."[3]

---

1. Peter Gay, *The Enlightenment: The Science of Freedom* (New York: W. W. Norton, 1996). See also Ernst Cassirer, *The Philosophy of the Enlightenment*, trans. Fritz C. A. Koelln and James P. Pettegrove, updated ed. (Princeton: Princeton University Press, 2009).

2. Ted Peters, *God as Trinity* (Louisville: Westminster John Knox, 1993), 83.

3. Catherine LaCugna, *God For Us* (San Francisco: HarperSanFrancisco, 1993), 8, and *passim*, which she indicates comes from an article by D. Wendebourg, "From the Cappadocian Fathers to Gregory Palamas: The Defeat of Trinitarian Theology," *Studia Patristica* 17, no. 1 (1982): 194–197.

Beginning with the early debates over the Arian controversy, followed later by the separation into two categories "the one God" and "the Triune God" by Thomas Aquinas, LaCugna argues that there was a continual movement away from understanding the Trinity in terms of the economy of salvation (salvation history) in deference to addressing the nature of the divine in itself, in an infinite divine realm. Elizabeth Johnson concurs,

> This approach was finessed by the rational spirit of the Enlightenment, which produced an idea of God known today as classical theism. This is a solitary God viewed alone in "himself" (the theistic God is always referred to in male terms) and arrived at primarily through philosophical inference. Transcendence is stressed to the virtual exclusion of immanence or indwelling, God and the world having to connect over a huge ontological chasm. And the Trinity itself is defeated.[4]

The Enlightenment simply accelerated and focused a process of reflection that had been developing over centuries.

God was increasingly viewed as distant and unaffected by the events of the world. God was primarily a transcendent philosophical principle whose contact with creation had long since ceased, with no hint of compassion left. It is little wonder then that any discussion of God's relatedness to the world or to salvation was seen as weak and irrational wish fulfillment. In the theological community of the nineteenth century, the Trinity was seen at best as an appendage to theological reflection. Friedrich Schleiermacher (d. 1834 CE), considered the father of modern liberal Protestantism, sought to find an independent ground for theology and religious belief. He argued that the root of religious faith lies in a sense of "absolute dependence," which could not be reduced to either philosophical or ethical reasoning.[5] Indeed, religion had its own independent basis for reflection. This meant, of course, that he necessarily focused on the essential nature of God and connected all theological reflection to this foundational experience, further marginalizing the doctrine of the Trinity.

In his classic work *The Christian Faith*, Schleiermacher placed the Trinity at the end of the work, in the last few pages, so convinced was he that it

---

4. Elizabeth Johnson, "Trinity: To Let the Symbol Sing Again," *Theology Today*, 54, no. 3 (1997): 301–2.

5. Friedrich Schleiermacher, *On Religion: Speeches to Its Cultured Despisers*, trans. Richard Crouter (Cambridge: Cambridge University Press, 1996).

had little or no relevance to the life of faith.[6] Carl Braaten observes, "Friedrich Schleiermacher had no taste for the Trinity, regarding this church doctrine as 'not an immediate utterance concerning the Christian self-consciousness, but only a combination of such utterances.' He dealt with the Trinity only in the 'Conclusion' of his dogmatics, which only encouraged those who followed in his train to regard it as a highly problematic theologoumenon [theological opinion]."[7] Schleiermacher laid the foundational attitude toward the Trinity for much of later liberal Protestantism, seeing it as an artificially derived doctrine that had more to do with the "Hellenization of Christianity" (Harnack) than springing from the soil of the gospel. Braaten concludes, "By the time the Protestant tradition reached Karl Barth the doctrine of the Trinity was all but dead."[8]

This general philosophical framework represents a broad optimism during the nineteenth century regarding human ability both to understand and control the natural world, and increasingly the social world as well. Beginning with the Enlightenment, human reason had appeared to know no bounds. All was possible. With the emergence of Darwinism at midcentury, even the biological realm appeared to fall under rational clarity and potential control. By late in the century, increasingly harsh critiques of religious belief were coming from multiple directions. First comes the "fiery brook" of Ludwig Feuerbach (d.1872 CE, Feuerbach means "fiery brook" in German), who had argued that theology is simply anthropology writ large and projected onto the heavens.[9] Friedrich Nietzsche (d. 1900 CE) proclaimed that God is dead.[10] Karl Marx (d. 1883 CE) in economics and Sigmund Freud (d. 1939 CE) in psychology were both influenced by Feuerbach, especially his analysis that all human thought is exactly that, human thought, and so everything humans reflect on must be connected back to the knower. This was Feuerbach's take on Kant, except he went a step further, contending that all thought was a projection of human experience and that theology, in particular, could never know revelation and had simply projected a superlativized humanity on the cosmos and called it God.

6. Friedrich Schleiermacher, *The Christian Faith*, trans. H. R. Mackintosh and J. S. Stewart (Edinburgh: T&T Clark, 1928), 738–51.

7. Carl E. Braaten, "The Triune God: The Source and Model for Christian Unity and Mission," *Missiology: An International Review*, 18/4 (1990): 417–18; Schleiermacher, *The Christian Faith*, 738.

8. Braaten, *Triune God*, 418.

9. Ludwig Feuerbach, *The Essence of Christianity*, trans. George Eliot (New York: Harper Torchbooks, 1957).

10. Friedrich Nietzsche, *Thus Spoke Zarathustra: A Book for Everyone and No One*, trans. Adrian del Caro (New York: Penguin, 1961).

It was Feuerbach's analysis that caused Freud to come to understand religion as an "illusion," and Marx, drawing on his understanding of Hegel as well as Feuerbach, to see it as an "opiate."[11] This left humanity to its own designs, and by the end of the nineteenth century it was optimistically assumed that all human knowing of the natural world would soon be complete (physics, for example, simply had to work out the final implications of Newton's laws) and that rational social policy would lead to a form of paradise on earth. It is hard to imagine such unbridled optimism from the perspective of the twenty-first century, but we, of course, have the benefit of history. We know that the same rationalism that produced understanding of the natural world also produced mustard gas, the machine gun, the airplane, the tank, and the submarine. All this optimism was to come crashing down with the bombs and bombardments of World War I, the "War to End All War." Mustard gas was to suffocate human optimism in the trenches in Europe as a whole generation eventually lay dead in Flanders Field. If there was now to be hope for humanity, it could not come from human effort alone or simply be the product of human reason.

Modernism had not recognized the dark possibilities within the human soul and had denied the possibility that even human reason could be turned for evil and not exclusively serve the good. The lesson was not fully learned even at this time, for a second world war and an even darker use of reason for evil and destruction under the Nazi regime still lay ahead. At this time, however, especially in theological circles, the need for a source of hope beyond the self, beyond reason alone, was recognized. It was in the aftermath of World War I that Karl Barth was to speak first not of reason but of revelation and the need to return to the root experiences of the Christian faith, beginning foremost with the Trinity. The Trinitarian renaissance had begun.

2. Trinitarian Renaissance

The marginalizing of the doctrine of the Trinity, as well as the devastation of world war, led thinkers in both the Protestant and Roman Catholic traditions to reassess the relevance of the doctrine and to turn to the root experiences of the Christian faith recorded in the Bible. The most significant contributors to this renewal of thinking about the Trinity in the West[12] were the two

---

11. Sigmund Freud, *The Future of an Illusion*, trans. James Strachey (1928; repr., Eastford, CT: Martino Fine Books, 2010). Karl Marx and Friedrich Engels, *German Ideology, including Theses on Feuerbach* (New York: Prometheus, 1998); and Karl Marx, trans. Samuel Moore, *Das Kapital* (Billings: Synergy International of the Americas, 2007).

12. For the sake of focus and simplicity, throughout this work I have primarily dealt with thinkers and movements in the Western Christian Tradition. This is in no way intended to denigrate Eastern

Karls, Karl Barth for Protestantism and Karl Rahner for Roman Catholicism. Each thinker, in his own way, sought to revitalize reflection on the Trinity. To a great extent they succeeded, for the last half of the twentieth century saw a large outpouring of publications on the Trinity and increased creative reflection on the foundational Christian understanding of God. We will look briefly at these two renewal thinkers and then turn to two later relational theologians, Moltmann and Pannenberg, who made major contributions to new constructive theological understandings of the Trinity. Let us turn first, then, to Karl Barth.

A. KARL BARTH

Karl Barth (d. 1968 CE) had been deeply disturbed by the complicity of his liberal theological professors in their unreserved support of World War I and what was perceived to be the superiority of German culture. In light of this lack of self-criticism, Barth felt that theology must find an alternative basis for its reflection. Only truth that comes from outside the human condition (*extra nos*) could be a source of truth not subject to human distortion. He found the basis of such truth in Scripture and the divine revelation that it contained. Revelation, he argued, comes from outside the human condition; it is not something produced or deduced by humanity. Barth rejected all forms of natural theology, which attempted to reason to the existence of God from human observation and reflection on the natural world. He also rejected all forms of what he called "religion," which he defined as humanity's attempt to find God. The message of the Christian gospel was precisely that because we cannot find God, God has found us!

In the aftermath and cultural depression of World War I in Europe, a message of hope could not come from human action, especially reason, for that had ultimately not prevented but had even intensified the destruction of war. For Barth, there was a need to return to the foundational experiences of the Christian faith and their center in the revelation in Jesus Christ. Barth also concluded that God disclosed God's self in a threefold manner in these experiences, so that the Trinity was a direct result of Christian experience based on divine revelation. The Trinity was the way Christians experienced and therefore understood God. Barth thus began his magnum opus, the *Church Dogmatics*, with reflection on the Trinity. Far from being an appendage or afterthought, as it had been for Schleiermacher, the doctrine of the Trinity was

Orthodox Christian thought but simply to address the tradition with which most potential readers will be familiar.

essential to understanding divine revelation and was at the core of the Christian experience of God. It was this reprioritization of the importance of the Trinity that contributed to the renaissance of Trinitarian reflection in the twentieth century.

Barth grounded his theological method in revelation, stipulating, "The reality of God which meets us in revelation is His reality in all the depths of eternity."[13] What Barth meant by this is that in the scriptural accounts God reveals who God truly is and that this takes place in a threefold manner, which is the root of the doctrine of the Trinity. Ted Peters comments, "For Barth, trinitarian thought consists of an explication of the original revelation. It is an analysis of what is already there; it is not a synthesis or reconciliation of several elements that results in the construction of something new."[14] Barth assumes that God's word is identical with Godself. He states, "Thus, to the same God who in unimpaired unity is Revealer, Revelation, and Revealedness is also ascribed in unimpaired unity variety in Himself precisely this threefold mode of being."[15] Peters concludes, "Barth's method of analysis seeks a guarantee that in the very structure of divine revelation itself the threefoldness of the divine reality is uncovered."[16] This is critical, for the source of this understanding comes directly from God in divine revelation and is not the result of human reasoning or the product of human synthetic construction derived from observation of nature or revelation. Benjamin Leslie concludes,

> Barth's procedure is typically to raise the question of what makes a given actuality possible. In this case the actuality of the revealed Trinity is a possibility only because of the immanent Trinity which is already reality in God's eternity. This is merely a specific form, and perhaps the most paradigmatic form, of an answer that permeates Barth's entire theological project. The foundation of Christian truth claims can be found only in the truth itself.[17]

In this way, Barth short circuits natural theology and cuts across the Enlightenment approach to understanding ultimate truth. Ultimate truth is

13. Karl Barth, *Church Dogmatics*, trans. G. T. Thomson (New York: Charles Scribner's Sons, 1936), 548. Quoted in Braaten, "Triune God," 417.

14. Peters, *God as Trinity*, 86. See Barth, *Church Dogmatics* I/1:353–54, and 349.

15. *Church Dogmatics*, I/1:344, quoted in Peters, *God as Trinity*, 86.

16. Peters, *God as Trinity*, 211n12.

17. Benjamin Leslie, "Does God Have a Life? Barth and LaCugna on the Immanent Trinity," *Perspectives on Religious Studies* 24, no. 4 (1997): 380. See also, George Hunsinger, *How to Read Karl Barth: The Shape of His Theology* (New York: Oxford University Press, 1991), 57.

revealed; it is not derived, by reason or any other human process. Thus the task is then to proclaim this word of God and to speak a word of hope and grace that comes from beyond the human condition and is addressed to it, particularly in the forgiving love of God in Christ. When human reason had got human society and thought into such a destructive and depressing state, as after World War I, Barth sought another source for human hope and did not put any trust in the idea of human progress, rational or otherwise.

Since human reason is part of the human condition, and the human condition is the problem, then human reason cannot be part of the solution; it too needs to be redeemed. This redemption is to be found in Christ, who is the living word of God, which God speaks forth (*Deus dixit*) to humanity and is accessible only through the exercise of faith. For Barth, there is a closed circle of faith, which originates and ends with divine revelation leading forth out of God (Revealer) to Christ (Revelation) to the believers who embrace in faith (Revealedness), which in turn returns to God. Since this process starts and ends with God's revelation, some critics, as well as admirers, of Barth have referred to it as a "revelational positivism" (Pannenberg). Barth posits divine revelation as a given and does not attempt to justify it or derive it from any other source. It is its own justification, for it is the word of God over against that of humanity, and no human justification, finite as it is, will ever justify the infinite God.

Furthermore, this divine word has come to humanity, specifically in the incarnation of Christ, so it can be heard, received, and trusted. While Barth derives some of his theological inspiration from both Luther (power of the word of God) and his later expositor Søren Kierkegaard (the infinite qualitative distinction between time and eternity), the final formulation is all his own, and it became a powerful resource for preaching and theological reflection for close to fifty years in Protestant theology. While theology had struggled to justify itself in the face of Enlightenment rationalism, for Barth Enlightenment rationalism had to justify itself in the presence of divine revelation, which stands over against it in critique. For our purposes here, Barth reintroduced and reinvigorated reflection on the Trinity by returning first and foremost to its scriptural basis and arguing that there, in divine revelation, the threefoldness of God is disclosed and forms the basis for the later formulation of the doctrine of the Trinity. In effect, somewhat like Luther, Barth returned Christian theological reflection to its roots and reinstated the process that had given rise to the doctrine in the first place in the early church (see chapter 4). In Protestantism, the Trinitarian renaissance had begun, but a powerful voice was also to arise about thirty years later to serve the same function in Roman Catholic thought. The other Karl, Karl Rahner, was to make contributions that not only invigorated Roman Catholic reflection on the Trinity but also, through the ecumenical movement, were to benefit all Christian theology.

B. KARL RAHNER

Karl Rahner (d. 1984 CE) was troubled by the way that the doctrine of the Trinity had not only fell into disuse but even into downright confusion. Rahner laments, "Christians are, in their practical life, almost mere 'monotheists.' We must be willing to admit that, should the doctrine of the Trinity have to be dropped as false, the major part of religious literature could well remain virtually unchanged."[18] He further comments, "The Trinity occupies a rather isolated position in the total dogmatic system. To put it crassly . . . when the treatise is concluded, its subject is never brought up again. It is as though this mystery has been revealed for its own sake, and that even after it has been made known to us, it remains, *as a reality*, locked up within itself. We make statements about it, but as a reality it has nothing to do with us at all."[19] Rahner believed, as we have already discussed, that this condition began to develop back in the Middle Ages when Thomas Aquinas, most notably among others, separated "on the one God" (*De Deo Uno*) from "on the Triune God" (*De Deo Trino*). He concludes, "The treatise of the Trinity locks itself in even more splendid isolation, with the ensuing danger that the religious mind finds it devoid of interest. As a result the treatise becomes quite philosophical and abstract and refers hardly at all to salvation history. It looks as if everything which matters for us in God has already been said in the treatise *On the One God*."[20] Carl Braaten observes,

> It is not as though there is another different reality of God behind his revelation, as though the true essence of God inheres in his oneness, with his threefoldness lying at a lower level of metaphorical language. Only by overcoming the separation between the oneness and the threeness is it possible to connect the mystery of the Trinity with the nature of the church and its mission.[21]

The fact that most Trinitarian thinking had taken place independently or only loosely connected to the scriptural tradition had moved it further into philosophical abstraction, in which case it could not find connection with human experience. Yet it was precisely human experience of the divine through

---

18. Karl Rahner, *The Trinity*, trans. Joseph Donceel (New York: Herder & Herder, 1970), 10–11.

19. Ibid., 14.

20. Ibid., 17.

21. Braaten, "The Triune God," 417.

Christ and the life of the disciples recorded in the New Testament that had given rise to the understanding of the Trinity in the first place. Rahner also needed to return Trinitarian reflection to its roots.

Rahner's solution to this predicament was to formulate one of the most influential dictums in the history of Trinitarian reflection, "Rahner's Rule," which was to become axiomatic in later Trinitarian thinking; namely: "The 'economic' Trinity *is* the 'immanent' Trinity and *vice versa*."[22] This interpretation inextricably ties any understanding of God as Trinity to the history of salvation as recorded in the New Testament. Wolfhart Pannenberg clarifies the logic of this insight,

> The incarnation certainly cannot be thought of as making no difference to the eternal life of the one God. This was the insight that prompted Karl Rahner to develop his now famous thesis that the immanent Trinity and the economic Trinity are one. The reason is that the incarnation as well as the salvation of humankind and the final, eschatological consummation of the world belong to the divine economy. If, however, the incarnation also belongs to the immanent trinitarian life of God, then the immanent trinitarian life and the divine economy must be one.[23]

This places change and relationality right in the eternal essence of God. God cannot be related to historical change without in some respects being changed in the process, even in the immanent Trinity, that is, the divine essence.

Rahner understood this conclusion of his dictum but did not fully embrace its consequences. There was a sense in which he still wanted to hold onto the immutability of God even in the face of such reciprocal relationality. Ted Peters observes, "An implication that Rahner himself does not yet draw, but which Jurgen Moltmann and Robert Jenson later do, is that the eternal or immanent Trinity finds its very identity in the economy of temporal salvation events. . . . Rahner persists in the classical insistence that God's eternity is independent of historical self-constitution."[24] Yet interestingly, Peters continues, "Rahner assumes that the immanent Trinity is actually given to us already in the experience of grace. 'The Trinity is not for us a reality which can only be expressed as a doctrine. The Trinity itself is with us.'"[25] The full implications

---

22. Rahner, *The Trinity*, 22 (italics original).

23. Wolfhart Pannenberg, "Eternity, Time and the Triune God," in *Trinity, Time and Church: A Response to the Theology of Robert W. Jenson*, ed. Colin Gunton (Grand Rapids: Eerdmans, 2000), 66–67.

24. Peters, *God as Trinity*, 97.

of Rahner's bold advance in Trinitarian thinking, which he was not willing to draw out, was to be left to major relational theologians who were to follow.

Rahner was, however, able to help reinvigorate reflection on the Trinity, one of his goals, as well as help to form a bridging consensus in Trinitarian thinking across ecumenical lines. Rahner's Rule marks a decisive watershed in twentieth-century trinitarian thinking.[26] Both Protestant and Roman Catholic theologians today embrace it. Peters concludes, "By identifying the immanent with the economic relations, Rahner opens Barth's door a bit wider so that we might consider how the history of the incarnation as history becomes internal to the divine perichoresis itself. And along with the incarnate Son comes the world that he was destined to save, so that the whole of temporal creation enters into the eternity of God's self-relatedness."[27] Temporality and eternity are to be brought into relation within the very essence of God, and with that all of the strengths and weaknesses, successes and failures that compose historical existence enter into the very life of God. Among the most striking features of this new relationality was that suffering becomes a dimension of divine existence. As Jürgen Moltmann was soon to develop, following Luther, we now have the "crucified God."

3. Relational Trinitarianism

This fundamental relation of the immanent and economic Trinity results, as Walter Kasper points out, in two dangers, namely, collapsing the distinction to one side or the other.[28] First, we can misunderstand the identification if we interpret the economic Trinity as merely a temporal manifestation of an eternal immanent Trinity. History, however, does make a difference, such that the incarnation means that God exists in the world in a new way. Peters observes, "The incarnation implies that God really does become."[29] This has profound implications for understanding not only God's relationship to the world but also the world's relationship to God. What we now have is the emerging of a relational ontology (see chapter 3), which does away with the idea of a static substance as constituting existence and replaces it with dynamic relationships, which necessarily involve mutual influence and reciprocity of affect. This change is furthered by new understandings of the physical world,

25. Ibid.

26. Ibid., 102.

27. Ibid., 103.

28. Walter Kasper, *The God of Jesus Christ*, new ed. (New York: Continuum, 2012), 275–76, quoted in Peters, *God as Trinity*, 102.

29. Ibid.

brought about by the physical sciences, as dynamic and relative. So history counts. But there is a second possible misinterpretation, and that is to collapse the identity in the other direction.

The second misinterpretation is to assume that the immanent Trinity first came into existence through the economic, that it did not exist until the incarnation. In our Trinitarian discussion, this occurs if we focus only on the economic history of salvation and neglect the understanding that God is also more than such a history and cannot be fully, even if importantly, described by such a history. If the relationship of revelation to experience is understood in such a way that human finite experience in nature and history determines the meaning of the revelation of God, that there is no *ad intra*, no beyond of the divine in itself that is disclosed, then we collapse back into the human problematic and do not have a source of hope beyond the human self. While it is important to point out these two dangers, post-Barthian Trinitarian theologians do not understand the relation in these ways and so do not fall into either of the misunderstandings of the Trinitarian identity that Kasper is so concerned about.

The key is to understand that the word *experience* as used here does not refer to common or natural human experience but, rather, specifically to the Christian church's experience of Jesus Christ, which is tantamount to special revelation.[30] Understood this way, revelation need not be pitted against experience in some type of interpretive-reduction debate. At issue is the nature of freedom, particularly the divine, in such a way that the economic does not restrict the immanent and that God has freedom to effect whatever God sees fit. *The economic Trinity in history by relating to the immanent Trinity in eternity does not dictate its nature, only influences it.* Experience does not dictate the content of revelation but rather provides the context for its reception. Both human and divine freedom can be allowed as long as one does not collapse the relationship to either side of the revelation/experience distinction. Ted Peters helpfully clarifies, "The alleged split between revelation and experience is a nonissue in the current debate. . . . Genuine freedom does not require a timeless eternity. It only requires an open future."[31] It is such an open future that relational Trinitarians such as Jürgen Moltmann and Wolfhart Pannenberg assume, an understanding of the Trinity that is relational, dynamic, historical, and eschatological. Such an open relational future was, however, born out of the pain of war-torn lives in both Moltmann's and Pannenberg's cases.

---

30. Ibid., 214n45.
31. Ibid.

A. JÜRGEN MOLTMANN

Moltmann (b. 1926 CE) as a youth was forced into the German army toward the end of World War II and was taken prisoner, spending several years in a prisoner-of-war camp. While there, he said that "hope rubbed itself raw on the barbwire. A man cannot live without hope."[32] He saw men give up hope of ever being repatriated, take ill, lie down, and die. He realized, however, that there was a "hope against hope" that doggedly refused to give up and to envision an alternate future and avoid succumbing to the painful present. This was the realization of the power of the future and the beginning of "the theology of hope." His starting position is characteristic of all the new Trinitarian theologians: "If the biblical testimony is chosen as point of departure, then we shall have to start from the three persons of the history of Christ. If philosophical logic is made the starting point, then the enquirer proceeds from the One God."[33] In homage to Barth, all subsequent Trinitarian thinkers begin with the biblical testimony, which means that they begin by looking at the multiple ways in which the early Christian community experienced God in Christ. They do not begin with a philosophical principle and attempt to derive from it the nature of the Trinity. But the agreement with Barth ends there. There is a strong drive in Moltmann's thought to place the Trinity in the context of human history and by so doing introduce change, relationality, and even pathos into God. This is the context for the "crucified God," and this God is intrinsically Trinitarian. Here is one of Moltmann's greatest contributions to the Trinitarian renaissance. In contrast to the past, God is now understood to be a becoming God such that God's "being is in becoming."[34] This moves far beyond and in intentional distinction from the Greek philosophical heritage, which had so influenced earlier Trinitarian reflection. It moves from stressing divine unity to emphasizing divine plurality.

Moltmann is critical of both Barth and Rahner for overly emphasizing the unity of God to the denigration of the multiplicity of the persons of the Trinity. They both identify the divine subject with the unity and not the plurality. They are still too modern in their worldview. Moltmann sees this ending in a cold, independent divine subject who is distanced from the realities of human history and suffering, indeed, is distanced from the cross itself. God

32. Quoted in M. D. Meeks, *Origins of the Theology of Hope* (Philadelphia: Fortress Press, 1974), x–xi.

33. Jürgen Moltmann, *The Trinity and the Kingdom* (New York: Harper & Row, 1981), 149.

34. See, e.g., Eberhard Jüngel, *The Doctrine of the Trinity: God's Being is in Becoming* (Grand Rapids: Eerdmans, 1976); and Jüngel, *God as the Mystery of the World* (Grand Rapids: Eerdmans, 1983). For the sake of space, I will not be developing Jüngel's thought, which is an interesting elaboration of Barth but also moves beyond him.

becomes an absolute individual who simply expresses the one divine self in three modes, Father, Son, and Spirit.[35] Moltmann seeks something more in consonance with the biblical witness. He says, "If we search for a concept of unity corresponding to the biblical testimony on the triune God, the God who unites others with himself, then we must dispense with both the concept of the one substance and the concept of identical subject. . . . It must be perceived in the perichoresis of the divine Persons."[36] What Moltmann is advocating by emphasizing the divine plurality is what he calls a "social doctrine of the Trinity."[37] Ted Peters helpfully clarifies, "So Moltmann's method is to attempt to get behind the metaphysical substantialism of the pre-nicene and Nicene theologians and return to the original scriptural witness. The problem with the Nicene theologians is that they were beginning with the assumption of divine unity and then asking about the possibility of a divine plurality. . . . The Bible, Moltmann says in contrast, begins with the three living persons and then makes unity the problem."[38] It is for this reason that Moltmann argues that Christianity is not a monotheistic religion, but neither is it tritheistic. Christianity represents a new alternative, that of the Trinity, between monotheism and polytheism.[39] The Trinity represents what I have been calling *pluralistic monotheism* and each side of this relationship must be equally maintained, both unity and plurality.

By returning to Scripture, Moltmann argues that Christianity can also then affirm the pathos of God in Christ, that indeed we have to do with the "crucified God."[40] As a young man, enduring the horrors of battle and being held in a prisoner-of-war camp, Moltmann profoundly agrees with Dietrich Bonhoeffer's statement that "only a suffering God can help."[41] If God is distant, immune, or immutable in the face of human suffering, then God is simply irrelevant to the human condition. Moltmann did not find this to be the case in the scriptural witness. Far from fitting into the philosophical model of immutability, the God of the Bible is a God of pathos. We need to understand that God is a God of self-giving love (*agapē*). This is most clearly displayed in

---

35. Peters, *God as Trinity*, 105.

36. Moltmann, *Trinity and the Kingdom*, 149–50. Quoted in Peters, *God as Trinity*, 104.

37. Moltmann, *Trinity and the Kingdom*, 19.

38. Peters, *God as Trinity*, 104.

39. Ibid., 103.

40. Jürgen Moltmann, *The Crucified God: The Cross as the Foundation and Criticism of Christian Theology* (Philadelphia: Fortress Press, 1974). See also Moltmann, "The 'Crucified God' A Trinitarian Theology of the Cross," *Interpretation* 26, no. 3 (1972): 278–99.

41. Dietrich Bonhoeffer, *Letters and Papers from Prison*, ed. Eberhard Bethge (London: SCM, 1967), 361.

Jesus' statement on the cross, "My God, My God, why have you forsaken me?" (Matt. 27:46, from Psalm 22). Moltmann argues that this cry directly enters into God and affects the very heart of God. It is a Trinitarian event. He puts it this way: "The Spirit is the Spirit of surrender of the Father and the Son. He is creative love proceeding out of the Father's pain and the Son's self-surrender and comes to forsaken human beings in order to open them to a future for life. We have interpreted the cross in a trinitarian manner as an event occurring in the relationship between persons, in which these persons are constituted in their relationship to each other and so constitute themselves."[42] He further clarifies, "The material principle of the doctrine of the Trinity is 'the cross,' and the formal principle of the theology of the cross is the doctrine of the Trinity."[43] God suffers too while the Son is dying on the cross, and ultimately death enters into God. God does not die, but death is in God. The cross affects the very interpersonal dynamics of the Trinity such that as the Son suffers the entire Trinity suffers. This is what it means to say that, in a social doctrine of the Trinity, the "material principle of the doctrine of the Trinity is the cross."

Elizabeth Johnson observes that "the cross reveals God's inner nature to be the trinitarian event of self-giving love capable of suffering, thereby releasing the Spirit who fills all creation with life. Every time we make the sign of the cross while reciting the names of the trinitarian persons we testify to this truth."[44] She adds, "The holocaust was never far from Moltmann's mind as he worked out this thesis. Here the theology of the suffering God receives its deepest significance: 'there cannot be any other Christian answer to the question of this torment. To speak here of a God who could not suffer would make God a demon.'"[45] For Moltmann, "to know Christ and him crucified" is to know the very heart of God and to experience the love of God, which is the root of the Christian experience of the Trinity.

There are, of course, concerns with Moltmann's understanding of the Trinity. Ted Peters, for example, raises two major questions: first, whether the New Testament really affirms a plurality in relation to God rather than a unity; and second, whether a social doctrine of the Trinity can succeed at maintaining divine unity.[46] From a number of sources, it is clear that the New Testament emphasis is on the oneness of God and that "the biblical God is One subject, One Thou, One personal being."[47] It may be the case that Moltmann overstates

---

42. Ibid., 294–95.

43. Ibid., 295.

44. Elizabeth Johnson, *The Quest for the Living God* (New York: Continuum, 2008), 62.

45. Ibid.

46. Peters, *God as Trinity*, 108.

his opposition to monotheism, but he certainly does not seek polytheism. At the heart of his resistance to monotheism really lies his critique of monarchy. He rejects the connection between monotheism and monarchy so strongly because of all the exploitation and social injustice that has been perpetrated in the name of God by "divine right." Moltmann's theology is also a political theology and as such includes a strong social critique of what he views as the sociopolitical co-optation of Christianity during its long cultural history, most notably during Nazi-era Germany. In referring to Moltmann, along with Dorothy Soelle and Johann Baptist Metz, as political theologians, Elizabeth Johnson makes the helpful observation that "political theology as they developed it is wary of a privatized religion that focuses on an individual's religious experience and morality alone. Such a narrow view contributed to the failure of the churches to vigorously oppose Hitler, allowing a complacency that enabled faith to be bound up with an unjust social order."[48] One way to avoid personalized and individual co-optation of faith is to argue for a social conception of God. This conception also has significance for ecological theology, as the social is expanded to include nonhuman nature. Moltmann seeks to challenge the privatization of faith and instead to enable a social conscience in service to social justice. He would probably argue that personhood as we now understand it is social and that the individual and society relationally constitute one another (see chapter 3). Unity is intrinsically bound up with plurality, but they are not the same and cannot be reduced one to the other either way.[49] Peters finally concludes, "What the Moltmann theology should lead us to repudiate is that there exists some sort of second God, a trinitarian double, a ghostly immanence hovering behind while unaffected by the actual course of divine-historical events. Moltmann reminds us that the relationship between the eternal and the temporal is now broken and, further, God is present on both sides of the brokenness."[50] Moltmann reminds us that whenever we think of God we must also, as Christians, think of the cross and that the intrinsic shape of the Trinity is cruciform.

---

47. Claude Welch, *In This Name: The Doctrine of the Trinity in Contemporary Theology* (New York: Charles Scribner's Sons, 1952), 268. Quoted in Peters, *God as Trinity*, 108.

48. Johnson, *Quest*, 55–56.

49. Peters, *God as Trinity*, 109.

50. Ibid., 110.

B. WOLFHART PANNENBERG

It is rare that one gets a glimpse of the originating religious experiences of great theologians, but Pannenberg is an exception. He was not raised in a Christian home, so his transition to Christianity and to studying theology was not simple or direct but based on a profound religious experience as a young boy in war-torn Germany. He relates,

> The single most important experience occurred in early January 1945, when I was 16 years old. On a lonely two-hour walk home from my piano lesson, seeing an otherwise ordinary sunset, I was suddenly flooded by light and absorbed in a sea of light which, although it did not extinguish the humble awareness of my finite existence, overflowed the barriers that normally separate us from the surrounding world. Several months earlier I had narrowly escaped an American bombardment at Berlin; a few weeks later my family would have to leave our East German home because of the Russian offensive. I did not know at the time that January 6 was the day of Epiphany, nor did I realize that in that moment Jesus Christ had claimed my life as a witness to the transfiguration of this world in the illuminating power and judgment of his glory.[51]

This vision of the transfiguration of the world was to compel Pannenberg into the study of theology and to understand that all of the creation was to be connected with God. While studying with Barth, Pannenberg became convinced that Barth's understanding of the relationship of revelation to history was too restrictive. At first impressed with Barth, Pannenberg later observed, "On the other hand, I was troubled by the dualism involved in his revelational positivism. It seemed to me that the truly sovereign God could not be regarded as absent or superfluous in ordinary human experience and philosophical reflection, but that every single reality should prove incomprehensible (at least in its depth) without recourse to God, if he actually was the Creator of the world as Barth thought him to be."[52] Pannenberg could not tolerate the dualism that Barth's "revelational positivism" had created; indeed; he has spent his entire career connecting theological reflection to every area of human knowledge of creation, from cosmology to anthropology. For our purposes, however, it is his insistence on the historical nature of the Trinity that is of importance.

---

51. Wolfhart Pannenberg, "God's Presence in History," *The Christian Century*, March 11, 1981, 261.
52. Ibid.

Pannenberg agrees with Barth, Rahner, and Moltmann regarding the origins of the doctrine of the Trinity in scriptural witness but takes the importance of God's action in history even further. He draws out the ultimate conclusion, which Rahner had not, namely, "Rahner did not yet draw the consequence that the eternal self-identity could not be conceived independently of the salvation-historical workings of the Son and the Spirit."[53] For Pannenberg, even the eternal identity of God is inexorably bound up with history. The Christian God is Trinitarian precisely because this God is involved in history, which means God not only has a dimension of the past but also a dimension of the future. The future, specifically the realization of the kingdom of God, becomes the hallmark of Pannenberg's theology and his understanding of God's activity in the world. This is his basis for "revelation as history," the name he gives to his overall project.[54] God is moving through history to realize God's kingdom so that one understands the present as well as the past only from the perspective of the future, what God is intending to realize. This is, however, only accessible through history. He indicates, "There is no direct conceptual approach to God, nor from God to human reality, but God's presence is hidden in the particulars of history. . . . When I began to understand that one should not set history and eschatology, nor (therefore) history and God, in opposition to one another, the general direction of my further thought was determined."[55] Pannenberg's theology is a theology of the future kingdom of God, where the understanding of eschatology (the study of last or final things) informs our understanding of history. In this he is in agreement with Moltmann, although he does not develop the social dimension as fully for social critique. Pannenberg's theology is not primarily a political theology. It is in light of the future kingdom of God and its proleptic disclosure in Christ and his resurrection that we can begin to know the nature of God and the activity of the Spirit in the world.[56] Ted Peters observes that "without this kingdom, God could not be God."[57]

What this means for Trinitarian reflection is that God is constituted by the Trinitarian relations; unity comes from relatedness, not the other way around. The divine essence, *ousia*, is relationally structured. Rather than subsuming

---

53. Wolfhart Pannenberg, "Father, Son, Spirit: Problems of a Trinitarian Doctrine of God," *Dialog* 26, no. 4 (1987): 251.

54. Wolfhart Pannenberg, *Revelation as History* (New York: Macmillan, 1968).

55. Pannenberg, "God's Presence in History," 260.

56. Wolfhart Pannenberg, *Jesus—God and Man*, trans. Louis Wilkins and Duane Priebe (Louisville: John Knox, 1968), ch. 3, section 1, "The Proleptic Element in Jesus' Claim to Authority," 53–54.

57. Peters, *God as Trinity*, 135.

the diversity of relations under some form of unity of divine substance as the ancients had done, for example, Aristotle, now relations constitute identity, and any relationship to substance is derived from them (see chapter 2). Drawing on the thought of Hegel (d. 1831 ce, one of the few nineteenth-century thinkers to take an interest in the Trinity), Pannenberg understands that each person of the Trinity must sublimate (self-restrict) itself to allow for the divine unity. The Trinity is a unity of reciprocal self-dedication.[58] Indeed, Pannenberg thanks Hegel for this insight, referring to it as the most profound clarification of the inner Trinitarian perichoresis to appear in the history of Christian thought.[59] This inner self-giving of the Trinity produces relational unity and integrates the threefold aspect of divine relatedness in the world. Pannenberg represents a Trinitarian theology done within a relational ontology such that being is indeed to be found in becoming and becoming is understood only in light of the future kingdom of God. Revelation is not only in history but is itself historical within the history of God. Ted Peters summarizes, "What Rahner's Rule comes to mean in Pannenberg's theory is that for all practical purposes we need not distinguish between the Godhead *ad intra* and *ad extra*. Identity is dependent and relational on both counts. Pannenberg believes God's relation to the world is necessary for determining God's identity." However, this does not mean that God is fully determined by the world. Peters continues, "Pannenberg, no less than Barth and Jungel, emphasizes that God is free, and this implies that God is eternal and in that sense independent of the world."[60] As the ground for the future, God must necessarily be more than the present world in order to be the source of future possibilities and realization.

As I bring this discussion of relational and post-Barthian theologians to a close, it might be helpful to briefly summarize how Pannenberg differs from those who came before him. This will also suffice as a summary of where much contemporary relational Trinitarian thinking is at. Peters gives us a helpful, succinct summary in five points.

> 1. The idea of the Trinity cannot be deduced from a general concept of God; it depends on an analysis of the revelation in Jesus Christ that explicates what is implicit.

---

58. Ibid., 137.

59. Pannenberg, *Jesus—God and Man*, 2nd ed. (Louisville: Westminster John Knox, 1977), 179–83. Referred to in Peters, *God as Trinity*, 224.

60. Ibid., 139.

2. In contrast to the classic view, which makes the Father the cause of the Son and Spirit, a view that makes causation effective in only one direction, Pannenberg advocates mutual causation.

3. The self-differentiation through humble obedience on the part of the Son is paradoxically the source of the Son's divinity.

4. In contrast to the tradition, especially in the East, where the monarchy of the Father locates the source of all divinity in the first person, Pannenberg adds the dynamic of redemptive history through which the establishment of the kingdom of God provides acknowledgment and acclamation and, hence, divinity of relationship.

5. In Pannenberg's scheme, the Son and the Spirit share in the divine essence of the Father not just by being begotten or by processing from a divine origin but also by contributing to the kingdom of the Father that is entrusted to the Son and returned to the Father through the Spirit.[61]

These five commitments signal the significant changes in Trinitarian reflection that have occurred in the twentieth century, starting first with Barth and continuing through many additional thinkers, most of whom I have not had space to mention here.

These thinkers, however, form the heart of the Trinitarian renaissance, a change in thought that emphasizes the critical role of Scripture and thus revelation in understanding the Trinity but also that emphasizes this revelation has occurred in history and as such means that history and change have entered into the divine life. God is now both immanent and becoming, not just transcendent and being. In addition, this means that the incarnation is at the heart of God, such that God's love is cruciform and that God is a God of pathos and not apathy. Finally, in these newer understandings of the Trinity, existence as becoming is understood relationally, such that the persons of the Trinity mutually constitute one another and there is not a hierarchy of being that informs a hierarchy of leadership on earth. Divine right, as with divine love, must be seen and understood from the context of the cross, so that a cruciform Christ leads to a cruciform God and a cruciform church. In the more technical vocabulary, a theology of the cross, *theologia crucis*, leads to a church of the cross, an *ecclesia crucis*.[62] Indeed, what we have, especially in

---

61. Ibid.141–42, from Pannenberg, "The Christian Vision of God," 31–35.

62. See Douglas John Hall's *The Cross in Our Context* (Minneapolis: Fortress Press, 2003), esp. ch. 4, "The Crucified God," 75–90, and ch. 7, "The Church and the Cross," 137–55.

Moltmann and Pannenberg, is a Trinitarian theology of the cross, a *Trinitate crucis*. All of these elements will be important as we move to a discussion of the insights of contemporary physics, which will provide useful metaphors for further elaborating these divine Trinitarian relationships. This developmental context for Trinitarian thought will be referred back to as we enter into constructive theological reflection in part 3.

KEY TERMS

Crucified God
Dogma/Dogmatics
Economic Trinity
Immanent Trinity
Modernism
Noumenal
Phenomenal
Rahner's Rule
Rationalism
Revelation as History
Revelational Positivism
Social Trinity
Theologia Crucis
Theology is Anthropology

DISCUSSION QUESTIONS

1. What were the original goals of the Enlightenment? In what ways did these goals fall short, especially in light of war and the Holocaust?
2. How did the Enlightenment stifle discussion of the Trinity? What caused the conversation to begin again (i.e., the "Trinitarian renaissance")?
3. Compare and contrast the theology of Karl Barth and Karl Rahner. Do you find one theologian more helpful in understanding the Trinity?
4. Why does Moltmann focus on the idea of a "suffering God"? How does this affect his view of Christ?
5. In what ways does Pannenberg stress the relationality of the Trinity differently from Barth, Moltmann, and Rahner?

PART III

Science and the Trinity

7

Theology, Science, and Quantum Theory

*Science without religion is lame and
religion without science is blind.*

—ALBERT EINSTEIN

The human quest for meaning and purpose draws on both our inner and outer experiences and reflects on them with both intuitive insight and rational thought—in other words, through the creative interaction of faith and reason. Throughout most of the Christian theological tradition, faith and reason have been companions on this journey of life; they have been seen as complementary and not contradictory. As was shown earlier, the fracturing of this relationship is a relatively recent phenomenon, occurring over the past three hundred years, and is primarily a product of Enlightenment rationalism and Cartesian foundationalism. Today, as we face challenges and difficult decisions on many fronts, from global climate change to stem cell research, there is an essential need for both faith and reason, fact and value, to be constructively related. More to the point, how is theological reflection to be conducted in a society and thought world influenced, if not dominated, by science? We are now at a point in the relationship of theology and science that we have not seen for almost 350 years, since the beginning of the modern period.[1] The modern period can roughly be dated as beginning with the Treaty of Westphalia in 1648, which ended the Thirty Years War, until the moon landing in 1969. Religion was

---

1. Some of the material in this and the following paragraphs are revisions of earlier material found in my articles "The Sighs of God: Kenosis, Quantum Field Theory and the Spirit," *Word and World* supplement series no. 4 (2000): 182–91; and "Toward a Kenotic Pneumatology: Quantum Field Theory and the Theology of the Cross," *CTNS Bulletin* 19, no. 2 (1999): 11–16.

split off from science in this newly emerging worldview, with religion relegated to the inexact realm of subjective experience and emotions and science to the rational, objective world of physical reality. It was, in effect, the separation of fact from value (see chapter 3).

With the emergence of the philosophy of science and its critique of scientific study, including the groundbreaking work of Thomas Kuhn in *The Structure of Scientific Revolutions*,[2] the stage was set for a more constructive interaction of science and theology. Kuhn demonstrated that science too is contextual and that theoretical shifts have as much to do with the relevant scientific human communities (human judgment) as they do with empirical data. Science is not as neutral, objective, value free, and rational as the Enlightenment thinkers had wanted to believe. We now realize that fact and value cannot be separated, for all facts are value laden, contextual truths. It is interpretation (hermeneutics) that transforms raw data into meaningful fact, by placing that data in a meaningful theoretical context, which is itself value laden (see chapter 3, fig. 2). This is true as much in science as it is in theology. Therefore, over the last fifty years, a conversation has developed between science and religion, particularly in academic theology.[3] This exploration has led to extensive reflection on different ways of relating the two. We will begin this chapter by exploring these ways before turning to the relationship between Newtonian and Quantum mechanics and finally focusing on quantum entanglement itself. This chapter is intended to provide background for the following chapter where the constructive theological use of entanglement will be developed.

1. RELATION OF THEOLOGY AND SCIENCE

A. BARBOUR: FOURFOLD TYPOLOGY

The classical typology for this relationship was first proposed by Ian Barbour, who identified four types: conflict, independence, dialogue, and integration.[4] *Conflict* is the position most often popularly portrayed in the media. It provides good sound bites but does not result in either good science or good theology!

2. Thomas S. Kuhn, *The Structure of Scientific Revolutions*, 2nd ed. (Chicago: University of Chicago Press, 1970), especially chs. 6–10.

3. The seminal work in this field is Ian Barbour's classic text *Issues in Science and Religion* (San Francisco: Harper, 1966), published one year after the discovery of the cosmic background radiation by Penzias and Wilson that has led to confirmation of big bang cosmology.

4. See Ian G. Barbour, *Religion in an Age of Science: The Gifford Lectures 1989–1991* (San Francisco: Harper & Row, 1990), vol. 1, ch. 1.

Conflict results from an ideological stance (on either side, biblical literalism or scientific materialism), which does not seek mutual understanding but rather dominance or conversion. The operative assumption is that the alternative sources provide rival answers to the same questions and are therefore competing theories of explanation. If science and religion are seen as discrete fields of study answering different, while complementary, questions, then conflict need not be the result. That is the approach of the independence model.

The *independence* model, which was popular in the 1950s and early 1960s, seeks mutual respect and integrity by affirming separate realms of investigation but does not seek common ground for mutual interaction or edification. Still prevalent in many university science departments today, this position is a step beyond conflict but ignores questions regarding disciplinary and methodological boundaries. It also does not recognize or encourage the serious interaction needed to address the complex, integrated problems of today, such as global climate change. Therefore most scholars in the field of science and religion have attempted over the last several decades to move beyond the independence model. *Integration* seeks a common worldview that allows for the mutual connections of theology and science, like in the medieval "scholastic synthesis." The diversity of positions found within individual disciplines in both science and theology currently makes this a very difficult possibility, although there are some, such as Ian Barbour, who are making the attempt. Therefore the position that has been most systematically utilized over the last forty years is one of relevant *dialogue*, which stresses mutual integrity and understanding. Indeed, the goal has been to simply get scientists and theologians talking to one another again. This effort has been constructive and essential for better understanding and cooperation and has been successful in restoring mutual trust among participants on both sides of the dialogue. After several decades of interaction, however, the conversation is now entering a new phase, in which dialogue is no longer enough. The crises of our time demand more.

B. RUSSELL: CREATIVE MUTUAL INTERACTION

One of the more interesting proposals for moving beyond dialogue but still remaining short of integration is that of "hypothetical consonance." Ted Peters writes regarding his and Robert John Russell's understanding of this concept,

> What we found to be inchoate and just asking for articulation is the assumption of hypothetical consonance. It is the assumption that both science and theology are concerned about the truth. And, we assume, one truth cannot contradict another truth. Somewhere in

the darkness of what is not-yet-known, we assume, lies a connection between the natural world as seen through scientific glasses and as seen through the eyes of faith.[5]

"Consonance" moves beyond dialogue because it carries with it the connotation of a resonance and mutuality that affirms more than simple interaction.[6] "Hypothetical," of course, affirms that the consonance is not yet fully achieved but that there are glimmers and glimpses of it that prompt further exploration.

Recently, one of the most serious constructive proposals for moving beyond dialogue toward hypothetical consonance is that of Robert John Russell in what he calls creative mutual interaction (CMI for short).[7] Russell's proposal suggests eight ways that science and theology can interact. The first five are ways that science can inform theology, and the last three are ways theology can inform science. For true "mutual interaction" to occur, the interaction has to move in both directions. Clearly, however, the majority of the discussions and writings thus far have moved from science to theology, which is the main theme of this text. The relationship does indeed need to go both ways, with theology contributing to science, but that topic is for another day.[8] Russell's eight ways are as follows.

> 1. Scientific theories may serve as data that places *constraints* on theology.
> 2. Scientific theories may serve as *supporting* data for theology in so far as they are explained theologically.
> 3. *Philosophical interpretations* of scientific theories may serve as data for theology.

5. Ted Peters, "Robert John Russell's Contribution to the Theology and Science Dialogue," in *God's Action in Nature's World: Essays in Honor of Robert John Russell*, ed. Ted Peters and Nathan Hallanger (Aldershot: Ashgate, 2006), 7.

6. For a deeper exploration of the concept of consonance, see Ted Peters, ed., *Science and Theology: The New Consonance* (Boulder, CO: Westview, 1998).

7. The most detailed development of these ideas is in Robert John Russell, "Eschatology and Physical Cosmology: A Preliminary Reflection," in *The Far-Future Universe: Eschatology from a Cosmic Perspective*, ed. George F. R. Ellis (Philadelphia: Templeton Foundation Press, 2002), 266–315. See also Russell, "Bodily Resurrection, Eschatology, and Scientific Cosmology," in *Resurrection: Theological and Scientific Assessments*, ed. Ted Peters, Robert John Russell, and Michael Welker (Grand Rapids: Eerdmans, 2002), 3–30 . Assessments of Russell's position can be found in Peters and Hallanger, *God's Action in Nature's World*; see especially part 1, "Creative Mutual Interaction Between Science and Theology."

8. For an analysis of the need for theology to inform science to fully affirm CMI, see the article by Philip Clayton, "'Creative Mutual Interaction' as Manifesto, Research Program and Regulative Ideal," in Peters and Hallanger, *God's Action in Nature's World*, 65–76.

4. Scientific theories may serve as data for theology when they are incorporated into a *philosophy of nature*.

5. Scientific theories may function *heuristically* in theology by providing conceptual, experiential, practical/moral, or aesthetic inspiration.

6. Theology may provide some of the philosophical assumptions underlying science.

7. Theological theories may function heuristically in the construction of scientific theories.

8. Theological theories may lead to "selection rules" within the criteria of theory choice; that is, for choosing among existing scientific theories that all explain the available data, or for deciding what set of data the theory should seek to explain.[9]

The first five ways provide a framework to begin to think through the role of science in theology. It would be helpful, then, for the reader to keep these CMI ways in mind as we move through the remaining material in part 3. It is especially the *supporting* and *heuristic* roles that will be employed in the next chapters as concepts from quantum physics are used to metaphorically inspire reflection on the Trinitarian understanding of perichoresis. For further clarification, I would like to briefly address each of these five ways in order.

I. CONSTRAINTS

In our contemporary, individualistic, freedom-oriented society, to say that anything puts *constraints* on the self or one's thought is not a popular notion. The real issue is, what are the limits of such constraint? Here the suggestion is that science helps us comprehend the world to which God is related. Insofar as the theologian seeks to relate God and the world, some understanding of the world is necessary, and science can assist in that understanding. The constraint for theologians comes in no longer being able to define the natural world in any way they see fit, particularly in regard to the biblical narrative. This leads to the second way, where science can *support* theology.

II. SUPPORTING

Physics, and to a lesser extent cosmology and biology, have been helpful to theology by providing more open understandings of the natural world. The quantum world is a world of probability and therefore of indeterminacy and

9. Russell, "Eschatology and Physical Cosmology," 286.

complementarity. Today the classical world of substance and mechanism (the clockwork universe) has given way to a world of dynamic and indeterminate processual relations. Physical reality is more like clouds than clocks, to borrow a metaphor from Sir John Polkinghorne.[10] This cloudy, supple, winsome world in which we now understand ourselves to exist is far more interdependent and subtle than was believed before and is much more amenable to theological reflection than was the Newtonian world of mechanistic external relations. In such a postmodern scientific worldview (Newton is considered the "modern" and "postmodern" supplements Newton with relativity and quantum theory), one can come to see God related to the physical cosmos, to intentionally borrow from sacramental imagery, as working "in, with, and under" the physical processes of the universe. In such a context, science can indeed *support* theology while not ever proving theological claims.

III. PHILOSOPHICAL INTERPRETATION

The above illustrations also indicate how the *philosophical interpretation* of scientific theories can help provide data for theological reflection. For example, the very nature of a physical existent as approached by physics has been redefined from a substantialist to a relational ontology. The openness of quantum relationality can philosophically allow for the presence of the divine spirit in the world without supernatural intervention or violation of natural law. To borrow an analogy from John B. Cobb Jr., just as the mind can be in the brain without displacing the neocortical tissue, so too God can be in the world without displacing natural processes.[11] (We will refer to this as the "panentheistic analogy" in chapter 8.) More recently, Robert John Russell has argued for what he calls "noninterventionist objective divine action" (NIODA), according to which God acts within the natural processes of the world without violating such processes. Russell observes,

> The old choice was based on classical physics and modern, reductionist philosophy. Today, because of changes in the natural sciences, including quantum physics, genetics, evolution, and the mind/brain problem, and because of changes in philosophy, including the move from reductionism to holism and the legitimacy

10. For further elaboration, see John Polkinghorne, *Serious Talk: Science and Religion in Dialogue* (Valley Forge, PA: Trinity Press International, 1995), especially ch. 2, "Understanding Quantum Theory."

11. John B. Cobb Jr., *God and the World* (Philadelphia: Westminster, 1969), especially ch. 3, "The World and God."

of including whole/part and top/down analysis, *we can now understand special providence as the objective acts of God in nature and history and we can understand these acts in a non-interventionist manner consistence with science.*[12]

As alluded to, the philosophical interpretation of biology also opens up a world of historical, dynamic change, which, while rife with suffering and loss, does allow growth and creative emergence. The concept of static perfection, inherited from the Greek philosophical tradition, is now replaced by a dynamic sense of perfection, which is much more amenable to biblical thought. The biblical conception of a dynamic God acting in history and related to the suffering of the creation is intelligible in the postmodern scientific worldview.

IV. PHILOSOPHY OF NATURE

For Russell, a *philosophy of nature* encompasses the philosophical implications of the understanding of space, time, matter, and causality in contemporary physics and cosmology.[13] It focuses on the nature and meaning of a physical existent, indeed, of what it means to "be" in a physically real sense. Whether working through quantum processes in "bottom-up" causality or through supervenient chaos theory in a "top-down" causality, there is room for God to act in the natural world without supernatural intervention. These types of philosophical theories open up a great deal of possibility for articulating divine presence in the natural world without violating natural law. Such an open philosophy of nature can be the beginning point for the formulation of a *theology of nature*, which is essential to the task of theological reflection and will be assumed in later chapters.

V. HEURISTICALLY

Finally, in terms of constructive theology, perhaps the most interesting way that science can relate to theology is *heuristically*, by "providing conceptual, experiential, practical/moral, or aesthetic inspiration."[14] There are many terms and images that the wider society has adopted from science and that are used in everyday speech, but this way suggests something more substantive, informing

---

12. Robert John Russell, "Does the 'God Who Acts' Really Act in Nature?," in Peters, *Science and Theology*, 79 (italics original), quoted in Peters, "Robert John Russell's Contribution," 10.

13. Here I agree with Nancey Murphy's understanding of the term in Russell's thought as she develops it in her article, "Creative Mutual Interaction: Robert John Russell's Contribution to Theology and Science Methodology," in Peters, *God's Action in Nature's World*, 49n5.

14. Russell, "Eschatology and Physical Cosmology," 286.

the very ideas and constructive concepts that we *think with*. This way calls for a metaphorical and analogical appropriation of scientific concepts by theology. As we shall see in the next chapter, in quantum theory there are several concepts that may prove helpful as metaphors in theology for understanding the relationship of God and the world in a panentheistic model.

2. QUANTUM CHALLENGES TO NEWTON

For over two hundred years, Newton reigned supreme. The billiard-ball, mechanical understanding of the physical world had dominated physics, and by extension philosophy. The world consisted of extended bits of matter in motion, which had external relations to one another and which could be understood objectively and rationally, expressed in mathematical form. Newtonian physics still works for everyday experience, but as research advanced to the ever smaller and faster particles, cracks began to appear in the Newtonian understanding. Newtonian physics had made three basic assumptions, all of which were to be called into question at the beginning of the twentieth century.

A. NEWTONIAN MECHANICS

The power of Newton's analysis lay in its the ability to break down whole phenomena into parts and then understand the interrelationship of all the constituent parts. The method was largely reductionist, and its motto was "Divide and Rule."[15] All physical objects were analyzed as matter in motion. Newton found that these bits of matter behaved in a predictable, lawlike manner that was expressible in mathematical formulation, hence the name "formalism." We are familiar with the effect of letting the air out of a blown-up balloon. It whizzes all around until the air is expended. That is Newton's third law of motion, for every action there is an opposite and equal reaction. The air rushing out of the balloon one way pushes the balloon the other. It is hard to imagine now, several centuries later, what a revelation it was to discover that the natural world was regular, predictable, and followed rationally discernible laws that could be expressed mathematically. It was, if you will, like nature was one huge machine that behaved in intelligible ways. Newtonian mechanism was born. Physical existence consisted of little pieces of billiard-ball like matter, *particles*, which interacted in measureable and predictable ways. It was only a matter of time, so it was believed, before physical reality would be

---

15. John Polkinghorne, "The Demise of Democritus," in *The Trinity and the Entangled World: Relationality in Physical Science and Theology*, ed. John Polkinghorne (Grand Rapids: Eerdmans, 2010), 2.

fully understood and there would be little left for physicists to do. Such was the optimism at the end of the nineteenth century.

By the end of the nineteenth century, another new model was also making headway, that of *waves*, which were also interpreted in mechanical ways. Thomas Young had demonstrated in his famous double slit experiment in 1801 that light interfered with itself, much like two interacting waves on a pond, producing a wave interference pattern, indicating that light displayed wavelike properties. By early in the twentieth century, however, through Einstein's theory of the photoelectric effect, discussed in the next section, light was also shown to display particle-like behavior. This created the puzzling situation where light seemed to display two distinct and conflicting models of matter simultaneously. How could light be both a wave and a particle at the same time? This was the context in which the Newtonian worldview began to break down, and the stage was set for relativity theory and the quantum revolution. It would be helpful, therefore, to specify what in particular was challenged in Newtonian mechanics and its philosophical extensions made by Enlightenment thinkers. It is this worldview that has been called by many the "modern" worldview[16] that was challenged in the twentieth century, giving rise to the "postmodern" worldview. So what was challenged? Three critical areas of understanding were called into question.

First of all, Newtonian mechanics had a *realistic* epistemology. The theories were believed to describe the world as it *really is*. As Ian Barbour observes, "Space and time were held to be absolute frameworks in which every event is located, independently of the frame of reference of the observer."[17] The calculations and observations were considered to be objective characteristics of the real world. Second, Newtonian physics was *deterministic*. Any future structure of a system of matter in motion could, according to Newtonian physics, be predicted based on knowledge of its present state. Barbour observes, "The universe, from the smallest particle to the most distant planet, seemed to be governed by the same inexorable laws."[18] Third, Newtonian physics was *reductionistic*; that is, it held that the smallest parts determine the behavior of the whole. The whole *is* the sum of its parts. Barbour concludes, "All three of these assumptions—realism, determinism and reductionism—have been challenged by twentieth-century physics. The changes in concepts and assumptions were so great that it is not surprising that Kuhn uses it as a prime example of a scientific

16. Ian Barbour, "Physics and Metaphysics," ch. 7 in *Religion and Science: Historical and Contemporary Issues* (San Francisco: HarperSanFrancisco, 1997).

17. Ibid., 165.

18. Ibid.

revolution, a paradigm shift."[19] He is speaking here of the great philosopher of science Thomas Kuhn, who in his work *The Structure of Scientific Revolutions*[20] pointed out the dynamics of change within relevant scientific communities such that the field was dramatically altered. In a scientific revolution, the governing theories and models collected into a coherent paradigm of explanation undergo radical shifts, and a new paradigm for the field is formed. The emergence of quantum theory and relativity theory were such paradigm shifts. They forever changed physics and our understanding of the physical world. We are still working out the implications of these revolutions, not the least of which is how we reconcile these two new paradigms. We will look briefly, then, at each of the revolutions, because they are essential for understanding the emergence of quantum entanglement.

B. QUANTUM MECHANICS

Quantum mechanics is the name given to the field in physics that studies the very small: the forces and structures of energy and matter below the atomic level. The term *mechanics* is inherited from Newton and refers to the regular nature of rationally discernible and mathematically expressible physical processes. The paradigm of the Newtonian "machine," discussed above, is behind this imagery, but it is the breakdown of this organizational image that brings about the end of the modern worldview. *Quantum*, as explained below, comes from the work of Max Planck, who very early on hypothesized that energy does not exist on an incremental continuum but rather exists in packets, which he named "quanta" to indicate discrete energy levels rather than a continuum. It all began with the discovery of the dual nature of light as both a wave and a particle, what is now known as wave–particle duality.

I. LIGHT, WAVES, AND FIELDS

The problem with Newtonian theory came down to the problem of light.[21] In 1801, Thomas Young, the physician, linguist, and member of the Royal Society in London, conducted his famous "double slit experiment," which verified the wavelike nature of light.[22] Young showed that when a bright light was passed

---

19. Ibid., 166.

20. Kuhn, *Structure of Scientific Revolutions*.

21. For a nice, readable account of the cracks that developed in Newtonian mechanics, see John Polkinghorne, *Quantum Theory: A Very Short Introduction* (Oxford: Oxford University Press, 2002), ch. 1, "Classical Cracks," 1–14.

22. For an interesting account of Thomas Young and his "double slit" experiment, see Amir D. Aczel, *Entanglement* (New York: Penguin, 2003), ch. 3, "Thomas Young's Experiment," 17–28.

through a piece of paper with two slits cut into it, the resulting pattern on a screen behind the paper displayed the classic interference patterns of waves. When peaks in a wave connect, they amplify one another; and when a peak and a trough interact, they nullify each other, giving alternating bands of light and dark on the screen. That is exactly what Young found, and this seemed to settle the issue that light was a wave. Mechanical waves, however, need a medium through which to travel, to be conveyed, and so the "luminiferous ether" was hypothesized as a medium to convey light waves from distant stars.

In the Newtonian view, mechanics requires a medium, such as the direct contact of a bat hitting a ball. The exception was gravity. Gravity seemed to violate this requirement and did not fit neatly into the mechanistic model. For Newton, gravity seemed to require action at a distance, which was difficult to reconcile with a mechanistic system. While he was able to describe gravity mathematically, it challenged the mechanistic models of the time, for it implied that a force could be conveyed without a medium. But it can. A good example is a magnet's magnetic field, which is spread out around the magnet from positive to negative poles. Iron filings, for example, need not come into direct physical contact with the magnet to be affected by its magnetic force, nor need there be any medium conveying the force. Neither does a compass needle require a medium to point to magnetic north. So forces can be conveyed without direct physical contact, and something can be influenced by a field of force simply by being placed within it.

By the last quarter of the nineteenth century, it was also understood that electricity and magnetism were both waves and produced fields that, thanks to the brilliant work of James Clerk Maxwell in 1873, were combined into what is now known as the electromagnetic field. Maxwell, however, still employed a mechanical model for waves and assumed that the fields required a medium to be conveyed and therefore supported the luminiferous ether hypothesis. As an analogy, imagine pushing water in a bathtub so that it eventually produces waves that travel across the tub. A medium (water in this case) has to be there to be pushed in order for waves to be generated, and in such a wave field, everything is local or situated at a particular point. Later on, however, it was discovered that Maxwell's equations (he was a pure mathematical theorist) worked even without the ether, and in contemporary physics the luminiferous ether has been dropped as an unnecessary assumption. Electromagnetic fields do not require a medium to be propagated.

But at the time the problem remained: if light was a wave that traveled through the ether, we should be able to calculate the speed of the impact of the earth's movement, which is also traveling through this ether, on the speed of light itself. That is, should there not be a differential in the speed of light depending on whether one is measuring the velocity moving with the earth as opposed to the opposite direction, ostensibly against the ether? As any canoeist knows, going with or against the current makes a lot of difference in the effort (energy) needed. If one is paddling upstream, it takes more energy and power to go at the same speed than one would achieve with less energy going downstream. So if the same energy is expended both directions, one should go faster with the flow than against it. The same thing was assumed for the speed of light. That is what Albert Michelson and Edward Morley attempted to discover in the 1880s. What they found, however, was that the speed of light remained constant no matter which direction they were measuring it.

II. QUANTA AND PHOTOELECTRIC EFFECT

This began to raise questions about the existence of the luminiferous ether, and when added to the problems of calculating the energy released in black-body (a perfect emitter/absorber of electromagnetic radiation in all wave lengths) radiation, including in ultraviolet light (known as the "ultraviolet catastrophe," in which the energy was calculated to be infinite),[23] serious issues were raised concerning the wave nature of light. At this point, Max Planck suggested that radiation might also be released in packets of energy of a definite size. The *quanta* of the energy would be in direct proportion to the frequency of the radiation.[24] The constant of proportionality became known as Planck's Constant. But how seriously should physicists take these quantum phenomena? The stage was set for Einstein.

The year of 1905 was an incredible year for Einstein. In this one year, he made three great discoveries, which he was to spend the rest of his life elaborating. For our purposes in understanding the emergence of quantum theory, his work on the photoelectric effect is most crucial. He had discovered that when a bright light is shone on a piece of metal, it knocks electrons out of the metal. This was first believed to be caused by the energy of light waves striking the electron and giving it enough energy to escape from the metal. As Polkinghorne puts it, "On a classical way of thinking, the electrons would be agitated by the 'swell' of the light waves and some could be sufficiently disturbed to shake loose from the metal."[25] It was then thought, again according to the classical view, that the intensity of the beam but not its frequency (wavelength) would influence the amount of electrons emitted. The opposite

23. Polkinghorne, *Quantum Theory*, 6–8.

24. Ibid., 7.

25. Ibid., 9.

was found to be the case, however. Below a certain frequency, no matter how bright the light, no electrons were emitted, and above certain frequencies, no matter how weak the beam, some electrons were released. Polkinghorne continues, "Einstein saw that this puzzling behavior became instantly intelligible if one considered the beam of light as a stream of persisting quanta. An electron would be ejected because one of these quanta had collided with it and given up all its energy. The amount of energy in that quantum, according to Planck, was directly proportional to the frequency."[26] These quanta of light came to be called *photons*. A major step toward the development of quantum mechanics had been taken.

III. WAVE-PARTICLE DUALITY AND COMPLEMENTARITY

Now, however, there was a major problem in understanding light. In verified experiments, light displayed either wave or particle behavior. These were two exclusive paradigms, normally not associated with each other. Something was either a wave or a particle, *but not both*! Light defied the logic of the law of the excluded middle. A new paradigm was needed, and that emerged in the amazing years of 1925 and 1926, which is when the real birth of quantum theory took place. Leading up to these *anni mirabilis*, in 1911 Ernest Rutherford and some younger colleagues had been experimenting with some positively charged particles that they called "alpha-particles." Used to bombard helium, these particles helped to reveal the atomic nucleus and develop the solar-system model of the atom. Niels Bohr, in 1913, was to take this model and add to it the idea of discrete orbitals such that electrons could only assume discrete distances from the nucleus based on the amount of energy they contained. Bohr applied to atoms similar principles to those Planck had applied to radiation. The Bohr atom was born. With the discovery in 1923, by Arthur Compton, of the scattering of x-rays by matter, reinforcing the particle nature of light, the stage was set for the development of quantum theory.[27] But there was still the enigma of this dual paradigm of light, and for that the concept of complementarity and the superposition of the wave function would have to be developed.[28]

In the third volume of his lectures on quantum mechanics, Richard Feynman asserts that superposition is *the* essential quantum mechanical phenomenon. John Polkinghorne goes on to observe, "It is the superposition principle—the fact that in quantum theory you can mix together things that in

26. Ibid.

27. Ibid., 10–13.

28. Polkinghorne, *Serious Talk*, 18. For a very concise and clear overview of quantum theory, see ch. 2 of Polkinghorne's book, titled, "Understanding Quantum Theory." 17–33.

classical physics are simply separate and cannot be mixed—that, at the level of formalism, is the thing that makes the difference between quantum theory and classical mechanics."[29] Light is the prime example of complementarity because one way of observation demonstrates wavelike behavior and another particle-like. (The same could be said for the electron.) The "double slit" experiment and the "photoelectric effect" have to be reconciled. Both are true and yet conflicting. Ian Barbour observes, "Waves are continuous and extended, and they interact in terms of phase; particles are discontinuous, localized, and they interact in terms of momentum. There seems to be no way to combine them into one unified model. . . . This same *wave-particle duality* is found throughout atomic physics."[30] He goes on to observe, however, "The paradoxical element in the wave-particle duality should not be overemphasized. We do not say that an electron is both a wave and a particle, but only that it exhibits wavelike and particlelike behavior; moreover we do have a unified mathematical formalism, which provides for at least probabilistic predictions."[31] The wave function involves superposition such that when a particular measurement is made, the wave function collapses into a particle. Superposition, then, has to do with the nature of the wave function. *Particles are quanta of the field described by the wave function.* There is, however, an interplay here where distinct models must be simultaneously affirmed. Niels Bohr, the great philosophical father of quantum theory, termed this duality and other pairs of sharply contrasting sets of concepts the complementarity principle. Within complementarity, Bohr affirmed several additional themes. Barbour summarizes,

> Bohr emphasized that we must always talk about an atomic system in relation to an experimental arrangement; we can never talk about it in isolation, in itself. We must consider *the interaction between subject and object* in every experiment. No sharp line can be drawn between the process of observation and what is observed. . . . Bohr held that it is the interactive process of observation, not the mind or consciousness of the observer, that must be taken into account.[32]

And also,

---

29. Ibid.

30. Ian Barbour, *Religion and Science: Historical and Contemporary Issues* (San Francisco: HarperSanFrancisco, 1997), 166–67 (italics original).

31. Ibid., 170.

32. Ibid. 166–67.

Another theme in Bohr's writing is the *conceptual limitation* of human understanding. . . . Bohr shares Kant's skepticism about the possibility of knowing the world in itself. If we try, as it were, to force nature into certain conceptual molds, we preclude the use of other molds. Thus we must choose between complete causal *or* spatiotemporal descriptions, between wave *or* particle models, between accurate knowledge of position *or* momentum. The more one set of concepts is used, the less the complementary set can be applied simultaneously.[33]

Bohr's complementarity has been debated since it was first articulated, and while different philosophical conclusions can be drawn, the need for complementary models and theories has not gone away. This need was heightened by Bohr's friend and colleague Werner Heisenberg and his discovery of the principle of uncertainty.

IV. HEISENBERG UNCERTAINTY PRINCIPLE

The Heisenberg Uncertainty Principle implies that to measure the position of an electron, for example, we cannot measure its momentum, and vice versa.[34] That is to say, we cannot determine both position and momentum to the same level of accuracy for a given particle. The measurement of one excludes the measurement of the other because it determines what questions can be answered. The first measurement determines all the following relevant questions. You are asking the wrong question if you ask why we can't we measure momentum if we know position. Physicist Bryan Luther puts it this way: "Say you tell a friend you have bought a car. He responds with the question, 'Great! What kind of fruit is it?'"[35] By observing that it is a car, you have determined the type of questions (say position) that can be asked. The first question determines what subsequent questions can have meaning. Another analogy might be like peering through a pair of binoculars at some object and focusing one lens such that as that eyepiece comes more into focus the other eyepiece becomes more blurred. You can see through one (position) or the other (momentum) with extreme precision, but not both at the same time. One measurement precludes the other. This, of course, led to a great deal of controversy and debate about the meaning and implications for the nature of physical existence.

33. Ibid., 167–68 (italics original).
34. Ibid., 170–71.
35. Personal conversation, Concordia College, April 5, 2013.

Light, for example, is understood to involve two different and distinct physical paradigms simultaneously, what is known as a "wave-particle duality." Wave-particle duality, however, does not mean that a photon or subatomic particle is both a wave and particle simultaneously, but that it could manifest *either* a wave or a particle aspect depending on circumstance. We say that one is "superimposed" on the other. The superposition is in the field itself such that the particles are the quanta of the field as described by the wave function in a specific measurement. How do a wave and particle exist superimposed? The currently received explanation is called the Copenhagen Interpretation. The Copenhagen Interpretation was first posed by physicist Niels Bohr in the 1920s. Josh Clark, writing for the website *How Stuff Works*, puts it this way:

> A quantum particle doesn't exist in one state or another, but in all of its possible states at once. It's only when we observe its state that a quantum particle is essentially forced to choose one probability, and that's the state that we observe. An electron, for example, can behave sometimes as a wave and sometimes as a particle, but never both together, just as a tossed coin may fall either heads or tails up, but not both at once. This state of existing in all possible states at once is called coherent superposition. The total of all possible states in which an object can exist makes up the object's wave function. When we observe an object, the superposition collapses and the object is forced into one of the states of its wave function.[36]

Bohr, the leader of the Copenhagen Interpretation, admonished those who would ask whether an electron *really* is a wave or a particle. He denounced the question as meaningless or without context (like asking, "What is north of the North Pole?"). To observe the properties of an electron is to conduct some sort of measurement. Experiments designed to measure waves will see the wave aspect of electrons. Those experiments designed to measure particle properties will see electrons as particles. No experiment can ever measure both aspects simultaneously, and so we never see a mixture of wave and particle.[37] But how is the wave function collapsed? It is possible that he affirmed either that quantum mechanics involves some unknown mechanism in moving from the microscopic to the macroscopic systems that collapses the wave function or,

---

36. Josh Clark, "How Quantum Suicide Works," *How Stuff Works*, http://science.howstuffworks.com/innovation/science-questions/quantum-suicide.htm.

37. Ian Barbour, *Religion and Science*, "Complementarity," 167-70. See also Polkinghorne, *Serious Talk*, 18-25.

even more unsettling, that it was about what we can know, not about what is. The collapse is not indicative of the creation of an observer-determined reality. As Richard Waite observes, "His [Bohr's] theory denied the possibility of a unified, observer-independent field. His own interpretation, the heart of his Copenhagen philosophy, implies that quantum phenomena can only be described by pairs of complimentary perspectives."[38] This condition led to Einstein's challenge to quantum theory.

3. QUANTUM ENTANGLEMENT

The quantum world defies commonsense and is counterintuitive, which is why it has undermined the modern (Newtonian) worldview so foundationally. Einstein was not happy with this and believed that the quantum world was determinate and that any indeterminacy was the result of theoretical incompleteness. For Einstein, quantum indeterminacy was *epistemological* and not ontological. For Niels Bohr and Werner Heisenberg, it was *ontological*; that is, indeterminacy was real and had nothing to do with incompleteness in the theory. This led to one of the greatest debates in the history of physics, and as you can see, it had as much to do with philosophical assumptions (the world is real and determinate vs. the world is real and indeterminate) as it did with experimental evidence. This is the context in which Einstein uttered his famous comment in correspondence with Max Born, "Quantum mechanics is certainly imposing. But an inner voice tells me that it is not yet the real thing. The theory says a lot, but does not really bring us any closer to the secret of the 'old one.' I, at any rate, am convinced that He is not playing at dice" ("Der Alte würfelt nicht"; "The Old One [God] does not play dice").[39]

A. THE EPR EFFECT

This debate finally led Einstein, in 1935, to enlist the help of two colleagues at Princeton, Boris Podolski and Nathan Rosen, to formulate what they thought was a conclusive thought experiment to prove that quantum theory was incomplete. This is a highly technical discussion that I do not claim to fully understand, but let me give you the gist of it. EPR (so named by using the last names for Einstein and his two Princeton colleagues Podolski and Rosen) argues that if quantum indeterminacy is true, then, because of superposition (two states present at the same time), if a split particle were sent in opposite directions, its potentialities would still remain entangled until one part of the

---

38. Richard Whaite, "Niels Bohr," *Center for Theology and the Natural Sciences*, CTNS.org.

39. Max Born, *The Born-Einstein Letters* (New York: Walker, 1971), 91.

particle was measured. Once that measurement occurred, then the movement (e.g., spin) of the other part of the particle would immediately be known, for it is the opposite of the measured particle, even though it could be light years away. This would seem to require either superluminary (faster than the speed of light) communication, which violates the special theory of relativity (which assumes the speed of light is constant and cannot be exceeded; to do so would be to have infinite mass) or would imply that there was action at a distance, which violates Einstein's understanding of discrete material individuals, which have only local and contiguous causal effects. For Einstein, the choice was either to reject special relativity and the limit it placed on all causal processes and connections and accept "spooky action at a distance" or to believe that quantum mechanics was an incomplete theory. He chose the latter. The EPR Effect, as it became known, was intended to disprove quantum indeterminacy because its proposers never thought that such an experiment would be successful. This in turn would show quantum mechanics to be incomplete. At the time and for almost fifty years after, no such experiment was possible. But now it has been performed, particularly testing what is known as Bell's inequality, in 1982, by Alan Aspect at the University of Paris and since in various forms by other labs, especially Anton Zeilinger at the University of Vienna.[40] As a result, quantum indeterminacy and nonlocal relational holism are now seen as descriptive of the quantum world and experimentally verified. Entanglement is real and part of the nature of the quantum world.

B. BELL'S INEQUALITY

What is Bell's inequality, and how was such verification done? Bell's inequality very ingenuously sets up the conditions that would have to be met if a theory were strictly local in its character. The conditions would apply *only* if there were no nonlocal correlations. In effect, what Bell did was to show what would be needed to be observed if EPR was correct. John Polkinghorne, in *Quantum Theory: A Very Short Introduction*, sets up the description this way. We begin by having two particles, 1 and 2, with total spin (motion like the spinning of a top) of zero. This means that the two particles are opposite to one another. In three dimensions, there are three axis, x, y, and z, that could be measured, but quantum mechanics does not permit the measurement of x and y components of spin simultaneously because there is an uncertainty relation between them. He concludes, "Einstein argued that, while this might be the

---

40. See Kirk Wegter-McNelly, *The Entangled God* (New York: Routledge, 2011), ch. 4, section 1, "Experimental Evidence."

case according to orthodox quantum thinking, whatever happened to particle 1 could have no immediate effect upon the distant particle 2. In EPR thinking, the spatial separation of 1 and 2 implies *the independence of what happens at 1 and what happens at 2.*"[41] This would assume no influence, no "spooky action at a distance," as Einstein referred to it. Kirk Wegter-McNelly further clarifies

> According to EPR (through Bell), there is a (fully classical but non-zero) limit on the amount of correlation that should be seen when measuring particles 1 and 2. There will be SOME correlation according to classical thinking, but only a certain amount. It must be less than a certain bound. THIS is the inequality. The inequality *does not* come from the measurements of 1 and 2 being different or unequal for any particular pair of particles. QM predicts that there will be *more* correlation present than the classical perspective allows, i.e., that the amount of correlation will exceed the classical bound or limit. Hence QM predicts a "violation" of Bell's inequality.[42]

Polkinghorne concludes, "Bell showed that if this strict locality were the case, there would be certain relations between measureable quantities (they are now called *Bell inequalities*) that quantum mechanics predicted would be violated in certain circumstances. This was a very significant step forward, moving the argument on from the realm of thought experiments into the empirically accessible realm of what could actually be investigated in the laboratory."[43] Using very sophisticated instrumentation in the laboratory, in 1982, Alan Aspect in France was able to vindicate quantum theory and negated the possibility of a purely local theory as advocated by Einstein.

Over the ensuing decades, these results have been confirmed using many different types of particles (including single photons by Anton Zeilinger at the University of Vienna) over many different distances and removing as many variables as possible.[44] Polkinghorne concludes, "It had become clear that there is an irreducible degree of non-locality present in the physical world. Quantum entities that have interacted with each other can remain mutually entangled, however far they may eventually separate spatially. It seems that nature fights back against a relentless reductionism. Even the subatomic world cannot be

---

41. Polkinghorne, *Quantum Theory*, 78 (italics original).

42. Kirk Wegter-McNelly in personal email correspondence, September 6, 2013.

43. Ibid., 79.

44. See Kirk Wegter-McNelly, *The Entangled God* (New York: Routledge, 2011), ch. 4, section 1, "Experimental Evidence."

treated purely atomistically."[45] He goes on to conclude that "the EPR effect's implication of deep-seated relationality present in the fundamental structure of the physical world is a discovery that physical thinking and metaphysical reflection have still to come to terms with in fully elucidating all its consequences. . . . One must acknowledge that a true case of action at a distance is involved, and not merely some gain in additional knowledge. Putting it in learned language, the EPR effect is ontological and not simply epistemological."[46] Bohr and Heisenberg were right.

C. *Veiled Reality*

This does, however, create a "veiled reality," as the French physicist and philosopher of science Bernard d'Espagnat refers to it. Veiled reality is an understanding of "independent reality" that is not fully accessible to human comprehension. He writes,

> But then, if radical idealism (neo-Kantianism) as well as all the cryptoradical-idealisms that proceed from it are to be rejected, that is, if the notion of "something" (perhaps, but not necessarily, a set of "things," for language betrays us here: perhaps events, or minds, or Mind, or gods, or God, or what not; let us just say "something") the existence of which is not dependent on (does not boil down to) *our* existence is considered as logically necessary, and if, on the other hand, it is realized that all the ontological theories are too speculative, that is the detailed features of this "something" are beyond our reach, then only two possibilities remain: either this "something" is altogether unknowable, a "pure X," or it is such that we can get, or guess, some knowledge about it, *but merely general or merely allegorical*. Our claim in this section is that rather convincing arguments favor the second branch of this alternative over the first.[47]

It would seem that in relation to both the ultimate character of physical reality in physics and the nature of God in theology, human comprehension is driven to analogy and metaphor. The appropriation of metaphorical concepts in quantum mechanics for use in constructive theology, then, is not only appropriate but may indeed build on their use in physics itself.

---

45. Ibid.

46. Ibid.

47. Bernard D'Espagnat, *Veiled Reality: An Analysis of Present-Day Quantum Mechanical Concepts* (New York: Addison Wesley, 1995), 355 (italics original).

In the following chapters, we will discuss and appropriate two concepts from quantum physics metaphorically to develop the model of "entangled Trinitarian panentheism." They are nonlocal relational holism called *entanglement* and *complementarity* understood through the concept of *superposition* of the wave function. Both concepts are essential to understanding the very counterintuitive nature of the subatomic realm that quantum physics describes. They also transform our understanding of the nature of physical reality, disclosing it as interrelational, interconnected, and interdependent. Such understanding can go a long way toward revising our understanding of the relation of God and the world, encouraging the model of panentheism, as well as the relationship of God as Creator, Redeemer, and Sanctifier. What will be undertaken is simply an ongoing example of theologians using the best understanding and language of the time to help explicate our relationship to God, as was seen in part 2. John Polkinghorne summarizes the current situation regarding physical existence this way.

> Science today faces a problem not totally dissimilar to that addressed by those early Trinitarian theologians. The physical world is not so atomized that we can understand it fully by an examination conducted constituent piece by constituent piece. Nor is it so inextricably relationally integrated that until one is able to comprehend the totality, one cannot understand anything at all. . . . Like theology in its different sphere, science has to struggle with the problem of reconciling unity with diversity. In fact, all theoretical engagement with issues of relationality has to find some way of combining connection with separation, since it is only to the extent that one can recognize a distinction between two entities that one can speak of their being in mutual relationship."[48]

Now it is time to turn to the theological significance some of these concepts in quantum mechanics and relativity theory might have for understanding the Trinity as unity-in-diversity, and for this the theological model of panentheism will be most helpful.

---

48. Polkinghorne, "The Demise of Democritus," 13.

KEY TERMS

Bell's Inequality
Creative Mutual Interaction
Copenhagen Interpretation
EPR Effect
Four-Fold Typology
Heisenberg Uncertainty Principle
Newtonian Mechanics
Paradigm Shift
Photons
Quantum
Quantum Mechanics
Realism
Veiled Reality
Wave-Particle Duality

DISCUSSION QUESTIONS

1. In what ways do scientific fields utilize hermeneutics, or interpretation, when utilizing data? What process(es) must take place as scientific data become scientific fact?

2. Discuss Kuhn's understanding of scientific pursuit. Why does Kuhn defend the idea that "science is not as neutral, objective, value free, and rational as the Enlightenment thinkers had wanted to believe"?

3. How is hypothetical consonance different from other interactions between science and theology?

4. How do physicists understand wave-particle duality? What makes this process of observing wave-particle duality unique? Explain how this may be helpful in theological reflection.

5. In what ways does quantum entanglement challenge the accepted scientific paradigm? What are the implications of theoretical physics as a "hard" science?

8

Perichoretic Trinitarian Panentheism

In him [God] we live and move and have
our being.

–St. Paul at the *Agora* in Athens,
Acts 17:28

What are we a part of that we might not even be aware of? That was the question Loren Eiseley took away from his encounter with the web of the yellow and black orb spider discussed in chapter 1, spider thoughts circumscribing a spider universe. How do we develop our own understanding, and how different are we in circumscribing our own universe? That is the focus of this chapter, in which I will be constructing a new theological understanding of the Trinity in regard to the contemporary scientific understanding of physical existence. The previous seven chapters have, in some ways, all been preparation for this and the following chapter. We needed to consider the process of theological reflection and its use of metaphor and analogy as well as the emergence of the doctrine of the Trinity both in historical and contemporary reflection before we turned to the current models of quantum physics. Having now done that, the goal of this chapter is to formulate a constructive theological argument for the use of these major concepts in physics as metaphors for reflection on a panentheistic model of the Trinity. Why the Trinity? Because at its heart lies the central divine mystery of the Christian tradition. Philip Clayton observes, "The singular beauty of the Christian doctrine of God lies in the incredible richness of the innertrinitarian life."[1] The doctrine attempts to preserve the integral mystery of Christ as the incarnation

---

1. Philip Clayton, "Panentheist Internalism: Living within the Presence of the Trinitarian God," *Dialog: A Journal of Theology* 40, no. 3 (2001): 214.

of a God who is related to the creation in multiple ways. The Christian tradition moves from the experience of three to one, not one to three.

What I would like to argue at this point is that perichoresis and entanglement can function as parallel metaphors, with quantum entanglement and superposition helping to explicate for today the meaning of divine energy, activity, and relatedness within a panentheistic model of God.[2] This would allow us to talk about Trinitarian entanglement in such a way that the inner life of the Trinity is entangled even as their functions become discrete in relation to creation. This would also mean that the Spirit is always connected to the activity of the Father and Son in creation and that the Father and Spirit are connected to the Son in incarnation, including crucifixion and resurrection. Divine entanglement becomes a way of understanding the perichoretic expression of divine love and grace in the creation. This also grounds both hope and the eschatological (final end) fulfillment of creation within the entangled eternal life of God. To quote Rahner's Rule, "The economic Trinity [God disclosed in revelatory acts in the creation] is the immanent Trinity [God in the Godhead itself]."[3] Particles that are once interrelated can never be fully separated; so too the mutually indwelling activity of the Trinity can never be dismembered. The proposal is this: *Perichoresis as entanglement can be understood as the energy of the divine Trinity through which the creation is expressed. The immanent Trinity exists in superposition with the economic Trinity and evolves within the entangled life of God with the creation, thus supporting a panentheistic model of God.* An entangled understanding of the Trinity does indeed give rise to an understanding of God in which we "live and move and have our being."

We will walk through this process in stages so that the pieces can be fitted more carefully together. We will begin by revisiting the understanding of metaphor and looking at the most important metaphors that arise for theological appropriation out of quantum entanglement. We will then turn to the connection between entanglement and perichoresis from the Trinitarian tradition and explore whether this helps to further unpack for contemporary understanding this ancient conception of divine energy. This will allow us to address more fully the theological model of panentheism and what this model

2. See Kirk Wegter-McNelly, *The Entangled God: Divine Relationality and Quantum Physics* (New York: Routledge, 2011). In ch. 6, he does briefly, referencing my earlier work, support the understanding of entanglement as mutual indwelling leading to an enriched understanding of the Trinity, but his overall focus is on the relation of God and creation. He does not further develop the Trinity nor place it in a wider panentheistic model, which I am doing here.

3. Karl Rahner, *The Trinity*, trans. Joseph Donceel (New York: Herder & Herder, 1970), 22, quoted in John Polkinghorne, *Exploring Reality* (New Haven: Yale University Press, 2007), 103.

might have to say regarding an entangled understanding of God and the world. Returning to the model of creative mutual interaction (CMI) discussed in the last chapter, it is especially the *supporting* and *heuristic* roles that science can play for theology that will be employed in this and the following chapter as concepts from quantum physics are used to metaphorically inspire reflection on the Trinitarian understanding of perichoresis. We will close with a discussion of perichoretic Trinitarian panentheism as a whole.

In the Christian faith, we have to do with a God who is believed to have entered time, nature, and history in such a way as to disclose to us the divine heart of love, mercy, and forgiveness in the midst of suffering and death. It is only from revelation in history that we can begin to construct any reflection on God, for only there is God to be encountered by human beings in their becoming of existence. God in God's self we of course have no access to and need not pretend to know, for there is mystery upon mystery. Even in trying to conceptualize our own experience and perception, we are driven to metaphor and symbol because the intrinsic nature of physical reality in itself apart from our perception of it is not disclosed to us. It is a "veiled reality." How much more that of the intrinsic nature of divine reality? The goal here then is a modest one: to employ contemporary thought for the understanding of the Trinity in such a way that some element of our own experience, including the scientific, of the world and perhaps the transcendence immersed within its immanence can briefly be given to thought. This is to do Trinitarian reflection from below, if you will, from the so-called economy of God and not from above, the internal, "immanent" nature of God. Hopefully, this will also help demonstrate the constructive mutual interaction of theology and science. Let us begin, then, with the metaphor of entanglement.

1. ENTANGLEMENT METAPHORS

When we turn to quantum theory, the reality of analogical and metaphorical construction becomes even more pronounced and unfamiliar. The quantum world defies common sense and is counterintuitive, which is why it has undermined the modern worldview so foundationally. The term *entanglement* was first coined by Erwin Schrödinger to describe the peculiar connection between quantum systems. He writes:

> When two systems, of which we know the states by their respective representatives, enter into temporary physical interaction due to known forces between them, and when after a time of mutual influence the systems separate again, then they can no longer be

described in the same way as before, viz. by endowing each of them with a representative of its own. I would not call that *one* but rather *the* characteristic trait of quantum mechanics, the one that enforces its entire departure from classical lines of thought. By the interaction the two representatives [the quantum states] have become entangled.[4]

Entanglement is simply another way of addressing the fact that physical reality is interconnected at the deepest levels we currently know and that there is a superposition of states that is complementary (Bohr) rather than contradictory, as in classical (Newtonian) physics. By way of summary, let me briefly talk about two aspects of this cloudy world that will be helpful for our reflection on the Trinity; nonlocal relational holism (entanglement) and complementarity (superposition).[5]

A. NONLOCAL RELATIONAL HOLISM (ENTANGLEMENT)

During the time of Newton, with the exception of gravity, which is still most vexing, all forces were expected to be contact forces. A contact force takes place, for example, when a bat hits a ball and the force of the bat is transferred to the ball. It is a kinetic (active) energy transfer. But gravity seemingly implied the effect of one body on another without direct contact. This conundrum was at least partially resolved by the discovery in the nineteenth century of what are called fields of force, of which gravity was believed to be one. The breakthrough came by means of the work of Michel Faraday and James Clerk Maxwell, who discovered the electromagnetic field and contributed to the formation of classical field theory. It was this discovery that eventually led to the development of radio, television, and telecommunications, among other technological advances.

The development of field theory in the nineteenth century also led to the idea of the luminiferous ether, which was believed to be the medium through which this field was conveyed, especially for light. As John Polkinghorne observes, however, "Relativity theory abolished the idea of the ether as the

---

4. Quoted in Jeffrey Bub, "The Entangled World: How Can It be Like That?," in *The Trinity and an Entangled World: Relationality in Physical Science and Theology*, ed. John Polkinghorne (Grand Rapids: Eerdmans, 2010), 19–20 (italics mine).

5. For a succinct, nonspecialist overview of quantum theory, see John Polkinghorne, *Serious Talk: Science and Religion in Dialogue* (Valley Forge, PA: Trinity Press International, 1995), ch. 2, "Understanding Quantum Theory." Material in this chapter also comes from my earlier article, "Quantum Perichoresis: Quantum Field Theory and the Trinity," *Theology and Science* 4, no. 2 (2006): 137–50.

carrier of fields and concentrated on the fields themselves as being fully physical entities, possessing energy and momentum just as material particles do."[6] He goes on to clarify, "However, classical fields, though they are spread out through space and vary in time, nevertheless are local entities in a causal sense. What happens in the neighborhood of a point can be altered without inducing immediate changes elsewhere, so even fields can be considered bit by bit."[7] While this is true for classical fields at a more macro level, when we turn to the micro, the subatomic, level of the quantum field, this is not true. This opens the door to the discussion of nonlocal relational holism.

At the subatomic level, we enter the counterintuitive world of the quantum and find that everything is entangled, resulting in nonlocal relational holism, "together-in-separation," as Polkinghorne refers to it. (See the more detailed discussion of quantum entanglement in the previous chapter.) Everything is interconnected at the subatomic level. Polkinghorne continues,

> Quantum fields, whose properties were first discovered by Paul Dirac, exhibit both wavelike properties (because of their space–time extension) and also particlelike properties (because their energy comes in discrete packets). Particles and fields are concepts that are fused in contemporary physics. Modern thinking pictures an entity such as an electron as being an excitation in the universal electron field, a concept that subtly modifies a purely atomized notion of electron nature. This field theory idea neatly explains why all electrons manifest exactly the same properties. They are related by their common origin in the electron field.[8]

Particles, as Polkinghorne likes to comment, are "more like clouds than clocks." They form as particles emerge out of the field of the quantum vacuum, which is present before any energy excitation and gives rise to particles. In a sense, the quantum field itself is the foundational wave function that exists everywhere. When energy is dropped into the field, it excites into a particle. Particles are "quanta" of the field excitation, so the wave function is the particle in all its probability amplitudes but has no specificity until measurement occurs. The wave function contains information that could yield many different possible states. The potentiality of all the probable states within the wave function makes

6. John Polkinghorne, "The Demise of Democritus," in Polkinghorne, *The Trinity and an Entangled World: Relationality in Physical Science and Theology*, 3.

7. Ibid.

8. Ibid.

entanglement possible. When a measurement is made, a randomly chosen particle state excites from all the possible states. While particles are distinct, they are simply excitations in the quantum field and will continue only as long as the energy of the excitation is conserved, which might be indefinitely. As an analogy, one might think of a spring, which, when compressed (the energy excitation), will continue to bounce forever in a (hypothetical) frictionless space. The energy imputed into the system will remain unless interacted with because the energy has to remain somewhere. This is true, for example, with light particles, or photons.

Nonlocal relationality has been demonstrated through the interrelational mixing of the potentialities of paired photons, for example by Anton Zeilinger at the University of Vienna, which carries with it some form of "action at a distance" or connectedness between particles, which is known as "entanglement." Once a pair of particles or a divided single particle is entangled, they remain connected no matter where in the physical universe they travel. Second, according to holism, the part seems to derive from the whole. The whole is more than the sum of its parts and perhaps even influences the nature of the part. This is central to the concept of emergence, particularly as it is found in evolutionary biology, but more on that later. Particles come in and out of existence as excitations within the field of the quantum vacuum, like ripples on a pond of energy. A photon is a quantum of the electromagnetic field and an electron a quantum of the electron field. These characteristics emerge when the "wave-particle duality" is brought to bear on the field excitation. One could say, in a sense, that the universe is not "filled" with the quantum vacuum but is "written" on it.[9] It is this realm of field that gives rise to holism, which permits action at a distance and grounds the understanding of nonlocal relational holism. It is truly togetherness-in-separation.

B. COMPLEMENTARITY AND SUPERPOSITION

Entanglement also involves complementarity, which is the current received explanation for the nature of light, the wave-particle duality. This is what Niels Bohr is referring to when he says that two seemingly mutually exclusive models are both necessary and thus must complement one another even if the current theoretical framework does not explain how. In saying this, however, physicists do not mean to say that light, for example, is both simultaneously but rather that one or the other will result depending on what type of measurement the

---

9. Ian Marshall and Danah Zohar, *Who's Afraid of Schrodinger's Cat?* (New York: William Morrow, 1997), 304.

observer is making. How is this possible? As explained above, and in chapter 7, the answer is that the particle is a "quanta" of the field excitation, which results from the wave function collapsing into a specific probability state upon measurement. Depending on the field and wave function involved, different types of particles may be excited. A photon is a particle that excites from the wave function of the electromagnetic field. Depending on what you are seeking to measure, you will find either a wave or a particle. This is the strange dualism of wave-particle duality, which complementarity attempts to name.

In the history of theology, there is an interesting example of a similar type of logic that defines simultaneity. It was utilized by Nicholas of Cusa, a fifteenth-century cardinal in what is now Germany who was also a philosopher, mathematician, astronomer, diplomat, and spiritual director. He was probably one of the most brilliant thinkers of his age. In seeking to provide guidance for the meditative prayer of monks under his care, he wrote the beautiful book *The Vision of God*. When he sent this book to the monks, he also had commissioned a painting of Christ that was to be painted in such a way that the eyes of the figure followed the viewer. Physicist Arthur Zajonc picks up the story here.

> He then suggested that the monks hang the painting in the refectory [dining hall], and that they go in twos to view the painting. The monks were to stand on opposite sides of the large room. Each monk would experience the figure as looking at them, a strange situation to contemplate. Then Cusa asked that the monks should walk towards one another reflecting all the while that the single pair of eyes not only were following him but also were simultaneously following his companion—an impossible fact. Cusa termed this the "coincidence of opposites." The exercise was designed to break the tyranny of logical thinking (or *ratio*) schooled on sensate reality in order to prepare the student for another and higher mode of experiential knowing he termed *intellectus* or *visio*, the vision of God.[10]

While our primary task here is not contemplation, Nicholas of Cusa's use of the painting can give us a helpful example of superposition from another field. The one set of eyes seems to view two different places at once. Indeed, if there were even more monks arrayed along a line in front of the painting, each monk would find the eyes gazing at him as well. In other words, there is a continuum of being viewed within the viewing range of the portrait. The

---

10. Arthur Zajonc, *Meditation as Contemplative Inquiry* (Great Barrington, MA: Lindisfarne Books, 2009), 63–64.

gaze is simultaneously at all the points along the continuum and at each one at the same time. This is analogous to a wave function, which is not localized throughout a range of positions until viewed and then collapses into a distinct particular at a specific point in space-time. Cusa's "coincidence of opposites" can also be interpreted today as superposition, which plays an important role in understanding the nature of entanglement.

This simultaneity of states has come to be understood as a specific example of the even more fascinating theory of the entangled state of a wave function. These entangled states will be appropriated as a metaphor for the theological concept of perichoresis and the discussion of God's relation to both God's self (the immanent Trinity) and the world (the economic Trinity). Kirk Wegter-McNelly observes,

> The most surprising element of quantum entanglement, interpreted in terms of relational holism, is that an entangled system can carry a definite value of a particular property even though its parts lack a definite value of the very same property. Primarily for this reason "entangled" is an apt term to describe the relational "seat" of divinity within the trinitarian God. The deity of the Trinity resides not in the persons as *distinct* from one another but within and among the persons as they are *related* to one another, i.e., in the relationality that constitutes them and binds them to one another.[11]

We now need to more carefully explore the metaphorical appropriation of entanglement as a way of illuminating the perichoretic relationship of the Trinity.

2. Perichoretic Relational Holism (Entanglement)

Perichoresis is the ancient Greek word that several early church fathers used to describe the inner relationship of the three persons of the Trinity. As developed in chapter 5, the earliest formal use was in the Greek-speaking East by the Cappadocian Fathers of the fourth century (Basil the Great, his brother Gregory of Nyssa, and their mutual friend Gregory of Nazianzus) and later elaborated by John of Damascus in the eighth century. Perichoresis directly flows from the decision at the Council of Nicaea in 325, and reaffirmed at the Council of Constantinople in 381, to formalize the use of the word *homoousios* ("same substance"). If the Son or Logos is divine, then the three must interrelate in

---

11. Wegter-McNelly, *The Entangled God*, 219–20 (italics original).

some way. It was said that the three "mutually indwell" with one another and while distinct in function are inseparable in being. Perichoresis comes most directly from *perichōreō*, meaning to "encompass" often interpreted as "mutual indwelling." An associated word, *perichōreuō*, means to "dance around" and is often preferred in theology because of its dynamic connotations. "Encompass" would appear to be an analogous metaphor to entanglement as "together-in-separation." Indeed, John Polkinghorne makes a brief passing comment to that effect in his book *Exploring Reality: The Intertwining of Science and Religion.* He observes, "A quantum physicist immediately thinks of the faint physical analogy of the non-local entanglement of the EPR effect."[12] I much prefer the Greek words over the Latin *circuminsessio* (from *circum-in-sedere*, "to sit around," preferred by Thomas Aquinas), which has the connotation of stasis or permanence between the persons of the Trinity and the substantialism it implies. I also like the companion meaning, which gives the image of a "dance of the divine." So the Greek has a more dynamic and even playful connotation to the relationship of divine love within the immanent Trinity. The Trinity is indeed a dancing God. The ancient Triquetra image attempts to convey this dynamism as well as interrelatedness.

Figure 3.

As you can see, the "parts" flow in and out of one another in a continuous way; no separation is possible, though distinction is. Were it to be done in three dimensions, it would be a threefold form of a Möbius strip, in which the inner and outer flows smoothly in and out of one another with one continuous surface.

So, too, the persons of the Trinity flow in and out of one another in a continuous, dynamic energy exchange of becoming. They are entangled in

12. John Polkinghorne, *Exploring Reality*, 106.

Figure 4.

their mutual becoming, and as the external creation relates to them they manifest in one of the three expressions of the divine mystery. As you look at figure 4, depending upon which one you focus on, you will see something different. Your observation determines what you will see and yet all three possibilities are there at the same time. It is a representation of superposition.

3. Perichoretic Complementarity and Superposition

If we now turn to the other main explanatory ideas from quantum physics, complementarity and superposition, we begin to see how this may enrich our understanding of the Trinity. Recalling the wave-particle duality of light from our earlier discussion, complementarity means that these states exist together in potentiality, but *it is how we view the phenomenon that determines what we find*. Measurement (observation) determines whether we derive a wave or a particle. It depends on what we are seeking to measure. This is of course related to the "is–is not" character of metaphor. Superposition may help us to understand how the Trinity can be three distinct *hypostaseis* but with one *ousia*. Complementarity can help explain why we address one person or another depending on what theological question we are asking or the specific context (measurement) out of which we are coming, for example, suffering, joy, or hope. It depends on what we are seeking. Remember that the Trinity emerged from the multifold experiences of the divine that the early Christian community experienced. They affirmed God as the source and origination of all existence inherited from the Jewish tradition. When we look for origins, we find Creator. But we are not always looking for origins. Sometimes we are looking for forgiveness and for hope. We are looking for "good news" (gospel), and the early Christian community found this present in Jesus as the Christ, the anointed one of God. If the divine is entangled, that is, interrelated and interdependent with multiple potentials such as a wave function, then the same entangled divine reality can be experienced as incarnation, not just origination.

The two are superimposed on one divine reality. Finally, the community also experienced, within the community itself, the sustaining spirit, the "Comforter," the "creative Spirit," as the ongoing presence of the divine within the midst of the community. This too is an expression of divine entanglement whereby a different experience is called on as the basis for reflection on the divine, another expression of divine relatedness. Yet in all three, origination, incarnation, sanctification, they confessed the same God at work. *The immanent Trinity exists in superposition with the economic Trinity.* Much like a particle is within the wave function in its potentiality, the economic Trinity is superimposed on the eternal potentiality of the immanent Trinity and emerges in particularity in relationship to the creation. The immanent Trinity is the eternal potentiality of the divine for multiple forms of relatedness and experience by humanity and the wider creation. We find in God, depending on what we are seeking (metaphorically, "measuring") what we need to find as the simultaneous entanglement of the divine love finds expression in the creation that it has made possible. This is not to say that humanity simply finds in God what it wants, much less that it creates the divine reality, but rather that the divine reality expresses itself in multiple ways, which humanity is only occasionally able to discern from diverse, finite perspectives. Light is wave and particle, but it is our finite observation that forces the measurement of one or the other. Likewise, the divine is Triune, but our finite experience cannot possibly contain the infinite in its multiplicity. We experience it, instead, as a perichoretic mystery, dare we say, as a perichoretic superposition. Finally, as we move to elaborate the understanding of the Trinity within the creation, this dynamic entanglement must now be connected with the understanding of panentheism. *Perichoresis may be conceived as the mutual indwelling energy of the divine Trinity through which the creation is created and which evolves within the life of God as entangled superposition.* This gives rise, in turn, to a coherent, panentheistic model of the divine.

4. Perichoretic Trinitarian Panentheism

As was mentioned earlier in chapter 3, panentheism[13] means that God is in the world but is more than the world. The world is not divine but is totally related to the divine. Indeed, one might say that the world exists in God so that God is always present (immanent) in the world but that God is also more than (transcends) the world as well. The divine is present "in, with, and under" the

---

13. F. L. Cross and E. A. Livingstone, eds., s.v. "Panentheism," in *The Oxford Dictionary of the Christian Church*, 3rd ed. (Oxford: Oxford University Press, 2005), 1221.

material forms of existence but is not limited to them. Martin Luther, who had a sophisticated and nuanced understanding of divine presence, employed a simple grain of wheat to illustrate this type of relationship. He observed,

> How can reason tolerate that the divine majesty is so small that it can be substantially present in a grain, on a grain, over a grain, through a grain, within and without . . . entirely in each grain, no matter how numerous these grains may be? And how can reason tolerate that the same majesty is so large that neither this world nor a thousand worlds can encompass it and say "behold, there it is"? . . . Yet, though it can be encompassed nowhere and by no one, God's divine essence encompasses all things and dwells in all.[14]

It is now time to take a closer look at this model of panentheism and why it should be considered a useful model for the God-world relationship in our time before turning to how the concept of entanglement can help elaborate this model and our understanding of the perichoresis of the Trinity. We will look first at the challenges to divine action in modern theism (see also chapter 3), then to the major elements of panentheism before turning to Trinitarian panentheism.

CHALLENGE

As has been pointed out earlier, the rise of the natural sciences severely challenged classical supernatural interventionist theism. Less and less was appeal to the divine needed to explain natural phenomena. This later gave rise to "God of the gaps" theories, which have been significantly discredited in the last century.[15] If God is primarily appealed to as a source for explanatory knowledge and human knowledge grows to close many of the knowledge "gaps," then eventually God as an external source of knowledge would have little, if anything, to do or explain. This is also connected to the problem of external relations. In the classical worldview of Newtonian science, objects have only external relations, that is, they are forces reacting on matter from the outside like two billiard balls hitting against one another. While there is a kinetic energy transfer from one ball to the other that sets the second

---

14. Martin Luther, WA (Weimar Ausgabe) 23.134.34–23.136.36, quoted in Elizabeth Johnson, *Quest for the Living God* (New York: Continuum, 2008), 188.

15. Alister McGrath, *Surprised by Meaning: Science, Faith, and How We Make Sense of Things* (Louisville: Westminster John Knox, 2011), 52–53. This is a fine introduction to many of the issues relating faith and contemporary science.

ball moving, the two balls do not enter into one another so as to have an internal relationship. Rather, the relationship is purely external and does not affect the internal make-up of either ball. If science can explain (theoretically) all these external interactions, then there is no need to appeal to an additional supernatural object, "god" for explanation. This "modern" worldview still lives on in much of the scientism and the so-called new atheism of our time, where a material explanation is seen as not only necessary but also sufficient. If science cannot answer the question, then the question is not worth asking. This, of course, leaves out a lot, but for our purposes it presents one of the most serious intellectual challenges to theism. There are also other challenges, such as the existence of evil and suffering and human moral ambiguity, but for our purposes the reason that classical theism has been so under attack is because it is not intellectually coherent in a scientific and technologically mediated world. As we saw in earlier chapters, the "modern" worldview also has its limits, such as the impossibility of separating fact from value, the impossibility of a purely objective description, and the moral ambiguity of reason, which can be employed to serve means of mass destruction as readily as that of constructive understanding. Reason, and therefore scientific analysis, is not morally neutral but morally weighted. Enlightenment, rationalist optimism came crashing down in the trenches of World War I at about the same time that a scientific revolution was occurring that significantly revised Newtonian physics and the modern worldview built on it. The objectivist and substantialist understanding of physical reality was undermined with the emergence of relativity and quantum theories, which also opened the way to a new understanding of theism.

The twentieth century saw the demise of substance and the rise of relationality as a way of understanding existence at all levels of complexity. Along with relationality came the possibility of internal and not just external relationships in an evolutionary process of development with emergent complexity. This has been a game changer in understanding the relationship of God and the world. John B. Cobb Jr. wrote extensively about this in an early work titled *God and the World*.[16] Philip Clayton has more recently employed what he calls the "panentheistic analogy,"[17] the relationship of God and the

---

16. John B. Cobb Jr., *God and the World* (Philadelphia: Westminster, 1969), ch. 3, "The World and God."

17. Philip Clayton, "Panentheism in Metaphysical and Scientific Perspectives," *In Whom We Live and Move and Have Our Being*, ed. Philip Clayton and Arthur Peacocke (Grand Rapids: Eerdmans, 2004), 81–84.

world understood as analogous to the relationship of mind and body. Clayton observes,

> Thus the analogical relationship suggests itself: the body is to mind as the body/mind combination—that is, human persons—is to the divine. The world is in some sense analogous to the body of God; God is analogous to the mind which indwells the body, though God is also more than the natural world taken as a whole. Call it the panentheistic analogy (PA). The power of this analogy lies in the fact that mental causation, as every human agent knows it, is more than physical causation and yet still a part of the natural world. Apparently no natural law is broken when you form the (mental) intention to raise your hand and then you cause that particular physical object in the world, your hand, to rise. The PA therefore offers the possibility of conceiving divine actions that express divine intentions and agency without breaking natural law.[18]

What Clayton is describing here is an internal relationship where the world is already within God such that God does not have to be made present or injected into the world to be present (supernatural intervention) but rather is already there (noninterventionist). God can thus influence the affairs of the world from within without having to suspend or violate natural law. Indeed, natural law is one of the ways in which God relates and directs the natural world. This is a form of being-in-relation where indeed the whole is more than the sum of its parts and emergent complexity allows for new action and agency. Here levels of explanation will become important and indicate the constructive relationship between science and theology.

By way of illustrating the importance of levels of explanation, let's bake a cake[19] (see also chapter 2). Sciences such as chemistry or physics can tell you what the cake batter is made of (its chemical composition) and what will happen when these ingredients are baked for a specified amount of time and heat (physics). What they cannot tell you is why the cake is being baked. Is it a birthday cake or a wedding cake, for example? The first type of explanation is what philosophers refer to as secondary causation. Something already exists, and this tells you *how* this material is behaving. The other type of explanation is the *why* question of meaning or purpose; this is the realm of philosophy

---

18. Ibid., 84.

19. Alister McGrath, *Surprised by Meaning*, 43–44. This is a fine introduction to many of the issues relating faith and contemporary science.

and theology, which has to do with primary causation. We need both types of analysis to tell us what something really is. For a complete explanation, the secondary level must be supported by the primary level, even though they are on different levels of explanation and employ different methodologies. Neither science nor theology alone is adequate. Connecting this to the panentheistic analogy means that one can explain the occurrences within the natural world in terms of secondary causes without challenging any primary causes within theology. The mental "decision" to raise your hand, expressive of mental purpose, does not violate the neurophysiology of the body in its conduct, but neither is it fully explainable by that conduct. This allows for the action of God in the world describable by natural science without violating its laws in a way that modern theism could never accommodate. But what does this panentheistic model fully consist of, and how does the understanding of relationality and emergence help articulate it? To these questions we turn in the discussion of the elements of the model.

B. ELEMENTS

There are many contemporary theologians who employ a panentheistic model for the God-world relationship,[20] and of course there is some variation among them. Denis Edwards, arguing for a Trinitarian form of panentheism, concisely summarizes for our purposes some of the most common elements.[21] We will list these and briefly describe each element.

---

20. Many books and authors could be listed here; a few classic examples suffice. Sally McFague, *The Body of God: An Ecological Theology* (Minneapolis: Fortress Press, 1993); Rosemary Reuther, *Gaia and God: An Ecofeminist Theology of Earth Healing* (San Francisco: HarperSanFrancisco, 1992); Philip Clayton, *God and Contemporary Science*, Edinburgh Studies in Constructive Theology (Grand Rapids: Eerdmans, 1998); Denis Edwards, *The God of Evolution: A Trinitarian Theology* (Mahwah, NJ: Paulist Press, 1999); Arthur Peacocke, *Theology for a Scientific Age: Being and Becoming—Natural, Divine, and Human*, Theology and the Sciences (Minneapolis: Fortress Press, 1993); Joseph Bracken, SJ, *The One in the Many: A Contemporary Reconstruction of the God-World Relationship* (Grand Rapids: Eerdmans, 2001); David Ray Griffin, *Reenchantment without Supernaturalism: A Process Philosophy of Religion*, Cornell Studies in the Philosophy of Religion (Ithaca, NY: Cornell University Press, 2000). A fine anthology is the coedited work by Philip Clayton and Arthur Peacocke, *In Whom We Live and Move and Have Our Being*.

21. Edwards does distinguish his panentheism from process theology, particularly over the nature of transcendence. See *How God Acts: Creation, Redemption, and Special Divine Action* (Minneapolis: Fortress Press, 2010), 62. While I am approaching this subject mainly from a process perspective, the differences are not critical for the present level of discussion, and I do have some sympathy with Edwards's Rahnerian position, as can be seen from the text.

1. Panentheism is understood in Trinitarian terms—in this form of panentheism, the universe is understood as being created from within the shared life of the Trinity.

2. It understands God as wholly other to creatures and, precisely as such, as radically interior to them. Divine transcendence and immanence are not polar opposites but presuppose each other.

3. The spatial image is of all-things-in-God. God is not literally some kind of container.

4. God is understood as a creator who enables creatures to have their own proper autonomy and integrity. There is an infinite difference between God's *creatio continua* (primary causality) and all the interacting connections and causal relationships between creatures (secondary causality).

5. It sees creation as a free act of divine self-limitation. Love involves free self-limitation, making space for another, and God can be thought of as supremely loving in this way.

6. This model understands creation as a relationship that affects God as well as creatures. This means that the relationship is real on the side of God as well as that of creatures. Each affects the other in a reciprocal relationship.[22]

What we see here is the interconnection of creational existence between divine initiative and response characterized by self-giving (agape) love. Edwards observes, "The Spirit is the interior divine presence empowering the evolution of the universe from within, enabling a universe of creatures to exist and become."[23] This is key to the panentheistic model in that God is already present within the universe that divine love is making possible. God is thus closer to us than we are to ourselves; God is radically interior to us. Edwards comments that it is precisely because God is understood as transcendent that God can be thought of as immanent in creatures in a way that is not possible for created being. It is because God is wholly other that God can be *interior intimo meo*—"closer to me than I am to myself."[24] But while God is intimate, God is not only the relationship. Then there would be no distinction. It is precisely because there is a distinction between creature and Creator (avoiding pantheism) that intimacy is possible. In this way, the creation can mirror the Triune Creator

22. Denis Edwards, "A Relational and Evolving Universe Unfolding within the Dynamism of the Divine Communion," in Clayton and Peacocke, *In Whom We Live and Move and Have Our Being*, 200–2.

23. Ibid., 200.

24. Ibid.; and Augustine, *Confessions* 3.6.11.

in its unity-in-diversity. If the character of the immanent Trinity is being-in-relation, in community, then it should be no surprise that the creation this Triune Creator makes possible is also being-in-relation and communal. In reflecting on the Trinitarian understanding of God, Edwards observes,

> When such a God creates a universe it is not surprising that it turns out to be a radically relational and interdependent one. When life unfolds through the process of evolution, it emerges in "patterns of interconnectedness and interdependence that 'fits' with the way God is."[25]

The universe unfolds within the life of God. Here the turn to incarnation within the Christian understanding of the Trinity is crucial, for the incarnation is the most intimate relationship of the Creator with the creation and the heart of the Christian witness.

Love is a wondrous and confusing thing. It leads one to the heights of joy in celebration and the depths of despair when it is lost. So too with God insofar as this very human analogy has any symbolic reference. Love creates, but it also frees, and to have an autonomous creation there has to be the self-restricting of divine love and power to allow for an individuated, responsive creation to become possible. Even as this creation flows out of the plenitude of divine love, as Bonaventure saw, the love must, as Hegel saw, also "sublimate" (self-restrict), to allow for the object of that love, just as this sublimation allows for the reciprocal relationality within the immanent Trinity. But this sublimation or self-restriction does not mean the absence of God in a panentheistic model, only a self-differentiation within the divine becoming. God is not absent from the world, God's love is self-restricting to allow for the reciprocal love of the creation. In the panentheistic model, this self-restricting is internal to God and to Trinitarian relationality.[26] So the "space" the self-restricting of the Creator creates is within God, for all relations are within God even though they are not God. God does not leave the world void of divine presence. Evolution takes place within God. In clarifying this connection, the metaphor of entanglement can make a contribution.

---

25. Edwards, *The God of Evolution*, 28.

26. Here is a partial response to Kirk Wegter-McNelly, who contends that the idea of kenosis or self-limitation would mean that God absences himself from the world. In a panentheistic model, the self-restriction occurs within God and so does not remove divine presence but simply redefines it in a way that allows for the free response of the creation. It is a way for the divine plenitude of love to not overwhelm the very creation that the divine fullness is making possible.

C. EXPRESSION

Philosophical theologian Philip Clayton, in an excellent article titled "Panentheist Internalism: Living within the Presence of the Trinitarian God," as well as in a later article titled "Kenotic Trinitarian Panentheism,"[27] develops the significance of the panentheistic model for contemporary Christian thinking, particularly in relationship to science. In what he calls the "panentheist wager," Clayton observes, "What if—so the panentheist wager goes—God does not intervene *into* the natural processes, but rather is already in them? What if the processes of nature *just are* God at work?" He continues, "This theological approach allows us to take the qualities we find in nature—the creativity, beauty, order and lawfulness—and to ascribe them to the agency of God. But we can only do this if we learn how to think God and the world together more closely than theism has traditionally done."[28] This is exactly what I think the understanding of entanglement allows us to do.

God's self-restriction in order to make room for the creation, for an "other" within the divine life, does not mean that God is totally separate from the creation. God is not absent from the world but transcendently immanent in its entirety in a way that no finite creature can be. Entanglement affirms an ongoing relatedness between two particles that have once interacted. By metaphorical extension, this also could apply to God and the creation. God is other than the creation by being its source but is still related and interconnected to it in its ongoing development. *Entanglement gives metaphorical identity to the manner in which panentheism models God's relationship to the creation.* The foundational interconnectivity between God and creation is such that not only does one influence the other but they also exist in a communitarian relationship that mirrors the divine communion of the internal Trinity. The creation is the economic extension of the immanent Trinity into panentheistic otherness, allowing for communion that includes origination, redemption, and sanctification. *It is pluralistic monotheism.* Creational existence is communal, just as the divine life is communal, because it is part of the divine communitarian life. Moltmann, Clayton, Edwards, Peacocke, and Zizioulas all affirm this communitarian existence.[29] What I am adding here is simply the additional metaphor of entanglement to explain the interconnectivity of the divine

---

27. Philip Clayton, "Panentheist Internalism: Living within the Presence of the Trinitarian God," *Dialog: A Journal of Theology* 40, no. 3 (2001): 208–15; and Clayton, "Kenotic Trinitarian Panentheism," *Dialog: A Journal of Theology* 44, no. 3 (2005): 250–55.

28. Clayton, "Panentheist Internalism," 209.

29. See Clayton and Peacocke, *In Whom We Live and Move and Have Our Being*; as well as Polkinghorne, ed., *The Trinity and the Entangled World*; and Polkinghorne, ed., *The Work of Love: Creation*

perichoretic communion. Entanglement provides a physical metaphor for the divine together-in-separation nature of that communion.

"Mutual indwelling" gives rise through the divine energy of communal love to the existence of the creation as a communitarian focus or object of that love. It is an expression of the divine "plenitude" that Bonaventure described. Perichoresis as entanglement means that this "mutual indwelling" gives rise to togetherness-in-separation with the creation. God could never be separated from the creation, for God is entangled through the divine love that makes the creation possible in the first place. *Self-restriction does not lead to absence but to entangled transcending immanence. It is a self-offering and not a self-emptying of the Creator.* God does not need to be made present in the world, for God is already there, as panentheism affirms. Clayton observes, "It makes more sense that God would create other centers of activity within the divine presence if it is God's eternal nature *already* to contain multiple centers of activity. Surprisingly, this natural partnership between panentheism and Trinitarian thought is rarely acknowledged."[30] This is the heart of social Trinitarianism as developed by the early church as a way of acknowledging the divine community of love and its expression into the creation. (See Augustine, Bonaventure, and Luther, for example, as well as Moltmann more recently.) God is thus internally related to the creation not as one among many but as the ground on which the many can be related, for God is self-sufficient in a way that no creature can ever be. Clayton remarks, "In short, the divine has ontological self-sufficiency that no finite, contingent creature can enjoy. It is sufficient for God to be internally related in order for God to exist, but no finite creature exists as a result of being internally related."[31] This is the nature of contingency and of being created that ontologically distinguishes the Creator from the creature. Because God is the ground of all existence (remember the levels of explanation; this is the "why" level), God is the basis for unity within diversity. This could be understood as an extension of the unity found within the immanent Trinity as it is lovingly expressed in the economic Trinity giving ground to the creation itself. *Creatio ex nihilo* ("creation out of nothing") gives rise to a *creatio continua* ("continuous creation") because God remains entangled with the creation and would never abandon it or back out. God continues to sustain the creation both from within and without. Originating creation transitions into sustaining creation. To go back to our earlier discussion, God is superimposed

---

as Kenosis (Grand Rapids: Eerdmans, 2001), as well as Jürgen Moltmann, *God in Creation: A New Theology of Creation and the Spirit of God* (Minneapolis: Fortress Press, 1993).

30. Clayton, "Kenotic Trinitarian Panentheism," 252.

31. Ibid., 254.

on the creation as the field potential is present prior to the emergence of a particle. Entangled field potential as a description of panentheism explicates divine presence while still allowing for freedom within the created order. This freedom then allows for emergent complexity, which increases the freedom of response as well as diversity within the divine embodiment. God dances with the creation by being spiritually immanent within it, guiding it to increased levels of complexity through the natural processes of existence. The dancing God is the God of evolution. Within the panentheistic model, as Denis Edwards points out, "evolution takes place within God."[32]

In this chapter, we have seen that science can provide metaphors that enhance theological understanding as they also help to improve the relationship between theology and science. The scientific entanglement metaphors of nonlocal relational holism and superposition have been used here both supportively as well as heuristically to develop a way of modeling the God-world relationship that is consistent with contemporary science. This is one of the goals of relating science and theology in creative mutual interaction. There are many additional issues that need to be developed, particularly as this entangled Trinitarian panentheistic model is related to each of the persons of the Trinity. What does entangled panentheism have to say about the nature of divine creation, and what are its implications for the environment? How does this model help to elaborate the understanding of the incarnation and its relationship to suffering within the creation? Can this model, in developing the understanding of the Spirit within the world, be a ground for community and hope? We will address each of these areas in the concluding chapter as we turn to more of the practical implications for what it means to understand ourselves and the world around us as dwelling within the divine. If God is as close to us as our next heartbeat, how then should we live? I close this chapter by asking you to simply take your pulse, and once you find your heartbeat, say to yourself with each beat the word grace . . . grace . . . grace. That is the creational grace of life itself that courses through our veins with every heartbeat and reminds us not only of the contingent nature of our existence but also its giftedness. It is the creational "green grace" of life itself which reminds us that we do not live from or for ourselves alone but within a much wider web of life in which everything is interrelated and mutually existent. It is the concrete love of God found beating within the human heart as our hearts mirror the living love and grace of God within our lives. We are with God in a more profound and intimate way than we can ever imagine or express. Ultimately, of course,

---

32. Edwards, *The God of Evolution*, 34.

all models, metaphors, and symbols will fail us as we seek to give expression to that which is beyond expression, more intimate and yet more distant all at once in the dialectic of divine life. Yet we are the universe become self-conscious and are able to ask and reflect on such existence in a way that itself mirrors the divine life we are called to image. It is most certainly true that it is within God that we "live and move and have our being."

Key Terms

Complementarity
Creatio Ex Nihilo
Creatio Continua
Electromagnetic Field
Field Theory
God of the Gaps
Measurement
Mind–Body Interaction
Non–Local Relational Holism
Noninterventionist
Panentheistic Analogy
Primary Causation
Secondary Causation
Superposition
Supernatural Intervention
Triquetra

Discussion Questions

1. What is significant about panentheism for creation? Why is it essential in an understanding of the Christian understanding of the Trinity?
2. What is the function of analogy and metaphor in theological reflection? In what ways do metaphor and analogy help us understand perichoresis?
3. How does entanglement lead to a relational understanding of God?
4. In what way is complementarity observed in light? How does Nicholas of Cusa's painting portray theological complementarity?
5. Do you think this entangled panentheistic model of God addresses the issues raised against modern theism?

9

The Entangled Trinity

*The material principle of the doctrine of
the Trinity is "the cross," and the formal
principle of the theology of the cross is the
doctrine of the Trinity.*

–MOLTMANN, *THE CRUCIFIED GOD*

Theologians of the church have always attempted to draw on the most
sophisticated language and understandings of their time in an attempt to clarify
and express the Christian faith. That task is no different today. In this final
chapter, then, we turn to unpack the threefold nature of the Trinity in more
detail, drawing on the earlier work in this volume. We will apply the model
of perichoretic (entangled) Trinitarian panentheism, from the last chapter, to
the specific work of the three persons (*hypostaseis*) to affirm the Christian
conception of the unity-in-diversity of God. No final or ultimate claims are
being made here, only that this model has heuristic value in explicating for
today the Christian experience of *pluralistic monotheism*. Let us begin with the
creation itself and our own participation within it.

1. ENTANGLED CREATION

*I believe that God has created me and
all that exists.*

–LUTHER, *SMALL CATECHISM*

When I first read the statement by Martin Luther quoted above, I was taken aback. "How arrogant," I thought. He places himself before all of creation and is concerned first and foremost about himself. As I studied more about Luther, however, I realized that that was far from the truth; indeed, the truth was quite the opposite. In his explanation of the first article of the Apostles' Creed, he clarifies our own existence, our own creation, body, mind, and spirit, is the most intimate experience of creation that we will ever have. It is through our own experience of being created that we have a window into the rest of creation. Our bodies are our little corner of the cosmos, from which we are then enabled to perceive the rest of the universe and all that it contains. It is from our experience of existing that we are then driven to ask the question why. Why is there something rather than nothing? Why does anything exist at all? It is in the fact of our own existing that we can begin to consider the existence of all. It is in our intimate experience of our own creation that we can begin to consider the nature of creation itself. It is in our own experience of created relatedness that we can consider the creational relatedness of God. Luther got it right. Reflection on creation begins with ourselves and our own giftedness into being through creational grace, which then gives us a vantage point from which to consider the giftedness of the rest of creation. It is indeed the pulse of grace . . . grace . . . grace.

A. CREATION AND COSMOLOGY

Borrowing from Bonhoeffer the method of *analogia relationis* ("analogy of relationship") rather than an *analogia entis* ("analogy of being"), we can understand that God exists as relationality and in effect the entangled Triune God relates the creation into existence.[1] Such creational potentiality proceeds out of a divine potentiality that grounds an entanglement with the potentiality of the creation. It is the plenitude of divine love (Bonaventure) overflowing into the creation, not God emptying God's self from presence. Here the Hegelian understanding of "sublimation" (self-restricting) comes into play. Just as each person of the Trinity must sublimate itself in order for the unity of the Trinity to occur, this divine unity must also sublimate itself in order to make "space" for the differentiation of creation. The creation must have autonomy if it is to be the object of divine love as well as reciprocate that love. In such a process, the divine remains entangled with the creation it has made possible. *Creation is the entangled expression of divine perichoresis turned outward in self-*

1. Kirk Wegter-McNelly, *The Entangled God: Divine Relationality and Quantum Physics* (New York: Routledge, 2011), 227.

distinction through self-offering. There is togetherness-in-separation between the divine unity and the creation. There is also a temporal dimension within this divine relatedness, as Edwards, drawing on Karl Rahner, observes: "God is now understood as *enabling and empowering the evolutionary unfolding of creation in a process of self-transcendence from within.*"[2] The continuing entanglement of God with the creation is one way in which God sustains the creation from chaos, an ongoing example of divine action, of *creatio continua*, continuing creation.[3] *Creatio ex nihilo* ("creation out of nothing") gives rise to a *creatio continua* because God remains entangled with the creation and would never abandon it. God is committed once the act of creation occurs.

As observed earlier, evolution occurs within God, including both cosmic and biological evolution. Contemporary understanding of the evolution of the cosmos has reintroduced the question of teleology (purposefulness) into cosmology. Current calculations and observations indicate that there are a number of variables that must come together in just the right amount at just the right time for there to have ever been a stable cosmos, much less intelligent life. This is the so-called fine-tuned universe, which raises the question of purpose or design. These variables include everything from the expansion rate of the universe to the formation of the elements and the particle/antiparticle ratio. The latter refers to the exceptional condition that for every billion antiprotons in the early universe there were a billion and one protons. The billion pairs annihilated each other to produce radiation with just one proton left over. Ian Barbour observes, "A greater or smaller number of survivors—or no survivors at all if they had been evenly matched—would have made our kind of material world impossible. The laws of physics seem to be symmetrical between particles and

---

2. Denis Edwards, "A Relational and Evolving Universe Unfolding within the Dynamism of the Divine Communion," in *In Whom We Live and Move and Have Our Being*, ed. Philip Clayton and Arthur Peacocke (Grand Rapids: Eerdmans, 2004), 209–10 (italics original).

3. The subject of "divine action" is currently a major focus in the science-theology dialogue, and so the literature is growing quickly. Polkinghorne, Peacocke, Russell, Clayton, Nancey Murphy, Tracy, and Barbour among others are writing on the subject. For a good overview of the issues and perspectives, see Robert John Russell, Nancey Murphy, and Arthur Peacocke, eds., *Chaos and Complexity: Scientific Perspectives on Divine Action* (Berkeley: CTNS, 1995); and Philip Clayton, *God and Contemporary Science* (Grand Rapids: Eerdmans, 1997), ch. 7–8. Also John Polkinghorne, "Creatio Continua and Divine Action," *Science and Christian Belief* 7, no. 2. (1995): 101–15; Lyndon Harris, "Divine Action: An Interview with John Polkinghorne," *Cross Currents* (Spring 1998): 3–14; and Robert John Russell, "Does 'The God Who Acts' Really Act? New Approaches to Divine Action in Light of Science," *Theology Today* 54, no. 1 (1997): 43–65. Russell prefers to approach this issue of divine action from the "bottom up," employing quantum theory, while Polkinghorne prefers to approach it "top down," employing chaos theory.

antiparticles; why was there a tiny asymmetry?"[4] This fine tuning continues into the nature and relationship of the four fundamental physical forces. Alister McGrath lists several additional fine-tuned constants.

> 1. If the strong coupling constant were slightly smaller, hydrogen would be the only element in the universe. This would not have allowed for the formation of carbon.
> 2. If the weak fine constant were slightly smaller, no hydrogen would have formed during the history of the universe. Consequently, no stars would have formed.
> 3. If the electromagnetic fine structure constant were slightly larger, the stars would not be hot enough to warm planets to a temperature sufficient to maintain life in the form we know it.
> 4. If the gravitational fine structure constant were slightly smaller, stars and planets would not have been able to form because they would have lacked the gravitational constraints necessary for coalescence of their constituent material.[5]

Sir Martin Rees, past president of the Royal Society of London and one of England's most distinguished scientists and cosmologists, indicates that there are "just six numbers," without which the fine tuning of the universe would not be possible. He lists

> 1. The ratio of the electromagnetic force to the force of gravity,
> 2. The strong nuclear force,
> 3. The amount of matter in the universe,
> 4. Cosmic repulsion,
> 5. The ratio of the gravitational binding force to rest-mass energy,
> 6. The number of spatial dimensions.[6]

The additional point to remember is that the variation in these constraints is very small, less than 1 percent or 1/1000th of 1 percent in some cases.

4. Ian Barbour, *Religion and Science: Historical and Contemporary Issues* (San Francisco: HarperSanFrancisco, 1997), 205.

5. Alister McGrath, *Surprised by Meaning: Faith, Science, and How We Make Sense of Things* (Louisville: Westminster John Knox, 2011), ch. 8, "The Deep Structure of the Universe," especially 59–60.

6. Martin Rees, *Just Six Numbers: The Deep Forces That Shape the Universe* (London: Phoenix, 2000), 2–4.

It would appear that our universe is no accident, but this flies in the face of much contemporary science that intentionally brackets out purpose. This has led some cosmologists to propose various theories of a "multiverse," which can mean an infinite number of universes. In such a multiplicity, the probabilistic odds would allow for such order to emerge by chance. With an infinite number of possible universes, one would eventually result in all the fine-tuning we perceive in our universe. A major problem with this theory is that such universes are not detectable within our universe, and such a multiplication blows the principle of parsimony (using the fewest number of terms to explain a phenomenon) and inference to the best explanation right out the window. Currently, cosmologists are left with either the clear possibility that our universe was designed or that it is one of an infinite number of undetectable universes.

It must also be remembered in both sets of examples given above that we do not know the full range of possible probability for each of these values, so it is not possible to assign a final probability. These are interesting values, and they give us a deep appreciation for the particular conditions of our own evolution, but ultimately, they cannot be used to prove design or purpose. Difficulty or proliferation of production cannot be used to verify purpose or design. For example, the universe has produced more black holes than human beings, and they last considerably longer (some up to 200 billion years), so one could say that the purpose of the universe is to produce black holes and that we just happen to be a very self-interested by-product.[7] This demonstrates the danger of trying to translate probability into causality, or as statisticians are fond of saying, "Correlation is not causation." Within the theological model of entangled Trinitarian panentheism elaborated in this volume the scientific unprovability of purpose does not present a serious problem; indeed, it is precisely what one would expect to find if God is active in the universe working through the present physical laws. In any scientific analysis purpose would be hidden, masked within the processes of nature itself. God is not intervening to create purpose from outside, externally, but directing it internally, from within the physical processes themselves. It is only when one moves to a more holistic level of explanation, such as in philosophy or theology, that the question of purpose can be addressed. It is only through faith that one can confess God's involvement in creation. The same issues arise when we turn to biological evolution.

---

7. Bryan Luther, physicist, conveyed in personal conversation, April 12, 2013.

B. CREATION AND BIOLOGY

Why is there an increase in biological complexity if survival is the primary constraint on biological evolution? The more complex a structure becomes, the more vulnerable it becomes, and yet here we are, and able to ask these questions. The fine-tuned cosmological context led Brandon Carter, in 1974, to propose the "Anthropic Principle," which exists in two forms.[8] This position was given fuller articulation by John Barrow and Frank Tipler in their landmark book *The Anthropic Cosmological Principle*.[9] The so-called weak form is really a simple statement of observation, that the universe is supportive of creatures such as us. If this were not the case, we would not be here to make such a statement. So it is a statement of the obvious. The second form is more interesting. The "strong" form states that the universe had us, or at least intelligent life, in mind all along, that the universe was designed with us in mind. This is, of course, a claim that goes beyond scientific verification, but it is interesting to pursue what developmental directions this analysis implies. Biologist-theologian Alister McGrath observes that this process begins with the formation of carbon, which requires the fusion of three helium nuclei in a twofold process, where two helium nuclei initially fuse to form beryllium, which then captures a third helium nucleus to create carbon. The beryllium midstage is unstable and short-lived, so it is remarkable that such a "double fusion" process occurs at all, and yet it is essential to get not only carbon but many of the other elements, including oxygen. Later discoveries showed that the energy levels of carbon and oxygen nuclei were "just right" to allow both to form in the proportions necessary for carbon-based life-forms. McGrath concludes,

> The origins of life are thus unquestionably anthropic. They depend upon the fundamental values of constants in nature being such that the universe is able to progress beyond the formation of atomic hydrogen and thus bring about nucleosynthesis of biologically critical elements. . . . The big bang, in itself and of itself, was not capable of producing the elements upon which life depends; carbon, nitrogen, and oxygen.[10]

---

8. The term comes from Brandon Carter, "Large Number Coincidences and the Anthropic Principle," in *Confrontation of Cosmological Theories with Observational Data*, ed. M. S. Longair (Boston: Reidel, 1974), 291–98.

9. John Barrow and Frank Tipler, *The Anthropic Cosmological Principle* (Oxford: Oxford University Press, 1986).

10. McGrath. *Surprised by Meaning*, 67–68.

Human beings, as well as the rest of nature, are literally star creatures. We are made of stardust; the heavier elements in our bodies require the thermonuclear fusion of stars that have gone supernova and spewed their material out into intersidereal space. This also reminds us that all existence, especially life, is interrelated, and that we exist in a biosphere that is interconnected and indissoluble, that we are entangled with all other existence. As self-conscious beings, we are also our fellow creatures' keepers. Interestingly, this is exactly what Genesis 2 reminds us of, that we are to be "keepers of the garden."

Within the panentheistic model developed here, this interdependence is essential and unavoidable, with a strong component of environmental stewardship. We are to care for creation, which means that we are to care for the expression of the divine in the natural world. We are called in the words of theologians Grace Jantzen and Sallie McFague to understand the world as "God's body,"[11] and to necessarily care for it as if it were our own. This is where the panentheistic model has its most significant relevance in relation to creation. We see that God, while othering the creation into existence, remains entangled with it. Creation, in other words, is from God and therefore cannot ever be truly separated from God. Relating this to the Trinity, we see that the Logos, which voiced forth the creation in the first place, is still connected to and continues to sustain the creation it has made possible. The communion of the Trinity flows out in creational grace and love to embody a physical communion of the cosmos. The creation is not divine, although it is related to the divine. The self-offering of God in creating allows for true relationship and community, by creating the "other" to which God can be related. God's own freedom and power make the creation what it is, not by withdrawing from but by fully relating to and creating it. (See Peters and Hewlett.) Being-in-relation means that communion is at the heart of God. Orthodox theologian John Zizioulas states, "It is communion that makes things be: nothing exists without it, not even God."[12] Catherine LaCugna in her magnum opus *God for Us* observes,

A nontrinitarian account of creation will always make it seem as if God is not *essentially* involved with the creature. This belies religious

---

11. Grace Jantzen, *God's World, God's Body* (Philadelphia: Westminster, 1984); and Sallie McFague, *The Body of God: An Ecological Theology* (Minneapolis: Fortress Press, 1993); McFague, *Super, Natural Christians: How We Should Love Nature* (Minneapolis: Fortress Press, 2000); and McFague, *A New Climate for Theology: God, the World, and Global Warming* (Minneapolis: Fortress Press, 2008).

12. John Zizioulas, *Being as Communion: Studies in Personhood and the Church* (Crestwood, NY: St. Vladimir's Seminary Press, 1985), 17, quoted in Edwards, "Relational and Evolving Universe," 204.

faith. A trinitarian doctrine of creation, on the other hand, thinks together divine relationality and created relationality. Divine relationality becomes the paradigm for every type of relationality in creation. And, every type of created relationality insinuates divine relationality.[13]

This "overflowing" of God into creation, however, is not a full disclosure of who God is. Just as in the cross, God remains hidden behind the masks of materiality. The creation too becomes *larva Dei*, the "masks of God." This means that, while in faith one may appeal to God as Creator, one cannot prove such a creation by observation of the natural world. Scientific analysis can neither prove nor disprove the presence of God in creation. In faith, however, one can be called to care for the creation and to see an intrinsic ecological ethic embedded in the theological model of panentheism. In caring for the body of God, we are caring for our body as well. In his book *Ecology at the Heart of Faith: The Change of Heart That Leads to a New Way of Living on Earth*, Denis Edwards elaborates the ecological implications of a panentheistic model in some detail, including how it can contribute to sustainability. (See Rasmussen.) Drawing on the thought of Danish theologian Niels Gregerson and his understanding of "deep incarnation," which has both biological and ecological implications, Edwards observes, "The cross of Christ reveals God's identification with creation in all its complexity, struggle and pain. Gregerson finds in the cross a microcosm of God's redemptive presence to all creatures that face suffering and death."[14] We take seriously the human biological nature of the incarnation and its interconnection with all of life. Gregerson describes it this way.

> In this context the incarnation of God in Christ can be understood as a radical or "deep" incarnation, that is, an incarnation into the very tissue of biological existence, and system of nature. Understood this way, the death of Christ becomes an icon of God's redemptive co-suffering with all sentient life as well as with the victims of social competition. God bears the cost of evolution, the price involved in the hardship of natural selection.[15]

13. Catherine LaCugna, *God for Us: The Trinity and Christian Life* (San Francisco: HarperSanFrancisco, 1993), 168.

14. Denis Edwards, *Ecology at the Heart of Faith: The Change of Heart That Leads to a New Way of Living on Earth* (Maryknoll, NY: Orbis, 2006), 59.

In this sense, the incarnation is an intensification of the self-offering process of creation. God loved the dinosaurs and the creative beauty they and other extinct species achieved. This value is preserved within the eternal life of God, never to be fully lost. Since living value requires some sentient subjectivity this also means that some form of subjective immortality is possible for all creatures within the divine life for all are part of the body of God. (See McDaniel and his "pelican heaven.") The loss to be found within the creation also affects God as well as the creative emergent novelty of new life. This intersection of the "green grace" of creation with the "red grace" of redemption is a prime example of the entanglement of the divine with the creation of the dynamics within the body of God itself. Here the perichoretic dynamism of the immanent Trinity intersects with the perichoretic dynamism expressed in the economic Trinity, and the form that that intersection takes is cruciform. The love of God for the world takes the form of a cross. George Murphy observes, "The most profound aspect of the cross is that *God himself* shares in the suffering of the world. In the Incarnation, God becomes a participant in the evolutionary process, sharing in the evolutionary history which links humanity with the rest of the biosphere."[16] Through the incarnation, the Creator further self-restricts and empties in order to enter the suffering "other" of the creation itself; this is the sublimation or kenosis (emptying) of the incarnation. Creation becomes cruciform for God. But because it is the suffering of God, suffering can be overcome in the divine life, providing hope for all creation. Let us now turn to the work of the Trinity in entangled incarnation.

2. Entangled Incarnation

The Spirit himself intercedes for us with sighs too deep for words.

—St. Paul, Rom. 8:26

---

15. Ibid.; also Niels Henrik Gregerson, "The Cross of Christ in an Evolutionary World," *Dialog: A Journal of Theology* 40, no. 3 (2001): 205, and "The Complexification of Nature: Supplementing the Neo-Darwinian Paradigm?" *Theology and Science* 4, no. 1 (2006): 5-31.

16. George Murphy, "'Chiasmic Cosmology' and the 'Same Old Story': Two Lutheran Approaches to Natural Theology," *Facets of Faith and Science*, vol. 4, *Interpreting God's Action in the World*, ed. Jitse van der Meer (Lanham, MD: University Press of America, 1996), 137 (italics original). See also Murphy, *The Cosmos in Light of the Cross* (New York: Trinity Press International, 2003).

It is in the frailty of life that we encounter the profound issues of suffering and death. While we may debate the problems of evil and suffering in theoretical ways such as those expressed in theodicy, as human beings we will ultimately encounter them in an existential and practical manner. Personal experiences of the processes of destruction undermine any simple explanation or justification for suffering. Suffering is the cost of freedom and autonomy within the creational space of God. The Christian tradition, while offering some intellectual explanations for the existence of evil and suffering via human free will as well as the free response of creation, ultimately offers not so much a Why? but a Who? as the answer to suffering. The creation is cruciform,[17] and thus too is the love of God. As Alfred North Whitehead once remarked, God is "the great companion, the fellow sufferer who understands."[18]

A. SIGHS OF SUFFERING

The angiogram scanner hummed smoothly as it passed over my bare chest in the catheter lab. As I lay there on the examining table with the traces of the lobster-based dye coursing through my heart, coronary arteries started to appear on the LED screen, looking much like the root structure of a daisy. As the scan proceeded across my chest, the images changed, capturing the movement of a human heart in rhythmic beat in real time. As the image moved to the left side of my heart, the left circumflex arterial root appeared to have been clipped off as if by a pair of scissors. As I turned to the cardiologist doing the exam, I muttered something to the effect, "That's not good is it?" He sighed and said, "No, it's not." At that point, I experienced what could only be called a high-tech encounter with mortality as I lay in the cool catheter lab watching my own beating heart on a computer screen, knowing full well that it was impaired to the point of being fatal. I began to shake uncontrollably, and I knew it was as much from the existential cold of confrontation with mortality as it was from the air conditioning in the lab. All I could do in the midst of such existential anxiety was emit a sigh as a prayer to God expressing petition and feeling beyond the capacity of human words to encapsulate or express. It was indeed a "sigh too deep for words."

---

17. Holmes Rolston, *Science and Religion: A Critical Survey* (Philadelphia: Templeton Foundation Press, 1987), ch. 3; see also Rolston, *Environmental Ethics: Duties to and Values in the Natural World* (Philadelphia: Temple University Press, 1989), ch. 4. For an eloquent treatment of evolutionary theodicy see Christopher Southgate, *The Groaning of Creation: God, Evolution and the Problem of Evil* (Louisville: Westminster John Knox, 2008).

18. Alfred North Whitehead, *Process and Reality: An Essay in Cosmology*, corrected ed., ed. David Ray Griffin and Donald W. Sherburne (New York: Free Press, 1978), 351.

"Sighs too deep for words." The profound existential simplicity of this phrase has always intrigued me. It is often in the sighs of life that the divine presence is needed and felt. While profound words and elaborate rituals may illumine the glory of God from time to time, it is in the daily dying of life, the perpetual perishing of existence, that the sighs of the Spirit seem a more appropriate manner for divine communication and presence. This is where the existential or personal dimension of divine entanglement interconnects with human need. It is where grace and forgiveness come in the knowledge that "God is with us," Emmanuel.[19] The "green grace" of the wood of creation provides the basis for the "red grace" of the cross of redemption. Here we enter the deepest heart of Perichoretic Trinitarian Panentheism. God enters most fully into the becoming of creation such that the becoming of God and the creation are entangled in dynamic mutual indwelling. It is deep incarnation.

B. THEOLOGY OF THE CROSS

At the heart of the Christian faith is the affirmation that God has become "Emmanuel" and, through St. Paul, this "with-us-ness" is understood as the kenotic self-emptying of God in Christ (Phil. 2:7). Kenosis (emptying) becomes a theological window through which to peer into the heart of divine love and as such reveals not only the manner of the incarnation but also the very nature of the Triune God. The kenosis of the Incarnation can be understood to characterize the spiritual presence of God in the world through nonlocal relational holism and superposition. God is always "with us" as the divine superposition within the midst of the creation. But in the incarnation, this superposition takes on a unique character as it "collapses" into the particularity of the incarnation, which is the presence of sanctifying, agapaic love in a particular time and place. With the incarnation, the Logos, which has been implicit within creation, becomes explicit, becoming transparent to the God with whom it exists. *The entanglement becomes explicit.* The communion of God becomes intimate communion with the world. "Sighs too deep for words" become embedded in the very character of God.

The principle of the incarnation is that the spiritual is manifest in the material, that the "Word became flesh" (John 1:14). Out of the incarnation flows God's justifying grace, forgiveness of sins, and the transformative hope of the resurrection. By becoming creature, the Creator has sanctified human

---

19. Part of this section draws on my earlier articles, "Theology of the Cross and Popular Culture," *Word and World* 23, no. 3 (2003): 253–62; and "Towards a Kenotic Pneumatology: Quantum Field Theory and the Theology of the Cross," *CTNS Bulletin* 19, no. 2 (1999): 11–16.

earthly existence, reconciling us not only to God but also to one another and the earth. The earliest scriptural analogy for conceiving this divine action is found in Phil. 2:6-8. Most biblical scholars believe it is a preexistent liturgical hymn that Saint Paul employs to express his understanding of *how* God could be present in human history.[20] It is also believed that he adds his own touch to this hymn by the addition of the phrase "even death on a cross" to characterize the depth of divine emptying. In the Christian tradition, the cross is the lens through which God is viewed, albeit "darkly."[21] The cross is a paradoxical and complex disclosure of the divine.[22]

In addition to God's paradoxical disclosure on the cross, there is a twofold hiddenness. First is the form of the opposite: power comes in weakness, victory in defeat, and life in death. Second is the totality of divine reality, God within God's self, the *mysterium tremendum et fascinans* (Otto), which is beyond the disclosure of God in Christ. God is more than God's self-disclosure in Christ. To draw on the panentheistic analogy again, one is more than one's body, and while the body can be analyzed, it can never fully disclose the mind. Human thought remains hidden in the interstices of our subjectivity. This distinction, then, gives us both a material and a formal principle for theological reflection. Formally, it tells us that the work of God on Calvary must be related to all Christian thought. The cross alone is our theology (*crux sola nostra theologia*) and also functions as a critical principle for the assessment of theological formulation. The material principle is the character of divine love as agape, or self-giving love, which I believe can be understood as the intimate entanglement of the love of God in particular superposition in the incarnation. The nature of human need through sin, suffering, and death become the lenses through which we view the functioning of the divine. Metaphorically, if you will, human suffering becomes the measurement through which the divine field potential of agapaic love "collapses" the wave function of agapaic love into the forms most particular to our need. This is the divine kenosis of the incarnation. God does not have to be made present, for God is always present, but the functional relationship within the immanent Trinity moves to economic expression in the incarnation. The Logos of creation becomes one

---

20. See Lucien Richard, *Christ: The Self-Emptying of God* (Mahwah, NJ: Paulist, 1997), especially ch. 4, "In the Form of a Servant: The Kenotic Hymn."

21. See Jürgen Moltmann, *The Crucified God: The Cross as the Foundation and Criticism of Christian Theology* (New York: SCM; Philadelphia: Fortress, 1974).

22. See George Murphy's articles, "The Theology of the Cross and God's Work in the World," *Zygon* 33, no. 2 (1998): 221–31; and "The Third Article in the Science-Theology Dialogue," *Perspectives on Science and Christian Faith* 45, no. 3 (1993): 162–68.

with the creation that it has made possible, entering ever more deeply into the biology and physical reality of human and creational life. This occurs not because of some flaw in God's plan or some external compulsion imposing itself on the divine will. No, this flows out of the omnipresent love of God within God's body itself as it seeks to heal and restore a part of itself. The Resurrection may then be understood as the proleptic disclosure of the future of the creation within the healing body of God. It is a glimpse of the power of the immanent Trinity within the realm of the economic.

How then does God remain distinct and yet become so intimately connected to the creation? This is where I believe the concept of kenosis is most effective. Indeed, I contend that with regard to the economic Trinity, the incarnation occurs as a *kenotic perichoresis*. When Philippians 2 says that Christ did not count equality with God a thing to be grasped but emptied himself, coming in the form of a servant, it does not say that Christ emptied himself of all divinity, only that Christ gave up the equal relationship with God. One could say that the Son kenotically gave up the Trinitarian perichoresis precisely in order to enter into the creation. *Christ kenotically emptied himself of the immanent perichoresis of the Trinity in order to enter into the economic perichoresis of the creation.* If the metaphors of non-local relational holism and entanglement are applied here, it might help clarify the ancient doctrine that "what can be said about the Father can be said about the Son except that the Father is not the Son." I would also add, "What can be said about the Son can be said about the Father except that the Son is not the Father." The theological reciprocity implied here affirms the divine affectability in both directions. The wholeness or holy otherness of God remains entangled with the particular embodiment even though it cannot be subsumed by that embodiment. God in God's self is more than Christ even though Christ is the human face of God. Christ is the full mirror of the *imago Dei* within the creation. This is why Paul refers to Christ as the "Last Adam" (1 Cor. 14:45). I believe perichoresis as entanglement can provide a useful metaphor for conceptualizing this, though certainly not explanations or proofs. Because of the ontological character of the finite human knower, metaphor and analogy may be all that we are ultimately capable of achieving.

To acknowledge ambiguity is to affirm the tensions of human life and the paradoxical character of human existence. The fight of faith is joined precisely in the midst of the ambiguity of human experience and moral decision making. To ignore or deny ambiguity is to deny ourselves and our experience of life. The ontological singularity of human existence must be constructively accounted for if a person is to grow and flourish in life.[23] At the heart of the Christian tradition, it is argued that in this solitariness one is not alone and that at the heart of spirituality is a self-transcending selfhood that enables a person to reach out beyond themselves. As Berdyaev once remarked, "To eat bread is a material act, to break and share it a spiritual one."[24] Jürgen Moltmann puts it this way: "The Spirit is the Spirit of surrender of the Father and the Son. He is creative love proceeding out of the Father's pain and the Son's self-surrender and comes to forsaken human beings in order to open them to a future for life."[25] A more critical awareness of the theology of the cross can assist believers in addressing the issues of the hiddenness of God in the world, the ambiguity of life, and suffering in human experience. A theology of the cross meets these concerns head on and does not deny them or simply explain them away. It does not try to "fix" everything in human life but places it in a wider context of meaning, including eschatological fulfillment in the kingdom of God, for Christ is the beginning of the new creation. The Spirit is the continuing self-offering, self-limiting, agapaic love of God sanctifying the creation toward life and fulfillment. An entangled Christology leads directly to an entangled Pneumatology, or understanding of the sanctifying work of the Holy Spirit. The green grace of creation, complemented by the red grace of redemption, then makes possible the blue grace of sanctification, of hope and peace in the spirit. Deep incarnation meets deep sanctification.

3. ENTANGLED SANCTIFICATION

When we dream alone, it is only a dream.
When we dream together it is no longer a
dream; it is the beginning of reality.

–DOM HELPER CAMARA,
CONTROLLING INTEREST

The floor was dirt. The walls were made of handmade mud bricks, and there was a bird's nest of electrical wiring hanging on the eve of the roof providing electricity across the barrio. There was raw sewage running down the middle of the dirt-packed street, and a single water tap provided water for possibly

23. Alfred North Whitehead once remarked that "religion is what the individual does with his own solitariness." Alfred North Whitehead, *Religion in the Making* (New York: Meridian, 1954), 16.

24. Quoted in Langdon Gilkey, *Shantung Compound* (San Francisco: HarperSanFrancisco, 1966), 229.

25. Jürgen Moltmann, "The Crucified God: A Trinitarian Theology of the Cross," *Interpretation* (1972): 294–95.

hundreds within a mile of the tap. This is a definition of "dirt poor," and yet within this material deprivation there was spiritual affluence. Colorful scarves were hung as window curtains inside, and through the open, glassless windows a light breeze gently blew, caressing the colors and animating them in its grasp. There was a poverty and a simplicity here on the outskirts of the Federal District of Mexico City that gave room for the spirit to work. The home was the location of a *Communidad de Base*, or Base Christian Community, where about two dozen members of the community gathered once a week to read Scripture, share experiences, and collaborate on how the Spirit would be moving them in the coming week to work for justice within their community. It was praxis, the integration of action and reflection, put into practice and flowing out of worship. It was a home base for Latin American theology of liberation.

I listened to the gathered community speak about their understanding of Scripture. While their interpretation seemed elementary, they were certainly not far afield. But it was when they turned to ask the follow-up question, "So what is the Spirit calling us to do today and this week to work for justice?" that the Spirit seemed to really enter the discussion. This was not something I regularly encountered in North America. They talked about joining teachers in their strike for higher wages down at the Zocalo, the historic center of Mexico City. They talked of going as a group to the person who sold propane gas to the barrio and ask him to better maintain his equipment because people were getting burned by faulty valves, otherwise they would take their business elsewhere. They mused about what it would take to get a concrete sewer down the street of their unincorporated area. Their discussion centered on what in North America might be called focused community organizing. But there was a difference. They were also concerned about the others affected by their actions, even the propane owner. They knew that all actions have multiple consequences, and for true liberation to occur it must liberate not only the oppressed but also the oppressor. The Spirit was moving through and within this community to enable works of peace and justice in a very concrete and local fashion. They were "dreaming together" so that social change could happen, as Archbishop Dom Heldar Camara had seen so many times before in his work against hunger and injustice in Brazil. The Spirit creates and exists in community, empowering for service in the world. The Spirit manifests the blue grace of hope and peace within the community of faith, even in the midst of difficult situations. This is the Spirit's animating of the life of faith. As the meeting broke up and the people left through the mud-brick door in their amazingly immaculate white ponchos and pants, the breeze gently drifted through the colorful window, reminding me that the Spirit will blow where it wills and that it is not subject to our control. To dream alone is only a dream, but to dream together is indeed the beginning of reality.

A. SPIRIT AND COMMUNITY

It is impossible to understand the Holy Spirit without community. The Spirit is the dynamic love within the communion of the Trinity itself, which is expressed in the Spirit's animating role within the creation and the wider human community. The immanent Spirit of the Trinity becomes *Spiritus Creator*, the creative Spirit in economic expression of the Trinity. The metaphor of the ongoing entanglement of the divine field potential toward the future with the creation's field potential could be a creative way of imaging the sanctifying activity of the Holy Spirit—in effect, a superposition of wave functions within the field that eventuates in providential presence in the midst of indeterminacy. *The Spirit is the ongoing entanglement of the Father and the Son with the creation, the sanctifying embodiment of the agapaic love of God, the blue grace of hope and peace.* The Spirit is the living force of the love of God within the creation, empowering it towards eschatological fulfillment. The Hebrew *ruach*, "breath" or "wind," as well as the Greek *pneuma*, "air," carry with them this understanding of an unseen force whose effects can be experienced. It would not be possible, however, to disentangle the spiritual presence in the "gossamer" of creation from all other causes and potentials in the field.

The difficulty here is that the field potentials in quantum theory are always indeterminate until measurement takes place.[26] All one can know is that the results will be correlated after measurement but not what the results will be beforehand. This is where entangled quantum potentials run head-on into quantum indeterminacy. Does this present an insurmountable obstacle to using quantum theory as a metaphor? I do not think so, if we realize that the creation is indeed free and at the same time that God is related to all the possible potentials of that creation. This, of course, does open up the possibility of abuse of this freedom, resulting in suffering and evil. Such occurrences are derivative from God through divine sublimation (self-limitation) but not directly caused by God. The material principle of agapaic love indicates God's willingness to enter into this suffering. True novelty is possible and is related to God, but it

---

26. This is one of Polkinghorne's reasons for preferring chaos theory over quantum theory to explain divine action. See "The Metaphysics of Divine Action," in Russell, Murphy, and Peacocke, *Chaos and Complexity*, as well as *Serious Talk: Science and Religion in Dialogue* (Valley Forge, PA: Trinity Press International, 1995), chs. 2 and 7. For Robert John Russell's argument on behalf of quantum theory, see "Does 'The God Who Acts' Really Act? New Approaches to Divine Action in Light of Science," *Theology Today* 54, no. 1 (1997): 43–65.

comes at a cost. Indeed, love is as interested in process as in outcome. Therefore God need not push for efficacy over growth, and divine self-limitation allows openness of outcome for the authentic reciprocity of love on the part of the creation.

This divine relation can also be analogous to measurement. If we posit divine becoming in relation to creation, God's self-understanding could constitute a measurement of the divine potential in relation to the creation in such a way that a correlate definiteness emerges in the creation. Divine phase potential could then be seen as a superposition on the creation's own phase potential. This could be a relational effect of divine entanglement and one possible role of the Spirit in creation ("particular providence for particular occasions," Whitehead). But one has to be careful here. I am not saying that God is the source of all measurement, otherwise there is no free will and God is the only responsible agent, and we are back in the middle of theodicy. What I am saying is that the understanding of entangled phase potentials may provide a helpful metaphor for theology in conceptualizing how divine influence could occur without dictating divine determinism. It would be one way of articulating the entangled relationship.

Also, because the two are entangled from the beginning, we do not have the need for a "causal joint" between divine action and the creation. They are part of the same holistic quantum potential. Instead, we might speak of a "causal potentiality" in which the entanglement brings forth respective quantifications from the quantum field. There is distinction as well as relatedness between God and the creation. This is the heart of a panentheistic relationship.[27] Joseph Bracken who, like myself, is attempting a neo-Whiteheadian position, modifying Whitehead in light of quantum field theory, refers to this as the "divine sensorium," where God is connected to all existence. He observes, "The divine nature is, thus, the ontological foundation for an all-embracing cosmic society with an ever growing corporate subjectivity represented in the first place by the three divine persons but likewise including all enduring personally ordered societies of finite actual occasions."[28] While he refers to the underlying stratum of existence as a "field of activity," I refer to it as quantum entanglement of field potentials and the basis for community. This community is also eschatological because the Spirit, as a ground for hope, is a living force for the future of the creation within the life of God. This necessarily leads to a

---

27. See Robert John Russell, "Cosmology from Alpha to Omega," *Zygon* 29, no. 4 (1994): 572.

28. Joseph Bracken, "Panentheism from a Process Perspective," in *Trinity in Process: A Relational Theology of God*, ed. Marjorie Suchocki and Joseph A. Bracken, SJ (New York: Continuum, 1997), 107.

wider understanding of faith as loving service in the world, the expression of Christian vocation (Luther).

B. SPIRIT AND VOCATION

Vocation addresses the practical from an existential context. It connects purposes and practices, ends and means, and does not allow them to remain separate. *Vocatio* ("calling") mirrors the involvement of the Creator in the creation. The principle impelling both creation and incarnation is the divine love of God. All existence is symbiosis, a life together, proceeding from God's love of creation and reconciled and restored through the incarnation of that love in Christ, which is animated by the Holy Spirit. Vocation is thus an expression of Trinitarian symbiosis. Such was Jesus' calling, and the Christian calling then follows on this symbiosis. The Christian is called (*klēsis*, as Paul uses the term, see Rom. 8:30 and 1 Cor. 7:20) to trust in the promise of God through faith and live out this faith through loving service to one's neighbor through symbiotic life in the world. It is to care for the life of God by caring for the life of the neighbor and the wider creation. What, then, would it mean to exercise vocation in the context of the entangled Trinitarian panentheistic model that we are pursuing here?

Vocation is animated by hope and the possibility of a better future for all. For the Christian, the Resurrection is the proleptic disclosure of this future for all creation and is the basis for hope. This hope is grounded in the power of the Spirit as it animates creation and human lives within it. The Spirit embodies the energy of the power of the future within the immediacy of the present. We always live our lives in the present, from which we remember the past and anticipate the future. It is easy to see how the past influences the present—causal efficacy sees to that. But the future also exercises an influence on the present by means of possibility and desirability. *It is in light of what might be that one can become empowered to challenge and change what is.* The power of hope grounds a prophetic vision of the future. If one has no vision of the future, one is left within the status quo. With the vision of future possibilities, one can become empowered to challenge the present status quo and the conditions of oppression. A vision of future possibility is one of the most powerful ideas that humans can possess, and it is the source of liberation. When one realizes "This need not be!" one is empowered for change. The most devastating thing that can happen to any human being is to lose a sense of hope in the possibility of the future. This dialectic of the future allows persons to realize their situation could be otherwise and to work for change. This is what is at work in the base Christian community I described at the beginning of this section. An animating vision of the future is at the heart of the Christian understanding of vocation. Vocation thus participates in the dynamic power of the Spirit for life and growth within the creation. That is, it participates in the entangled field potential that is the divine love. In the panentheistic model developed here, we participate and contribute to the divine life and are animated by the divine field potential that God makes possible. Vocation therefore is for the earth and the world of today, so that, as Gustav Wingren summarizes, "human action is a medium for God's love to others."[29] We are drawn out of ourselves to consider the needs of others and the wider environment as we come to understand that we are all interconnected, that we are all entangled within the field of force which is the love of God. We are called to serve the other, whomever or wherever that might be, including persons of other faith traditions.

C. INTERFAITH COOPERATION

This model of panentheistic spirituality also has important possibilities for interfaith dialogue and cooperation. If the entire world is interconnected through God's body, then there is no part of the creation, including human cultures, that is without divine presence. This is not to say that all religions are the same but rather quite the opposite. Just as different organs in the human body have their specific functions and do not look alike but nevertheless contribute to the well-being of the whole, so too do diverse religious expressions. We are certainly all together in the one biosphere, and to address the environmental challenges of our time, we must find ways to cooperate and coordinate, including religiously, for mutual survival. Buddhist ecologist Stephanie Kaza in her book *Mindfully Green* encourages all persons, regardless of religious orientation, to follow the "Green Path." This includes reducing harm, being with the suffering, and embracing the deep view.[30] In calling for this kind of mindfulness, Kaza is calling for deep awareness of all that is happening around us and our part within it. At the heart of Buddhism is the understanding of the impermanent and yet deep interconnectedness of all existence. Mindfulness can be practiced by both the theist and the nontheist, and in the context of this volume, mindfulness can lead one to the awareness of the divine interconnectedness in all of existence, to the body of God. Both positions can lead to and affirm a global, ecological perspective.

---

29. Gustav Wingren, *Luther on Vocation* (Philadelphia: Muhlenberg, 1957), 180.

30. Stephanie Kaza, *Mindfully Green: A Personal and Spiritual Guide to Whole Earth Thinking* (Boston: Shambala, 2008).

Diana Eck, one of the leading theologians in reflecting on religious pluralism in America, observes that dialogue is essential to this process of mutual understanding and cooperation. She affirms that "Christians not only have a witness to bear; they also have a witness to hear."[31] True dialogue is entered into in a framework of mutual respect and integrity. The goal is not to convert the dialogue partner but to learn from them to increase one's own understanding perhaps leading to "mutual transformation" (John B. Cobb Jr., *The Emptying God*).[32] For Eck, neither exclusivism, which sees only one's own religion as true, nor inclusivism, which affirms the truth in another's position only insofar as it agrees with one's own, are acceptable. She affirms pluralism, which involves both commitment to one's own tradition as well as openness to hear from the other.[33] This is not relativism, which denies that any ultimate commitment is possible, and which is self-contradictory. If one denies there are any universal truths, a common tenet of thoroughgoing relativism, that is itself a universal truth and contradicts itself. Eck seeks interreligious understanding through pluralism precisely to lead to intercultural understanding and mutual cooperation. The model of entangled panentheism strongly supports such interreligious dialogue, for it affirms not only that we are connected within the one creation as the body of God but also that each religious tradition adds something significant to the understanding of that body, without which our understanding is significantly reduced. If someone is different from oneself, then that person has something to teach you. For the Christian, interfaith dialogue can certainly be understood as an activity of the creative Spirit moving for wholeness and health within the body of God.

If "to be" means "to be in relation" at the most fundamental levels of physical existence, then we have an interrelational and communitarian understanding of existence, upon which all other emergent structures of complexity are built. *Existence is community in relation.* The very nature of physical existence at the micro level points to a dynamic interrelationality that human community at the macro level can also embody. Humans are not single, isolated beings that exist in self-sustaining independence from everything else. Rather, we are becomings that exist in dynamic interrelationship to others in the wider ecology of existence. In other words, identity is a process, not a possession, and environment forms identity. We are constituted by the world around us as we also help to constitute it. Since all existence is interrelated, there

---

31. Diana Eck, *Encountering God: A Spiritual Journey From Bozeman to Banaras* (Boston: Beacon, 2003), 23.

32. Ibid.

33. Ibid., ch. 7.

is a sense in which dynamic, communal relations are at the core of all existence. For human becoming, community resides in trust and in the willingness to transcend self-interest for the sake of the other. It is empowered by that around which the community gathers; indeed, what it has in "common" to form the *communio*, the community.

In conclusion, I have been arguing that perichoresis and entanglement can function as parallel metaphors for the divine reality. We have been talking about Trinitarian entanglement in such a way that the inner life of the Trinity is entangled even as its functions become discrete in relation to creation. The pluriform expression of the grace and love of the economic Trinity in creation, redemption, and sanctification, however, is also unified through perichoretic entanglement with the mutual indwelling of the immanent Trinity. This would mean that the Spirit is always connected to the activity of the Father and Son in creation and that the Father and Spirit are connected to the Son in incarnation, including crucifixion and resurrection. *It is pluralistic monotheism.* To return to Rahner's Rule, "The economic Trinity (God disclosed in revelatory acts in the creation) is the immanent Trinity (God in the Godhead itself)."[34] Just as particles that have once interacted can never be fully separated, the activity of the Trinity can never be fully dismembered. The Spirit moves where it wills within the animated body of God, entangled perichoretic Trinitarian panentheism.

KEY TERMS

Analogia Entis
Analogia Relationis
Big Bang
Communio
Deep Incarnation
Fine-Tuned Universe
Green, Red and Blue Grace
Incarnation
Interfaith Dialogue and Cooperation
Kenosis
Larva Dei

---

34. Karl Rahner, *The Trinity*, trans. Joseph Donceel (New York: Herder & Herder, 1970), 22 quoted in John Polkinghorne, *Exploring Reality: The Intertwining of Science and Religion* (New Haven: Yale University Press, 2005), 103.

Multiverse
Pluralism
Strong Anthropic Principle
Teleology
Theology of the Cross
Theistic evolution
Theodicy
Vocation

DISCUSSION QUESTIONS

1. What do you think of the "fine-tuning" argument in cosmology and its relationship to the Anthropic Principle? Does the metaphor of entanglement clarify or confuse this relationship?

2. How do you understand the relationship of suffering to the nature of God? Does the understanding of "deep incarnation" help clarify this relationship?

3. What is the relationship between the divine Spirit and human community? Does a panentheistic model of God help to clarify this relationship?

4. Do you find the metaphors of entanglement and superposition helpful in clarifying the work of the Trinity in the creation?

5. What do you find most helpful or confusing about the relationship of science and theology in understanding the nature of God?

Conclusion

No one has ever seen God; if we love one another, God lives in us and his love is perfected in us. By this we know that we abide in him and he in us, because he has given us of his Spirit.

—1 John 4:12-13

As observed earlier, the human question of, "Why?" always hangs suspended between the finite and the infinite. Between logos and ethos we exercise our pathos, as we seek meaning before our own beginnings and after our demise. We encounter God through "masks," the masks of self-restriction, for that is the only way the infinite can enter into the finite without displacing it. It has been the contention of this volume that by metaphorically appropriating insights from quantum physics and connecting them with a panentheistic model of the Trinity, an understanding of the divine might be articulated with coherence and relevance to contemporary life. It is hoped that this might provide a way for us to understand a bit more of that divine mask and a way to perceive the self-offering, agapaic love of God behind it grounding hope for the future.

As stated in the introduction, the thesis of this study has been that perichoresis evolves within the Trinitarian life of God as entangled superposition, relating Creator and creation in mutual interaction, supporting a panentheistic model of God. The immanent Trinity exists in simultaneous superposition with the economic Trinity and evolves within the entangled life of God with the creation. Entanglement gives metaphorical clarity to the manner in which panentheism models God's relationship to the creation, including incarnation and sanctification. Superposition and non-local relational holism provide physical metaphors for the whole within the parts in such a way as to illuminate God's being both in the world and beyond it at the same time. In this communitarian model of the God-world relationship, we all exist in mutual simultaneous relationships with one another. To exist at all is to exist in relationship, and we are bound together by the interrelationality of God.

In summation, entangled Trinitarian panentheism may:

1. Through phase entanglement and non-local relational holism provide metaphors for the perichoretic activity of the Trinity immanently and economically in sustaining and sanctifying the creation from within a scientifically consistent panentheism;

2. Through quantum indeterminacy, affirm the freedom and openness of the creation in relation to divine self-limitation and the problem of suffering;

3. Provide a conceptual bridge between creation and the Trinitarian character of the divine life;

4. Contribute to the mutual understanding and interaction of theology and science;

5. Assist interested persons in deepening their understanding and appreciation for the divine mystery of the Trinity; and

6. Help provide a basis for interfaith dialog and cooperation as we collectively address the global issues of our time.

In Langdon Gilkey's *Shantung Compound*—a classic study of a community under pressure, a Japanese internment camp in China during World War II—he concludes that it was not the decline in physical resources that finally threatened their survival; it was the internees' inability to stop stealing from themselves and to transcend self-interest to foster the common good. Indeed, it was what the Judeo-Christian tradition calls *original sin*, inordinate self-centeredness and selfishness, that nearly destroyed them before the Allied liberation. It was the spiritual and not the material values that were essential and in short supply.[1] The meeting of physical needs can mask the absence of spiritual ones. When will our society learn to see beyond consumption? When will individuals be drawn out of themselves and into concern for others and the wider world of nature? The church, the synagogue, the temple, and the mosque all have important roles to play in fostering spiritual values that promote the common good, and today that common good is global.

As humans, we are always capable of experiencing more than we can communicate. Yet, we continue to seek expression and explanation in the hope that it will clarify our lives and connect us more completely to the world around us as well as the divine in the midst of life. Such has been the quest of this book. It has been an intellectual pilgrimage through the interpretive history of the doctrine of the Trinity as well as that of quantum theory. In the end, we have to do with a perichoretic God, who mutually indwells and continues to dance with the creation that the immanent Trinity voiced forth into life and the economic

1. Langdon Gilkey, *Shantung Compound* (New York: Harper and Row, 1966).

Trinity has remained entangled in dance with ever since. We are invited into the dance ourselves, "because he has given us of his Spirit."

Bibliography

Abrams, Nancy Ellen, and Joel R. Primack. *The New Universe and the Human Future: How a Shared Cosmology Could Transform the World.* New Haven: Yale University Press, 2011.

Aczel, Amir D. "Thomas Young's Experiment." In *Entanglement.* New York: Penguin, 2003.

Althaus, Paul. "The Trinity." In *The Theology of Martin Luther.* Minneapolis: Fortress Press, 1966.

Augustine. *Augustine: Confessions and Enchiridion,* edited by Albert Outler. Philadelphia: Westminster, 1955.

Barbour, Ian. *Issues in Science and Religion.* San Francisco: Harper, 1966.

———. "Models and Paradigms." In *Religion and Science: Historical and Contemporary Issues.* San Francisco: HarperSanFrancisco, 1997.

———. "Physics and Metaphysics." In *Religion and Science: Historical and Contemporary Issues.* San Francisco: HarperSanFrancisco, 1997.

———. *Religion in an Age of Science: The Gifford Lectures 1989–1991.* Vol 1. San Francisco: Harper & Row, 1990.

———. *Myths, Models and Paradigms: A Comparative Study in Science and Religion.* New York: Harper & Row, 1974.

———. *When Science Meets Religion: Enemies, Strangers or Partners?* San Francisco: Harper San Francisco, 2000.

Barnes, Timothy D. *Constantine and Eusebius.* Cambridge, MA: Harvard University Press, 1981.

Barrow, John, and Tipler, Frank. *The Anthropic Cosmological Principle.* Oxford: Oxford University Press, 1986.

Barth, Karl. *Church Dogmatics,* Vol 1, Part 1. Translated by G.W. Bromily. Edinburgh: T & T Clark, 1975.

Bellah, Robert, et al. *Habits of the Heart: Individualism and Commitment in American Life.* Berkeley: University of California Press, 1985.

Bonhoeffer, Dietrich. *Letters and Papers from Prison.* Edited by Eberhard Bethge. London: SCM, 1967.

Born, Max. *The Born-Einstein Letters.* New York: Walker, 1971.

Braaten, Carl E. "The Triune God: The Source and Model for Christian Unity and Mission." *Missiology: An International Review* 18, no. 4 (1990): 415–27.

Bracken, Joseph. "Panentheism from a Process Perspective." In *Trinity in Process: A Relational Theology of God*, edited by Marjorie Suchocki and Joseph A. Bracken, SJ. New York: Continuum, 1997.

Brooks, Rodney A. *Fields of Color: The Theory that Escaped Einstein.* Wanaka, NZ: Allegra Printing and Imaging, 2011.

Brown, Peter. *Augustine of Hippo: A Biography.* 2nd ed. Los Angeles: University of California Press, 2000.

Bub, Jeffrey. "The Entangled World: How Can It be Like That?" In *The Trinity and an Entangled World: Relationality in Physical Science and Theology*, edited by John Polkinghorne. Grand Rapids: Eerdmans, 2010.

Carter, Brandon. "Large Number Coincidences and the Anthropic Principle." In *Confrontation of Cosmological Theories with Observational Data*, edited by M. S. Longair. Boston: Reidel, 1974.

Clayton, Philip. "'Creative Mutual Interaction' as Manifesto, Research Program and Regulative Ideal." In *God's Action in Nature's World*. Aldershot: Ashgate, 2006.

———. "Kenotic Trinitarian Panentheism." *Dialog: A Journal of Theology* 44, no. 3 (2005): 250–55.

———. "Panentheism in Metaphysical and Scientific Perspectives." In *In Whom We Live and Move and Have Our Being*. Edited by Philip Clayton and Arthur Peacocke. Grand Rapids: Eerdmans, 2004.

———. "Panentheist Internalism: Living within the Presence of the Trinitarian God." *Dialog: A Journal of Theology* 40, no. 3 (2001): 208–15.

Cobb, John B., Jr. *The Structure of Christian Existence*. Philadelphia: Westminster Press, 1967.

———. "The World and God." In *God and the World*. Philadelphia: Westminster Press, 1969.

Cobb, John B., Jr. and Christopher Ives, eds. *The Emptying God: A Buddhist-Jewish-Christian Conversation*. New York: Orbis, 1990.

Creel, Richard. *Religion and Doubt: Toward a Faith of Your Own*. 2nd ed. New York, Prentice Hall, 1990.

Dabney, D. Lyle. *Die Kenosis des Geistes: Kontinuitat zwischen Schopfung und Erlosung im Werke des Heiligen Geistes*. Neukirchen-Vluyn: Neukirchener, 1997.

Dabney, D. Lyle, with Bradford Hinze. *Advents of the Spirit: An Introduction to the Current Study of Pneumatology*. Marquette Studies in Theology 30. Milwaukee: Marquette University Press, 2001.

Davies, Paul. *The Mind of God: The Scientific Basis for a Rationalistic World.* New York: Simon & Schuster, 1992.

Dawkins, Richard. *The God Delusion.* New York: Haughton Mifflin, 2006.

D'Espagnat, Bernard. *Veiled Reality: An Analysis of Present-Day Quantum Mechanical Concepts.* New York: Addison Wesley, 1995.

Eck, Diana. *Encountering God: A Spiritual Journey From Bozeman to Banaras.* Boston: Beacon, 2003.

Edwards, Denis. *How God Acts: Creation, Redemption, and Special Divine Action.* Minneapolis: Fortress Press, 2010.

———. "A Relational and Evolving Universe Unfolding within the Dynamism of the Divine Communion." In *In Whom We Live and Move and Have Our Being.* Edited by Philip Clayton and Arthur Peacocke. Grand Rapids: Eerdmans, 2004.

———. *Ecology at the Heart of Faith: The Change of Heart That Leads to a New Way of Living on Earth.* Maryknoll, NY: Orbis, 2006.

———. *The God of Evolution.* Mahwah, NJ: Paulist, 1999.

Einstein, Albert, and Leopold Infield. *The Evolution of Physics: From Early Concepts to Relativity and Quanta.* New York: Simons and Schuster, 1938.

Eiseley, Loren. "The Hidden Teacher." In *The Star Thrower.* New York: Harcourt Brace Jovanovich, 1978.

Erikson, Erik H. *Identity, Youth and Crisis.* London: Faber & Faber, 1974.

Ferre, Frederick. *Hellfire and Lightening Rods: Liberating Science, Technology and Religion.* Maryknoll, NY: Orbis, 1994.

Feuerbach, Ludwig. *The Essence of Christianity.* Translated by George Eliot. New York: Harper Torchbooks, 1957.

Fowler, James W. *Faithful Change.* Nashville: Abingdon, 1996.

———. *Stages of Faith: The Psychology of Human Development and the Quest for Meaning.* San Francisco: Harper & Row, 1981.

Fretheim, Terence E. *The Suffering of God: An Old Testament Perspective.* Philadelphia: Fortress Press, 1984.

Freud, Sigmund. *The Future of an Illusion.* Translated by James Strachey. 1928. Reprint, Seattle: Pacific Publishing Studio, 2010.

Gay, Peter. *The Enlightenment: The Science of Freedom.* New York: W. W. Norton, 1996.

———. Foreword to *The Philosophy of the Enlightenment,* by Ernst Cassirer. Translated by Fritz C. A. Koelln and James P. Pettegrove. Updated ed.. Princeton: Princeton University Press, 2009.

George, Murphy. "The Third Article in the Science-Theology Dialogue." *Perspectives on Science and Christian Faith* 45, no. 3 (1993): 162–68.

Gilkey, Langdon. *Shantung Compound*. San Francisco: Harper & Row, 1966.

Gore, Albert. *An Inconvenient Truth*. New York: Rodale, 2006.

———. "Climate and Civilization: A Short History." In *Earth in the Balance: Ecology and the Human Spirit*. New York: Houghton Mifflin, 1992.

Gregerson, Niels. "The Complexification of Nature: Supplementing the Neo-Darwinian Paradigm?" *Theology and Science* 4, no. 1 (2006): 5-31.

———. "The Cross of Christ in an Evolutionary World." *Dialog* 40 no. 3 (2001): 192–207.

———. "Grace in Nature and History: Luther's Doctrine of Creation Revisited." *Dialog* 44 no. 1 (2005): 19–29.

Gunton, Colion. *The Triune Creator: A Historical and Systematic Study*. Edinburgh: Edinburgh University Press, 1998.

Hall, Douglas John. "Against Religion," *The Christian Century*, January 11, 2011.

———. "The Crucified God" and "The Church and the Cross." In *The Cross in Our Context*. Minneapolis: Fortress Press, 2003.

Hanson, Bradley. "Faith and Theology." In *Introduction to Christian Theology*. Minneapolis: Fortress Press, 1997.

Hanson, R. P. C. *The Search for the Christian Doctrine of God: The Arian Controversy 318–381*. Edinburgh: T&T Clark, 1988.

Harris, Lyndon. "Divine Action: An Interview with John Polkinghorne." *Cross Currents* 48, no. 1 (1998): 3–14.

Haught, John. *God and the New Atheism: A Critical Response to Dawkins, Harris and Hitchens*. Louisville: Westminster John Knox, 2008.

———. *God After Darwin: A Theology of Evolution*. Boulder, CO: Westview Press, 2001.

Hawking, Stephen W. *A Brief History of Time: From the Big Bang to Black Holes*. New York: Bantom, 1988.

Helmer, Christine. *The Trinity and Martin Luther: A Study on the Relationship Between Genre, Language and The Trinity in Luther's Works (1523–1546)*. Mainz: Verlag Philip Von Zabern, 1999.

Hunsinger, George. *How to Read Karl Barth: The Shape of His Theology*. New York: Oxford University Press, 1991.

Irenaeus of Lyons. *Adversus Haeresus*. In *The Ante-Nicene Fathers*. Vol. 1. Edited by Alexander Roberts and James Donaldson. 1885–1887, www.ccel.org.

Jantzen, Grace. *God's World, God's Body*. Philadelphia: Westminster Press, 1984.

Jenson, Robert W. *The Triune Identity*.Philadelphia: Fortress Press, 1982.

Johnson, Elizabeth. *Quest for the Living God: Mapping Frontiers in the Theology of God*. New York: Continuum, 2008.

———. "Trinity: To Let the Symbol Sing Again." *Theology Today* 54, no. 3 (1997): 298–311.

Jüngel, Eberhard. *God as the Mystery of the World*. Grand Rapids: Eerdmans, 1983.

———. *God's Being is in Becoming: The Trinitarian Being of God in the Theology of Karl Barth*. Grand Rapids: Eerdmans, 1976.

Kasper, Walter. *The God of Jesus Christ*. New ed. New York: Continuum, 2012.

Kaza, Stephanie. *Mindfully Green: A Personal and Spiritual Guide to Whole Earth Thinking*. Boston: Shambala, 2008.

Kelly, J. N. D. *Early Christian Creeds*. London: Longmans, 1960.

———. *Early Christian Doctrines*. New York: Harper & Row, 1960.

Kohlberg, Lawrence. "Education, Moral Development, and Faith." *Journal of Moral Education* 4 no. 1 (1974): 5–16.

Kuhn, Thomas S. *The Structure of Scientific Revolutions*. 2nd ed. Chicago: University of Chicago Press, 1970.

Kung, Hans. *The Beginning of All Things: Scienc and Reigion*. Grand Rapids: Eerdmans, 2007.

LaCugna, Catherine. *God For Us: The Trinity and Christian Life*. San Francisco: HarperSanFrancisco, 1993.

Leslie, Benjamin. "Does God Have a Life? Barth and LaCugna on the Immanent Trinity." *Perspectives on Religious Studies* 24, no. 4 (1997): 377–98.

Luther, Bryan. Physicist. Personal conversation, April 12, 2013.

Luther, Martin. "Small Catechism." In *The Book of Concord*, edited by Robert Kolb and Timothy Wengert. 2nd ed. Minneapolis: Fortress Press, 2001.

———. "The Large Catechism." In *The Book of Concord*, edited by Theodore Tappert. St. Louis: Concordia, 1958.

Marshall, Ian, and Danah Zohar. *Who's Afraid of Schrodinger's Cat? All the New Science Ideas You Need to Keep Up with the New Thinking*. New York: Morrow, 1997.

Marx, Karl. *Das Kapital*. Translated by Samuel Moore. Seattle: Pacific Publishing Studio, 2010.

Marx, Karl, and Friedrich Engels. *German Ideology, including Theses on Feuerbach*. New York: Prometheus, 1998.

———. "Critique of the Gotha Programme." In *Marx/Engels Selected Works*. Vol. 3. Moscow: Progress, 1970.

Maslow, Abraham. *Religions, Values, and Peak-Experiences*. New York: Penguin, 1994.

McDaniel, Jay B. *Of God and Pelicans: A Theology of Reverence for Life*. Louisville: Westminster John Knox, 1988.

McFague, Sallie. *A New Climate for Theology: God, the World., and Global Warming*. Minneapolis: Fortress Press, 2008.

———. *Super, Natural Christians: How We Should Love Nature*. Minneapolis: Fortress Press, 2000.

———. *The Body of God: An Ecological Theology*. Minneapolis: Fortress Press, 1993.

———. *Metaphorical Theology: Models of God in Religious Language*. Minneapolis: Fortress Press, 1982.

McGrath, Alister. *Surprised by Meaning: Science, Faith, and How We Make Sense of Things*. Louisville: Westminster John Knox, 2011.

Meeks, M. D. *Origins of the Theology of Hope*. Philadelphia: Fortress Press, 1974.

Moltmann, Jürgen. "The 'Crucified God': A Trinitarian Theology of the Cross." *Interpretation* 26 no. 3 (1972): 278–99.

———. *The Crucified God: The Cross as the Foundation and Criticism of Christian Theology*. Philadelphia: Fortress Press, 1974.

———. *The Trinity and the Kingdom*. New York: Harper & Row, 1981.

Muilenberg, Gregg. "An Aristotelian Twist to Faith and Reason." *Intersections* (1997): 6–12.

Murphy, George. "'Chiasmic Cosmology' and the 'Same Old Story': Two Lutheran Approaches to Natural Theology." In *Facets of Faith and Science*. Vol. 4, *Interpreting God's Action in the World*, edited by Jitse van der Meer. Lanham, MD: University Press of America, 1996.

———. *The Cosmos in Light of the Cross*. New York: Trinity Press International, 2003.

———. "The Theology of the Cross and God's Work in the World." *Zygon* 33, no. 2 (1998): 221–31.

Murphy, Nancey, and George F. R. Ellis. *On the Moral Nature of the Universe: Theology, Cosmology, and Ethics*. Minneapolis: Fortress Press, 1996.

Nietzsche, Friedrich. *Thus Spoke Zarathustra: A Book for Everyone and No One*. Translated by Adrian del Caro. Cambridge, UK: Cambrige University Press, 2006.

O'Collins, Gerald. *The Tripersonal God: Understanding and Interpreting the Trinity*. Mahwah, NJ: Paulist, 1999.

Odahl, Charles Matson, *Constantine and the Christian Empire*. New York: Routledge, 2004.

Olson, Kenneth H. *Lens to the Natural World: Reflections on Dinosaurs, Galaxies and God*. Eugene, OR: Wipf & Stock, 2011.

Ord, Thomas Jay, ed. *The Polkinghorne Reader: Science, Faith and the Search for Meaning*. West Conshohocken, PA: Templeton, 2010.

"Panentheism." In *The Oxford Dictionary of the Christian Church*. Edited by F. L. Cross and E. A. Livingstone. 3rd ed. Oxford: Oxford University Press, 2005.

Pannenberg, Wolfhart. "Eternity, Time and the Triune God." In *Trinity, Time and Church: A Response to the Theology of Robert W. Jenson*, edited by Colin Gunton. Grand Rapids: Eerdmans, 2000.

———. "Father, Son, Spirit: Problems of a Trinitarian Doctrine of God." *Dialog* 26, no. 4 (1987): 250–57.

———. "God's Presence in History." *The Christian Century*, March 11, 1981, 260–63.

———. *Revelation as History*. New York: Macmillan, 1968.

———. "The Proleptic Element in Jesus' Claim to Authority." In *Jesus—God and Man*. Translated by Louis Wilkins and Duane Priebe. Louisville: John Knox, 1968.

Pelikan, Jaroslav. *The Christian Tradition*. Vol. 1, *The Emergence of the Catholic Tradition (100–600)*. Chicago: University of Chicago Press, 1971.

Peters, Ted, ed. *Science and Theology: The New Consonance*. Boulder, CO: Westview, 1998.

———. *God as Trinity*. Louisville: Westminster John Knox, 1993.

———. "Robert John Russell's Contribution to the Theology & Science Dialogue." In *God's Action in Nature's World: Essays in Honor of Robert John Russell*, edited by Ted Peters and Nathan Hallanger. Aldershot: Ashgate, 2006.

Peters, Ted, and Hewlett, Martinez. *Evolution From Creation to New Creation: Conflict, Conversation and Convergence*. Nashville: Abingdon, 2003.

Phan, Peter C., ed. *The Cambridge Companion to The Trinity*. Cambridge, UK: Cambridge University Press, 2011.

Piaget, Jean. *The Psychology of Intelligence*. London: Routledge & Kegan Paul, 1971.

Placher, William. *The Triune God: An Essay in Postliberal Theology*. Louisville: Westminster John Knox, 2007.

Polkinghorne, John. "Classical Cracks." In *Quantum Theory: A Very Short Introduction.* Oxford: Oxford University Press, 2002.

———. "Creatio Continua and Divine Action." *Science and Christian Belief* 7, no. 2 (1995): 101–8.

———. *Exploring Reality: The Intertwining of Science and Religion.* New Haven: Yale University Press, 2005.

———. "The Demise of Democritus." In *The Trinity and the Entangled World: Relationality in Physical Science and Theology,* edited by John Polkinghorne. Grand Rapids: Eerdmans, 2010.

———. "Understanding Quantum Theory." In *Serious Talk: Science and Religion in Dialogue.* Valley Forge, PA: Trinity Press International, 1995.

Polkinghorne, John, ed. *The Work of Love.* Grand Rapids: Eerdmans, 2001.

Rahner, Karl. *The Trinity.* Translated by Joseph Donceel. New York: Herder & Herder, 1970.

Rasmussen, Larry L. *Earth-Honoring Faith: Religious Ethics in a New Key.* Oxford: Oxford University Press, 2012.

Rees, Martin. *Just Six Numbers: The Deep Forces That Shape the Universe.* London: Phoenix, 2000.

Richard, Lucien. "In the Form of a Servant: The Kenotic Hymn." In *Christ: The Self-Emptying of God.* Mahwah, NJ: Paulist Press, 1997.

Richardson, Mark W., and Wesley J. Wildman, eds. *Religion and Science: History, Method, Dialogue.* New York: Routledge, 1996.

Ricoeur, Paul. *The Symbolism of Evil.* New York: Beacon, 1969.

Rolston, Holmes. *Environmental Ethics: Duties to and Values in the Natural World.* Philadelphia: Temple University Press, 1989.

———. *Science and Religion: A Critical Survey.* Philadelphia: Templeton Foundation Press, 1987.

Ruether, Rosemary Radford. *Gaia and God: An Ecofeminist Theology of Earth Healing.* San Francisco: Harper San Francisco, 1992.

———. *Women and Redemption: A Theological History.* Minneapolis, Fortress Press, 2012.

Rusch, William, ed. *The Trinitarian Controversy.* Sources of Christian Thought. Minneapolis: Fortress Press, 1986.

Russell, Robert John *Cosmology From Alpha to Omega: The Creative Mutual Interaction of Theology and Science.* Minneapolis: Fortress Press, 2008.

————. "Bodily Resurrection, Eschatology, and Scientific Cosmology." In *Resurrection: Theological and Scientific Assessments*, edited by Ted Peters, Robert John Russell, and Michael Welker. Grand Rapids: Eerdmans, 2002.

————. "Cosmology from Alpha to Omega" *Zygon* 29, no. 4 (1994): 557–77.

————. "Does 'The God Who Acts' Really Act? New Approaches to Divine Action in Light of Science." *Theology Today* 54, no. 1, (1997): 43–65.

————. "Eschatology and Physical Cosmology: A Preliminary Reflection." In *The Far-Future Universe: Eschatology from a Cosmic Perspective*, edited by George F. R. Ellis. Philadelphia: Templeton Foundation Press, 2002.

Russell, Robert John, Nancey Murphey, William R. Stoeger, S.J., eds. *Scientific Perspextives on Divine Action: Twenty Years of Challenges and* Progess. Vatican City:Vatican Observatory Publications and Berkeley: Center for Theology and the Natural Sciences, 2008.

Schleiermacher, Friedrich. *The Christian Faith*. Translated by H. R. Mackintosh and J. S. Stewart. Edinburgh: T&T Clark, 1928.

————. *On Religion: Speeches to Its Cultured Despisers*. Translated by Richard Crouter. Cambridge: Cambridge University Press, 1996.

Schwehn, Mark. *Exiles from Eden*. New York: Oxford University Press, 1993.

Selman, Robert L. *The Development of Conceptions of Interpersonal Relations*. Cambridge, MA: Harvard University Press, 1974.

Simmons, Ernest. *Lutheran Higher Education: An Introduction*. Minneapolis: Fortress Press, 1998.

————. "Quantum Perichoresis: Quantum Field Theory and the Trinity. *Theology and Science* 4 no. 2 (2006): 137–50.

————. "Theology of the Cross and Popular Culture." *Word and World* 23, no. 3 (2003): 253–62.

————. "The Sighs of God: Kenosis, Quantum Field Theory and the Spirit." *Word and World* supplement series 4 (2000): 182–91.

————. "Toward a Kenotic Pneumatology: Quantum Field Theory and the Theology of the Cross," *CTNS Bulletin* 19, no. 2 (1999): 11–16.

Sittler, Joseph. *Essays on Nature and Grace*. Minneapolis: Fortress Press, 1972.

Smart, Ninian. "Exploring Religion and Analyzing Worldviews." In *Worldviews: Cross Cultural Explorations of Human Beliefs*. 3rd ed. New York: Prentice Hall, 1999.

Southgate, Christopher. *The Groaning of Creation: God, Evolution and the Problem of Evil*. Louisville: Westminster John Knox, 2008.

Sponheim, Paul R. *The Pulse of Creation: God and the Transformation of the World*. Minneapolis: Fortress Press, 1999.

———. *Faith and the Other: A Relational Theology*. Minneapolis, Fortress Press, 1993.

———. *Faith and Process: The Significance of Process Thought for Christian Faith*. Minneapolis: Augsburg Publishing House, 1979.

Tillich, Paul. *Systematic Theology*. Vol. 1. Chicago: University of Chicago Press, 1973.

———. *The Dynamics of Faith*. New York: Harper Torchbooks, 1958.

———. *Theology of Culture*. New York: Oxford University Press, 1964.

Tracy, David. *The Analogical Imagination: Christian Theology and the Culture of Pluralism*. New York: Crossroad, 1998.

Vardy, Peter, and Julie Arliss. *The Thinker's Guide to God*. Alresford, UK: John Hunt, 2003.

Volf, Miroslav, and Michael Welker, eds. *God's Life in Trinity*. Minneapolis: Fortress Press, 2006.

Welch, Claude. *In This Name: The Doctrine of the Trinity in Contemporary Theology*. New York: Charles Scribner's Sons, 1952.

Wegter-McNelly, Kirk. "Experimental Evidence." In *The Entangled God*. New York: Routledge, 2011.

———. *The Entangled God: Divine Relationality and Quantum Physics*. New York: Routledge, 2011.

West, Cornel. *Race Matters*. Boston: Beacon, 1993.

Whitehead, Alfred North. *Process and Reality: An Essay in Cosmology*, edited by David Ray Griffin and Donald W. Sherburne. Corrected ed. New York: Free Press, 1978.

———. *Religion in the Making*. New York: Meridian, 1954.

Williams, Daniel Day. *The Spirit and the Forms of Love*. New York: Harper & Row, 1968.

Williams, Rowan. *Arius: Heresy and Tradition*. 2nd ed. Grand Rapids: Eerdmans, 2002.

Wigner, Eugene. "The Unreasonable Effectiveness of Mathematics." *Communication on Pure and Applied Mathematics* 13 (1960): 1–14.

Wingren, Gustaf. Translated by Rasmussen, Carl C. *Luther On Vocation*. Philadelphia: Muhlenberg, 1957.

Zajonc, Arthur. *Meditation as Contemplative Inquiry*. Great Barrington, MA: Lindisfarne Books, 2009.

Zizioulas, John. *Being as Communion: Studies in Personhood and the Church*. Crestwood, NY: St. Vladimir's Seminary Press, 1985.

———. "Relational Ontology: Insights from Patristic Thought." In *The Trinity and an Entangled World*, edited by John Polkinghorne. Grand Rapids: Eerdmans, 2010.

Index

CPSIA information can be obtained at www.ICGtesting.com
Printed in the USA
LVOW11s1908161213

365574LV00003B/5/P